FUN TIME, FAMILY TIME

FUN TIME, FAMILY TIME

Written by Susan K. Perry

Recipes by Andrea Chesman
Illustrated by Sandra Forrest

Produced by The Stonesong Press and
Alison Brown Cerier Book Development

AVON BOOKS  NEW YORK

FUN TIME, FAMILY TIME is an original publication of Avon Books. This work has never before appeared in book form. Because the level of maturity and dexterity varies from child to child, adult supervision and guidance are strongly recommended on a number of these activities and recipes. No child should ever attempt to use tools, stoves, ovens, kitchen appliances or cooking utensils without first securing permission from an adult.

AVON BOOKS
A division of
The Hearst Corporation
1350 Avenue of the Americas
New York, New York 10019

Copyright © 1996 by The Stonesong Press, Inc., and Alison Brown Cerier Book Development, Inc.
Produced by The Stonesong Press, Inc., and Alison Brown Cerier Book Development, Inc.
Published by arrangement with The Stonesong Press, Inc., and Alison Brown Cerier Book Development, Inc.
Cover illustrations by Keith Graves
Library of Congress Catalog Card Number: 96-9262
ISBN: 0-380-78772-5

Library of Congress Cataloging in Publication Data:

Perry, Susan K., 1946–
    Fun time, family time / Susan K. Perry ; recipes by Andrea Chesman ; illustrated by Sandra Forrest
        p.   cm.
    1. Family recreation.   2. Games.   3. Play.   I. Chesman, Andrea.   II. Title.
GV182.8.P377   1996
790.1'91—dc20

96-9262
CIP

First Avon Books Trade Printing: November 1996

AVON TRADEMARK REG. U.S. PAT. OFF. AND IN OTHER COUNTRIES, MARCA REGISTRADA, HECHO EN U.S.A.

Printed in the U.S.A.

OPM   10   9   8   7   6   5   4   3   2   1

Avon Books are available at special quantity discounts for bulk purchases for sales promotions, premiums, fund raising or educational use. Special books, or book excerpts, can also be created to fit specific needs.

For details write or telephone the office of the Director of Special Markets, Avon Books, Dept. FP. 1350 Avenue of the Americas, New York, New York 10019, 1-800-238-0658.

To my parents,
Frances and Daniel Selden—
We had fun, didn't we?

And to my children,
Simon John Lakkis and Kevin Michael Lakkis,
who have made me proud to be a parent,

And to my husband,
Stephen Perry,
my partner in love and fun
—SKP

To Rory and Sam,
who kid-tested all the recipes
—AC

CONTENTS

· ·

WHERE TO FIND THE RECIPES

INTRODUCTION

A few years ago, parents were told to focus on "quality time" with their children. Since then, experts on child development have found that children benefit less from a short time of intense interaction than from lots of informal shared moments throughout the day. Having supper together, playing a quick game, planning a birthday party, even picking up the house are opportunities for such shared moments.

In this book, you will find ideas that can help you create these moments for your family—to play together, laugh together, and build closeness and memories.

Because families today are so busy, the ideas are simple, quick, and *doable*. Included are suggestions for breakfast to bedtime, for celebrations of achievements and family milestones, for indoor games and simple crafts, for outdoor games and adventures, and for holidays throughout the year.

How will you know you've caught the spirit of play? If you feel like asking "Are we having fun yet?" you're trying too hard. Fun is when, in the middle of a game or conversation, you look straight into the eyes of your four- or six- or ten-year-old, or those of your adult partner, and feel a flood of warmth. You want the moment to go on and on!

This is not a book of formulas to follow. Rather, it should be viewed as a source to dip into. When you read a suggestion that makes you say, "That's a good idea," try it out. Not all of the activities will work for you. Skim all the chapters and sections, then mix and match whatever intrigues you.

The activities are not marked for specific ages because nearly all can be modified to suit the abilities and interests of children of all ages. You know your child better than anyone else does, so you'll know how to make it happen. Adaptable activities also serve the needs of families with children of several ages, since everyone can be part of the fun.

Families today come in all kinds and sizes. Whatever form your family takes, from traditional to single parent, from blended to extended, you'll find tips, ideas, and celebrations for bringing family members closer together.

The first part of this book is called "Making Every Day Special." In chapter 1, you'll find ways to give meaning to everyday routines by inventing your own family rituals. Chapter 2 offers practical suggestions for making dinnertime a highlight of the family's day. In chapter 3, you'll learn to think of household tasks in a new way. By seeking out the fun hidden in even the most mundane work, both you and your child will experience more play in your day. Chapter 4 points out opportunities to celebrate the specialness of your child and family.

Part 2, "Fun Inside and Out," is filled with things to make and do. Chapter 5 provides indoor games and pastimes that may be new to you. Chapter 6 suggests an array of arts and crafts you can share with your child. In chapter 7, the art of make-believe is explored with a multitude of ideas for pretend play that even a busy parent can get caught up in. Chapter 8 is filled with games for outdoors, whether you and your child find yourselves on the grass, on cement, in or near the water, or in the snow. Check out chapter 9 for adventures at nearby parks, beaches, and other outdoor locations.

Part 3 is devoted to holidays of one kind or another. In chapter 10, you'll find ways to celebrate your child's birthday to make it especially memorable. Chapter 11 covers holidays from Valentine's Day through Thanksgiving, while chapter 12 delves into old and new ways to celebrate the holidays that come at the end of the year and the start of the new year.

Many of the ideas throughout the book can become important rituals to observe each year, or each week—for example, the custom of lighting candles one night a week at dinner for a special reason, like the celebration of a child's achievement. Over the years, as lives have become busier and as families have spread out across the country, many traditions have been lost. Like many families, you may be on the lookout for new traditions that work for you.

Eating and cooking are favorite parts of many family activities and celebrations, so we've included recipes to complement the "together times" throughout the book. From snacks to holiday feasts, the focus is on the kinds of foods American families love to cook and eat today, including a wide variety of regional American specialties and ethnic dishes. Developed and tested specifically for this book, the recipes are easy and quick. Many offer suggestions for ways in which parents and children can cook the dish together.

Read on.

PART ONE

MAKING EVERY DAY SPECIAL

CHAPTER 1

....

EVERYDAY RITUALS

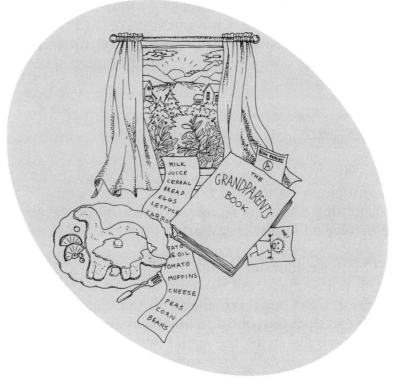

A ritual is something that your family does regularly, and that has a special meaning for you. Many families have found that small, simple rituals help them find and share the joys of even the most ordinary day. Creating and observing traditions is one of the most pleasurable parts of being a family. Rituals also fulfill an important psychological need by providing a sense of security and permanence in a changing world.

Any activity you do together week after week, or year after year, becomes a tradition that everyone in the family counts on. It seems that the younger a child is, the quicker he or she will turn a routine into a ritual. If you decide on the spur of the moment to stop at the library on the way home from your child's appointment with the dentist, your child is likely to want to do the same thing after the next dental appointment. Before you realize it, you have a new family tradition: "First the dentist, then the library—that's how our family does things."

A ritual can be a way to start the morning or end the day. It can be the creation of a special day, set aside from the normal routine, to celebrate every week, month, or year. It can be a way to smooth out the rough spots of a day, or a means of expressing the love you feel for each other.

WE ARE FAMILY

The moment two or more people join together into a family, rituals are born. Your family can tighten its natural bonds by finding ways to share your specialness, like designating a certain squeeze to mean love, or embarking on ongoing projects that involve all family members.

THE LOVE SQUEEZE A Westchester, California, family with three school-age children regularly uses a particular ritual to show their love for each other. One of them gives someone else three squeezes either on the hand or on the wrist to indicate "I love you." "We can do it anytime and anywhere and we don't have to say a thing," says the mother, who also uses the signal with her husband. Other families have used as their own love signals three quick kisses on the forehead, a kiss blown from each finger, or two winks of an eye.

SING A SONG TOGETHER Singing simple, familiar songs together is a tradition in many families. They can be childhood favorites, patriotic ditties, or popular songs. So that everyone can follow along without having to struggle to remember the words, type up the words and make copies for everybody. You can even compile these favorite sing-along songs into a booklet.

THEY'RE PLAYING OUR SONG Nothing binds a family together like sharing a smile when you hear the familiar strains of "your song." Maybe it's a song that seems to play over and over on the radio, or a kid favorite that Mom and Dad like too. It could be one that you first heard on a long car trip, or on the way to pick up your child's new bike. However it comes to be chosen, from now on, "That's our song!" Make a point of agreeing on "our park bench," "our ice cream shop," "our hiking trail," and so on. And why not "our tree," the large leafy one you all meet under when you're at the park?

FAMILY BULLETIN BOARD On some central wall, such as in a hall, install a bulletin board that anyone can add to at any time. Or use the refrigerator (stock up on magnets). Anyone can add clippings, jokes, cartoons, and ideas for places to go and things to do as a family.

GRAFFITI BOARD A wall or part of a wall devoted to your children's scribblings can become a real conversation piece over time. One couple allowed their youngsters free rein over an entire bathroom wall, limiting them to red and blue colored markers so their homespun graffiti would at least blend in with the color scheme of the wallpaper on the other three walls. If you can't spare a wall, hang a large white sheet or a large blackboard at child height in some out-of-the-way spot.

What should your kids write with markers or chalk on this graffiti board? Anything they want, though you might have to call a halt to language that would embarrass the family when others read the board. A toddler might add scribbles, an older child lots of stick-figure pictures. Older kids will probably enjoy inscribing comments about their friends, like "Dylan is a jock" and "Kylie loves Lou."

TOOT FOR ATTENTION Look for a whistle or small horn with an unusual sound that you can use for calling the kids in to dinner or for getting their attention at other times. One family uses a special whistle with a unique set of tones to call the kids back together when they're separated in a shopping mall.

GRANDPARENT BOOK If your children miss their grandparents because they live far away, help them remain connected with a special book to give to Grandma and Grandpa. Every Friday night, sit down with your kids and fill in a couple of pages of the book with details about the ordinary events of your kids' lives. The grandparents will love to know that Andrea participated in the class spelling bee and actually spelled *choreography* correctly; that Bobby learned to make his radio-controlled car jump curbs; and that the kids played "cat show" with Tiger and somehow got the family cat to walk across the carpet so the "judges" could grade her.

At each session, have your child draw a picture of what he's been doing and write a few lines he'd like to share with his grandparents. Either send the book to your folks or bring it with you next time you visit, so you can all talk about what daily life has been like for the kids since the last visit.

LET'S DO LUNCH A Long Beach, California, woman whose second husband doesn't enjoy eating out in restaurants makes a ritual of taking her two young children out to lunch every Thursday. Occasionally they opt for fast food, but more often she takes them to a regular sit-down restaurant with a variety of choices on the menu. The kids get to pick whatever they want, and they look forward all week to their special outing with Mom.

SUNRISE, SUNSET Every so often, round up the family and watch the stunning natural beauty of the sun rising or setting. You can look up sunrise and sunset times in your daily newspaper so you can plan ahead.

FRESH-START MORNINGS

Mornings can be a mad rush to get off to work and school as you urge on the slow dressers and throw lunches together. Some days that's just the way it is in every busy family. But if you want to get most days off to a more positive start, consider freeing up even a few minutes for a simple morning ritual.

Many families find that the secret to ending the morning rush hour is to get organized the evening before. Everyone lays out clothes for the next day, breakfast preparations are made, backpacks and diaper bags and briefcases are filled. For some families, it's even worth it to get up a few minutes earlier to have a more relaxed morning. Experiment with ways of putting a little ritual and good cheer into your mornings before you scatter for the day.

TOAST THE DAY If breakfast is the one meal when you're all together, even if only for a glass of orange juice, lift your juice glasses and clink them gently together. Take turns saying whatever day-brightening toast comes to anyone's mind, such as "Here's to a happy day," or "Here's to Mae-ling's spelling test," or "May those rain clouds disappear by the time of the soccer game!"

BREAKFAST SERIAL Keep a selection of books in the kitchen, and read to your child for ten or fifteen minutes a day while he eats breakfast. Choose a short story, a poem, or a chapter of a longer book.

WORD OF THE DAY At the start of breakfast, have your child close his eyes, open a dictionary at random, and point to any word. Read the word and its definition aloud. Now everyone in the family tries to use that word during breakfast. If it's a word that's new or unusual to you or your child, see whether it turns up again during the day, or later in the week, and report back to the family. Often once you become aware of a new word, it's amazing how often you'll notice it in your daily life.

LUNCH-BAG ART An efficient and pleasant morning ritual for your school-age child is having her prepare her lunch while you're making breakfast. Also, both preschoolers and primary-graders enjoy decorating their lunch bags with crayons or colored markers. These decorations don't need to be elaborate if time is short. Suggest that your child try out various ways of personalizing her bag—how many different ways can she write her name?

PRIVATE TIME TOGETHER Breakfast can be a time for you to spend one-on-one with a child. After she divorced, a

Pennsylvania secretary began having breakfasts alone with her son. When she remarried and they became a blended family, she decided not to change the ritual the two of them had enjoyed so much before. Her husband is often still sleeping when she and her son sit down to a simple breakfast. She sets the table the night before. They talk about the upcoming day and when she'll see him next. This time is especially important to her because her son spends weekends with his father.

PANCAKE ARTISTRY Every morning for the past five years, a father in Cerritos, California, has made his two children pancakes for breakfast. He shapes them like dinosaurs or his children's initials. You can do this by pouring the batter a little at a time from a spoon, instead of directly from the bowl. It's even easier to make French toast, shaping it with cookie cutters.

RECIPES FOR FUN: GOOD-START BREAKFASTS

Here are some recipes that are healthful, fast, and fun.

LOW-FAT APPLE BRAN MUFFINS
Yield: 12 muffins

For mornings when you need something quick to grab and eat on the run, these low-fat apple muffins are just the thing. They also work well as a snack to pack for a midmorning pick-me-up or as an after-school treat. In fact, these cinnamon-scented muffins are delicious any time of the day.

Children enjoy making muffins. They can take charge of greasing the muffin tins, chopping the apples in a food processor, measuring, and mixing—but don't let them overmix; the secret to light muffins is to mix the ingredients as briefly as possible.

2 cups cake flour (cake flour works best; 2 cups minus 2 tablespoons
  all-purpose flour may be substituted)
1 teaspoon baking powder
1 teaspoon baking soda
½ teaspoon salt
½ teaspoon cinnamon
1 cup light brown sugar, packed
½ cup liquid egg substitute or ½ cup egg whites
1 cup buttermilk
¼ cup canola oil
3 apples, peeled and finely chopped
1½ cups bran flake cereal

1. Preheat the oven to 350°F. Lightly grease a 12-cup muffin pan or coat with non-stick cooking spray.
2. Sift the flour, baking powder, baking soda, salt, and cinnamon into a medium-size mixing bowl.
3. In another medium-size bowl, combine the brown sugar, egg substitute, buttermilk, and oil. Stir until well combined.
4. Make a well in the center of the dry ingredients. Pour in the brown sugar mixture, the apples, and cereal. Stir just until the dry ingredients are well moistened. The batter will be lumpy; do not overmix.
5. Pour the batter into the prepared muffin cups. Bake for 20 to 25 minutes, until the muffins are golden and firm. Let cool for about 5 minutes before removing from the pan. These are delicious warm. They will keep for about 5 days in an airtight container.

FRUIT SMOOTHIES
Yield: 2 to 3 servings

A refreshing way to start the day! Pair whatever fruit or combination of fruits you have on hand with your favorite fruit juice. The ice makes it extra refreshing, but it isn't necessary, especially with frozen fruit. Let your children experiment with different combinations of fruit and juice.

1 cup diced or sliced peeled fresh, canned, or frozen fruit (berries or soft-fleshed fruits such as pineapple, melons, bananas, oranges, peaches, nectarines)

Unsweetened pure fruit juice (orange, pineapple, pear, apple, white grape juice, apricot)

½ cup vanilla or lemon yogurt

4 ice cubes (optional; do not use with frozen fruit)

1 banana

12

1. Pour the fruit into the blender. Add enough juice to cover the fruit. Add the remaining ingredients.
2. Process until smooth.
3. Pour into tall glasses and serve at once.

DECLARING EVERYDAY HOLIDAYS

Everyone loves a holiday, and there's no need to wait for those few big ones that everyone shares. You can declare your own family holiday anytime you feel like breaking the normal routine and having some extra fun. Try these for starters.

RED DAY, BLUE DAY At bedtime, anyone in the family can announce, "Tomorrow is Red Day." On Red Day, everyone in the family puts on some red clothes. Follow the red theme throughout the day in as many ways as possible. Draw something red. Make a dinner that includes something red. Make red gelatin for dessert. Before or after dinner, take a walk and look for red flowers, red cars, red bikes, red curtains, and so on. Read a red-covered book before bed.

SHAPE UP WITH SHAPE DAY Your preschooler will enjoy a shape-themed day. Circle Day? Serve round cookies for a snack, cut lunch sandwiches into circles with a cookie cutter. Your child can make a collage out of a collection of different size circles (including tiny ones from a hole punch) and play Count the Circles (or round things) in the house. Try a Square Day and a Triangle Day also.

FAMILY NIGHT Everyone in the family, from eight-year-olds on up, can take turns being responsible for that week's Family Night (adult help is always allowed). This means planning the dinner menu and deciding what the night's activities will be once homework and chores are completed. Activities can be anything from game playing to a group art project to watching a rented video. You can include out-of-the-house activities, such as going out to a movie, if you like. A few days before, a child planning the event should tell an adult if anything needs to be purchased ahead of time, such as materials for the art project or special food.

A parent should take the first turn, to model how it's done. Rules and limitations will evolve as time goes on, but for the plan to work, be open-minded and flexible about your kids' choices.

TALENT NIGHT Set aside one evening a month as Talent Night, during which all members of the family express themselves through one of their talents. Family members might sing or play a tune on an instrument, tell a story, or read something that has moved or amused them.

SNACK RITUALS

Snacks are an integral part of childhood—not just the "milk and cookies" halfway between lunch and dinner but the little munchies that make activities and games even more fun. Here are ideas for *where, when,* and *how.* For *what,* see the quick, easy, nutritious snacks under Happy Hour Treats in chapter 2.

HEAD 'EM OFF AT THE PORCH Ever notice how kids seem to demand something to eat the very minute they sail through the door after school? Consider heading your own hungry youngster off at the pass: make a point of having a snack waiting for him on the front porch or just inside the front door. Place a chair and a tray table, laden with the goodie of the day, where it can't be missed. Some families set aside a particular spot for after-school snacks, such as a corner of the garden, or seated on the floor at the coffee table in the family room. If you're home when your child gets home from school, sit down together and talk about the day's deeds. If you're at work, the waiting snack and a phone check-in will help your child feel that you're there in spirit.

WHEEL OF SNACK FORTUNE For a primary-grader, you can make even healthful snacks seem like prizes with a homemade wheel of fortune. Cut out a large circle of cardboard, draw dividing lines, and write the name of one snack in each section. Lay the circle on the floor. Your child then spins a small top over it before leaving for school in the morning. Whatever the top stops on is the snack of the day.

If your child is old enough to take responsibility for putting together his own refreshments, help by posting a list of possibilities on the refrigerator, and by making sure the ingredients are on hand.

PLASTIC POSSIBILITIES Next time you and your child are poking around a thrift shop, buy the most unusual bowl you can find and designate it "the snack bowl" for use only between meals. Whenever you have Game Night or Talent Night, serve popcorn or some other treat in this not necessarily beautiful, but memory-laden, bowl.

If you have more than one child, get each a special snack dish. One might be a large fish-shaped bowl, another a bunny plate.

WALK YOUR TALK A family in Idaho got in the habit of taking a short walk after school every day, during which they'd go over the events of the day and plan the evening. They offered their daughter a walking snack to take along, such as half a sandwich, some trail mix, or a cored apple filled with peanut butter or soft cheese.

STATION BREAK If you're concerned about your child's habit of snacking her way through several television programs in a row (studies show that kids who watch the most TV are the most overweight), agree on a few refreshment rules. For instance, from now on allow stocking up on snacks only during the station break between one show and the next, and only one time per night. Or limit eating to one half-hour program per evening. Some families prefer that their children not snack while they watch television, but they make an exception once a week for a special program the whole family enjoys together. One family likes to make a point of saving dessert for later in the evening, and serving it as a snack after homework is completed.

MAKING THE MOST OF WEEKENDS

Ahhh, the weekend. Time to catch up on chores? Sure, but also a great chance for parents and kids to spend some extra time together. Many families use longer stretches of weekend time to do something out of the ordinary.

RUN AWAY FROM HOME Almost everyone has the urge to "run away from home" once in a while, parents included. Make it a family outing! Choose a day, when no one will miss anything important. Begin by announcing to the family that you're all going to run away from home together for a day of fun, and that everyone is free of the usual responsibilities. Make a point of putting aside the chore list. Take a drive to a neighboring town, playing games in the car. Take an extra-long walk in your own town, stopping to eat at someplace different. Take in the circus on the spur of the moment. Pick up the ingredients for a picnic lunch, and spend a day at a state park—eating, playing catch, and walking in the sun-dappled woods. Don't come home until everyone is good and tired. Years from now, the kids will still be talking about the day the family ran away from home.

COOKIE DAY One working mother spends Saturday mornings baking cookies with her eight-year-old daughter. This is when their most open conversations take place (*and* the cookies are put to good use in school lunches).

GARDENING PLEASURES A father in Los Angeles likes to go out into the garden with his four-year-old son every Sunday at midday, after the usual chores are completed. Depending on what's needed that week, the child takes on the role of "seedman," "weederman," or "planterman." He really looks forward to these afternoons spent working with his dad.

SHARE THE SEASONAL BOUNTY A family in Florida bakes homemade pies with the fruits that grow in their extensive backyard garden. Then they deliver them to their neighbors. When the kids were preschoolers they each made tiny pies, but now they're old enough to make regular big pies.

SUN DAY On any nice, sunny Sunday, have a Sun Day picnic. Make a Sunshine Salad of oranges, apples, grapes, and bananas, and brew some Sun Tea (pour a gallon of water into a jug and add eight tea bags, cover the top of the jug with plastic wrap and set the jug in the sun for three or four hours). Now spread a blanket in a sunny spot and enjoy.

AND NOW FOR SOMETHING COMPLETELY DIFFERENT Once a month, declare a Fun Day and break your weekend routine by doing something that's brand-new for your family. For instance, you might read that it's cherry season and decide to go picking on the spur of the moment. Attend a dog show or an auction, or leisurely explore an antique mall, especially if you have older kids who are fascinated by old stuff. Other possibilities: hike in a new place, go ice-skating, have a Ping-Pong tournament.

THE WEEKEND BOX Even though your child gets up as early as ever on Saturday and Sunday mornings, it's possible to resolve the age-old dilemma of how to get some extra sleep for yourself. Whatever your child's age, involve him in choosing the contents of a special Weekend Box. In this box place playthings and other items to occupy him for an hour or so while you catch up on your sleep. After your child goes to sleep on Friday night, put the Weekend Box where he can reach it.

For a preschooler, you might put a couple of favorite toys in the Weekend Box, with or without asking him first ("Would you like to put this new toy from Grandma in the Weekend Box, so you can play with it on Saturday morning?"). A school-age child might enjoy choosing a few library books, a new puzzle, or some materials from an art supply store to be kept exclusively in the Weekend Box. Then, when you wake up, take an interest in what your child has been doing with the contents of the box. Change the box's contents as needed.

CHRISTMAS IN JULY When the summer doldrums hit, some families get a kick out of celebrating an extra Christmas in July. Hang and fill Christmas stockings with small summery toys and summer fruits. Make some holiday decorations and hang them up for the day. Play holiday music and exchange small gifts.

STOP THE CLOCK Once every two or three months (more often if you can), announce to the family on a Friday evening that the next day will be a Stop the Clock day. Be sure this is convenient for all members of the family so that no one will be missing an appointment or class. First, tape sheets of paper over all the clocks in the house, and put all your watches in a drawer. Plan some special fun things to do that aren't dependent on specific starting times (like movies are). Relax over breakfast, chat, peruse family albums, take a long walk, discuss what pictures you see in the clouds, play a leisurely game, and, in general, act as though you're on

17

vacation. Breaking the habit of clock-watching, even for a day or part of a day, is very liberating and relaxing for all ages.

RITUALS FOR THE ROUGH SPOTS

18

Conflict and occasional "blah" moods are absolutely normal in every family. The trick is to find workable ways to resolve the conflicts and shorten the negative moods. A little tender care provided by a loving family can work wonders.

WHEN THE GRUMPIES GET IN THE WAY OF FUN "To carp" is to complain. A carp is also a kind of fish. Put the two together for a lighthearted approach to some pretty heavy feelings. All you need is a plastic or cloth fish. Anytime someone in the family needs to express a complaint, vent some irritation, or simply be a grump for a little while, that person—-or someone who recognizes that person's need to let off a little steam—calls out "Carping Time." The person who's feeling grumpy holds the carp and says his or her piece without interruption. Anyone else who wants to then gets a turn, either to respond or to express other feelings.

THE PERKER-UPPER JAR Set aside a widemouthed jar, such as an unused cookie jar. Have the whole family brainstorm a list of on-the-spot and planned activities that are known to turn glum moods into perky ones. Write each on a slip of paper, fold, and drop into the jar. Continue to add slips whenever a new idea comes to mind. Now whenever anyone feels the need, all he or she has to do is dip into the Perker-Upper Jar for an idea guaranteed to deliver a smile. Here are some suggested perker-uppers:

☀ List ten things you like about your family.

☀ Talk to a plant.

☀ Take a bubble bath with a rubber ducky.

☀ Get rid of your old toothbrush, pencil stubs, or underwear and go out and buy new ones.

❋ Tell someone why you like him or her.

❋ Put music on and dance around the house until you're tired.

BARK IT OVER A family therapist wrote a letter to *The New York Times* not long ago in which she described her fantasy of "bark therapy." Here's how you can use this silly technique to defuse verbal battles in your own family. When two members of the family are having a trivial disagreement, either one of the arguers, or a third party, can suggest they "bark it out." Mimic the sounds of dogs barking at each other (which is what arguers sound like from a distance anyway). Start softly and get as loud as necessary. Before long, everyone will be laughing.

A NEW KIND OF TIME-OUT CHAIR Long after your kids are past the age when you might put *them* in their rooms for a time-out, the family can use the time-out concept in a different way. Designate a comfortable chair, preferably in a room of the house that isn't used constantly, as the Time-Out Chair. Anyone in the family who feels the need for a little alone time can then sit in that chair for as long as necessary. Whether it's a parent who's feeling overwhelmed or who needs some private time to think through a knotty problem, or a child who needs some space away from a sibling, whoever sits in this special chair has "diplomatic immunity" and must be left alone.

BOX OF CAVITIES In some families, battles over candy and other sweets can cause ill feelings. One family found a way to limit their child's consumption of candy by inventing the Box of Cavities. This is a shoebox, decorated by their child, which is kept all week on top of the refrigerator. Whenever any candy is brought into the house, it is automatically put in this box. Then, after lunch on Sunday, the child can dig into the box and eat his fill.

THE SICK-DAY TRAY Invest in an attractive bed tray that is brought out only when someone in the family is sick. The unlucky child or adult will feel a bit luckier when served snacks on this special tray. He can also use it to work on crafts, puzzles, or games.

AND SO TO BED

There's nothing more reassuring for a young child at the end of the day than to be tucked into bed by a loving parent. Those few minutes of transition time that you share with your child can make the experience of being left alone in a dark bedroom comfortable instead of scary. This is not the time for new activities that are too exciting. Rather, children need a familiar routine, evening after evening, to help them let go of their daytime wakefulness. Don't forget to include some low-key humor for a happy end to the day.

BATHTIME ROUTINES A preschooler's pre-bedtime bath can be more than a way to get clean. Since you can never leave a young child alone in the bath, put the time to good use by reading or telling a story. If your child is old enough to relish simple chapter books, bathtime is just long enough for one chapter. You might even speed the way to bed by offering to read one more chapter once she's tucked in.

Some children enjoy filling their bath with a great many plastic animals and other figures and then devising elaborate stories. You can join in on the story development, suggesting new twists and turns to the evolving plot.

Another bathtime ritual, especially good for Thursday or Friday nights, is to use the time to talk about your plans for the coming weekend.

READ IT AGAIN, WITH FEELING A Los Angeles museum docent found a way to expand the meaningfulness of her preschooler's usual bedtime story. After reading or telling the boy a story, she or her husband hands him a crayon, asks him how he felt about the story, and has him draw a picture about those feelings.

TELL A CHAIN STORY By the time your child is five or six, she can help you tell a continuing "chain story" at bedtime. Begin with "Once upon a time…" or "One day a little girl was walking in the forest [or the mall]…" After you've said a sentence or two, perhaps stopping in the middle of a sentence, it's your child's turn to continue the story. Then it's yours again. You might like to set a timer for five minutes for this process, and when the bell goes off, it's time for bed, no matter where the story has gone. The next night, continue approximately where you left off. Try to keep the story going with wild plot twists for as many days as your child shows interest. Start a new chain story whenever your child wants to.

SAY "TIMBER!" A woman in Long Beach, California, recalls her favorite bedtime ritual from her own childhood. She and her sister would get ready to sleep and then stand on their beds. Their mother would come in and say, "Timber!" Both girls would then drop themselves onto their mattresses, laughing happily.

GOODNIGHT MOON AND ROOM Lots of toddlers and preschoolers find the book *Goodnight Moon* a fitting end to the day. Some families use the popular book as a takeoff point for personalizing their own nighttime ritual with their children. Simply look around your child's room and say "good night" to everything you can see and name. Be as soothing or as amusing as you like, bidding good night to teddy bears and toy shelves, as well as light switches and specks of fluff on the carpet.

TURN THE TABLES AT TUCK-IN TIME Simply reverse all the usual bedtime rituals. Your child can read or tell you a story ("One more please!"), then get you a drink of water, give you a hug and a kiss or two, then neaten the blanket around you. Of course, you might end up having to pop out of bed to tuck your child in after all. Even so, it's a fun ritual, occasionally.

ESKIMO KISSES It's amazing how many ways kids can find to delay the moment when you finally leave them alone in their beds. One of their most irresistible delay tactics is to ask for extra hugs and kisses. One little boy insisted on Eskimo kisses (rubbing noses). Another wanted to know how butterflies and frogs kiss. Within a month, every kind of kiss known to animal—from the lightest to the loudest to the silliest—was exchanged between this daughter and her mother, with the greatest of glee. While you want your child to settle down, it's fun to see such imagination at work.

SAILING OFF TO SLEEP A family in Ohio found a way to make their son's bedtime something to look forward to. It also worked to keep him happily in bed once he got there. Before he'd settle into bed, whichever parent was putting him to bed that night would remind him that his bed was a boat on a lake and that he had to collect anything he might need for his voyage into sleep, including whichever dolls were to be his crew that night. His parent would join him on the bed long enough to talk about the passing clouds and the interesting fish swimming by. Once they imagined a water-skier passing by, leaving a frothy wake. Finally, the parent would "dive" off the bed and "swim" out the door.

22

CHAPTER 2

••

COMING TOGETHER AT DINNERTIME

Dinnertime may be the only time all day when the whole family is together in one place. While it's sometimes tempting to let everyone eat quickly and separately, many families find it gratifying to eat together as many nights of the week as they possibly can. The dinner hour is a ready-made opportunity to cement family bonds while talking about what each person did during the day. By coming together around the table to satisfy everyone's obvious hunger for food, you can at the same time satisfy family members' less articulated need for a connection to each other.

Make the most of this opportunity by building pleasant family interactions right into the mealtime experience. Soon you'll find that dinner isn't simply a necessity to get out of the way so you can get on with your evening but a special time to enjoy being a family.

TURNING THE WHINY HOUR INTO HAPPY HOUR

If you work outside the home, no doubt your kids jump all over you the moment you walk in the door or pick them up at day care. You want to be able to look forward to this time of reconnection after being away, but it's hard to make the transition so quickly. If you've been home most of the day, the hour before dinner is still probably the low point of everyone's day, the time when hunger and irritability set in.

If the hour is late, you may need to launch into dinner preparations at once. But the transition time will work much better if you can set aside even a few minutes of together time first. Consider instituting a Happy Hour for both you and your kids, even if the "hour" is only ten minutes. Snuggle up on the couch with your kids, share a nutritious snack, riffle through your mail, and chat with your child about his day. Once you've reconnected and your child no longer needs your attention so urgently, then you can think more calmly about dinner, homework supervision, and other plans for the evening.

Here are some other ways in which families have improved this important transition time.

SWITCH GEARS The more you can get out of your work mode and into your family mode *before* you get home, the better. Listen to music in the car, take a nap on the train, or walk home if you live nearby. Then when you get home, change into the most comfortable clothes you have. Consider asking your preschooler to help you choose which "play clothes" you'll wear. Some families find that a short before-dinner walk with the whole family works wonders for everyone's mood.

PLAN A SPECIAL ACTIVITY Make the before-dinner hour special for your child by planning a regular activity for that time every day. Set up Monopoly or another long-running board game on a card table and play for a half hour every day before dinner, while sipping on a fruit drink. Or help your child work on an elaborate puzzle or an ongoing craft project during that time. Some families keep a special supply of videotapes to watch with their kids during the homecoming hour. You might watch a half hour of a long tape per night, so that each evening the kids will look forward to the next portion of the story.

FAMILY TIME AT FIVE On some busy weekends, your family may be scattered and on their own all day, especially if you have older children or teens. On some such days in one family, a parent hangs a sign on the refrigerator announcing: "Family Time at 5. Be There!" Then the whole family gathers for drinks and goodies in the early evening. It may just be a glass of wine or juice and some cheese and crackers. Once in a while, there's something warm and scrumptious to go with a fire in the fireplace. Whatever the drink or food, it's a time to check in with one another and find out how the day has gone for both the kids and the adults.

RECIPES FOR FUN: HAPPY HOUR TREATS

If you and the kids have something to snack on before dinner, you'll all have more stamina to help you through that difficult transitional time. Having nutritious snacks available for the children to munch on while supper is being prepared will also prevent demands for candy or other inappropriate snacks. The trick is to be sure the snack is easy to prepare—better yet, preparable ahead of time—and healthful. Consider it *part* of dinner. If the snack involves action on the part of the children—dipping, for example—the eating is slowed down, and appetites are less likely to be completely sated.

Keep on hand a supply of short bamboo skewers for making kabobs of fruits or vegetables. Small children really enjoy the challenge of threading foods onto skewers and repeating patterns. They also enjoy spearing foods with toothpicks. Here are some finger foods that can involve the kids and keep pre-supper munchies healthful. These are also good ideas for snacks after school or playtime, or during family games or other activities.

26

☼ **Veggie Plate** A plate of celery sticks, sweet pepper strips, cucumber rounds, raw broccoli florets, cherry tomatoes, snow peas, and baby carrots or carrot sticks offers plenty of healthy choices for hungry children. To keep the children busy, suggest they make patterns out of their snacks. You can buy low-fat yogurt-based dips at the supermarket, or you can make your own dip.

☼ **Cottage Cheese Dip** Beat cottage cheese in a blender until smooth. Season to taste with salt and pepper, chopped chives, chopped garlic, curry powder, or chopped fresh herbs.

☼ **Peanut Butter Dip** Combine 3 parts peanut butter with 1 part soy sauce for an exotic dip with an Asian flair. Season with garlic or chives, if desired.

☼ **Stuffed Celery Sticks** Give the children cream cheese to spread on celery sticks. Or have them make "ants on a log" by stuffing the celery with peanut butter and dotting it with raisins.

☼ **Fruit Kabobs** Children like to make colorful kabobs with slices of banana, apples, peaches, and pears and cubes of pineapple, melons, and cheese. Grapes, whole strawberries, and orange sections are also good for skewers.

☼ **Dried Fruit** Provide barbecue skewers for kabobs of dried fruits. Or make a snack bowl of mixed nuts and dried fruits.

❋ **Cheese Skewers** Put out cubes of cheese with tiny pickles, apple wedges, or cherry tomatoes.

❋ **Melon Bowl** Provide a bowl of melon balls or melon cubes. Throw in grapes or whole strawberries, if you have them on hand. Give the children toothpicks to eat with; this slows down the eating and adds an element of fun to the snack.

TOOTHPICKS

❋ **Nachos** If a hearty snack is appropriate, let the kids make nachos, or just give them corn chips and cheese. They arrange the tortilla chips on a baking sheet, grate cheddar or Monterey Jack cheese, and sprinkle it over the chips. Spoonfuls of salsa over the cheese are optional. Melt the cheese under the broiler for 3 to 5 minutes.

Other healthy pre-dinner snacks include flavored popcorn, pretzels, cheese and crackers, peanut butter and crackers, and string cheese. Cracking nuts and removing the meat from the shells is a fun activity for little children. Although nuts are high in fat, they are also good protein sources—and the amount the children eat will be fairly small, because they have to crack the nuts first.

Here are some more quick appetizers the whole family can enjoy while supper is cooking.

CHEESY QUESADILLAS
Yield: 3 to 6 appetizer servings

Quesadillas (kay-sa-dée-yas), Mexican cheese turnovers, can be made by children with little or no help, especially if a microwave oven is available. Quesadillas make great appetizers, but they can also be served for supper as the main course—just garnish the plates with shredded lettuce and guacamole or avocado slices, and pass the salsa. Refried beans or Spanish rice makes a nutritious side dish.

2 tablespoons butter, melted
2 six-inch or eight-inch flour tortillas
4 ounces Monterey Jack cheese, grated
1 green onion, finely chopped
1 medium tomato, diced
2 tablespoons chopped green chiles or sweet green peppers
Garnish: sour cream, salsa, guacamole

1. If you don't have a microwave, preheat the oven to 375°.
2. Place one tortilla on a microwave-safe plate (or baking sheet, if you are using the oven). Sprinkle on the cheese and vegetables. Top with the remaining tortilla.
3. Bake until the cheese melts, about 2 minutes in the microwave on high (or 5 minutes in a 375° oven).
4. Cut into wedges. Garnish with sour cream, salsa, and guacamole as desired.

SWEET AND SPICY CHICKEN WINGS
Yield: 50 pieces

Jerk chicken, a Jamaican barbecue specialty, inspired the seasonings for these tasty morsels. The wings make great appetizers for kids, especially when you are planning to follow them with a meatless main course. The cooked wings freeze nicely and can be reheated in the microwave whenever you want to give the children something to munch on. You can also pack these along to take on picnics and in lunch bags. Don't forget the napkins!

¼ cup soy sauce
1 tablespoon chopped garlic
2 tablespoons sugar
1 teaspoon allspice
¼ teaspoon nutmeg
¼ teaspoon cayenne (or more to taste)
½ teaspoon cinnamon
½ teaspoon salt
5 pounds chicken wings

1. Preheat the oven to 425°. If the wings are attached to the drummettes, you may want to cut them apart to make them easier to eat. Bend the chicken at the joint to break the joint, then use a sharp knife to cut through the skin and joint. Both the wing part and the drummette can be used. If the wing tip is attached, use a sharp knife to cut it off; discard.
2. Lightly coat two baking sheets with nonstick cooking spray, or oil lightly. Combine the soy sauce, garlic, sugar, spices, and salt in a large bowl. Add the chicken wings and toss to coat. (The chicken can be refrigerated overnight at this point.)
3. Arrange on the baking sheets (do not crowd), and brush with any excess marinade. Bake for 30 to 35 minutes, turning and basting halfway through the cooking. Serve hot or at room temperature.
4. Freeze any extra wings. To serve, remove as many as desired. Reheat in microwave on high for 45 seconds per wing. You can reheat several wing parts at a time; just multiply the number of wing parts you are reheating by 45 seconds.

OLIVE CROSTINI

Yield: 4 appetizer servings

The whole family should enjoy these intensely flavored, mozzarella-topped toasts (*crostini* means "little crusts" in Italian), but if anyone is afraid of olives, make some plain, spreading a little olive oil on the bread and topping it with the mozzarella.

½ cup ripe pitted black olives
2 garlic cloves
1 teaspoon extra-virgin olive oil
8 slices French or Italian bread
8 slices mozzarella cheese

1. Preheat the broiler.
2. On a cutting board or in a food processor, mince the olives and garlic until the mixture is almost a paste. Spoon into a small bowl and mix in the olive oil.
3. Spread the olive paste on the bread. Top each piece of bread with a slice of mozzarella.
4. Broil just until the cheese melts, 3 to 4 minutes. Eat immediately.

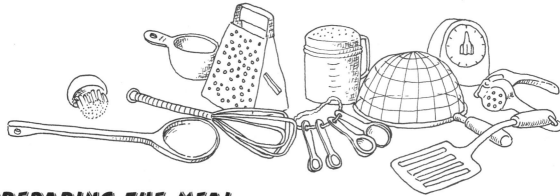

PREPARING THE MEAL

Kids are naturals in the kitchen. The whole process of turning something into something else, especially something that's yummy, is fun for a child. So, although it's often quicker to do it yourself (and sometimes, that's just what you'll need to do), you'll find there are wonderful benefits that derive from involving your child in meal preparation from an early age. Besides the shared fun, a lot of learning happens when a child follows a recipe or departs from one. And nothing builds confidence and self-esteem like being able to say, "I helped make dinner!"

To ensure that your child's kitchen experiences are safe ones, take a few simple precautions. Make sure that everyone washes their hands before beginning food preparation. Long hair should be tied back to keep it out of the cook's eyes and the food. Roll up long sleeves so they don't get in the way. Announce that the parent is in charge of the oven, the stove, and all sharp utensils. Turn pot handles in at the stove so no one knocks into them. And you should always supervise the use of electric appliances.

There are ways that even quite young children can be genuinely useful in the kitchen. Children's abilities vary widely, and you are the best judge of your own child's dexterity and patience. Nevertheless, here is a rough guide to the ages when children can perform some common kitchen tasks:

☀ **Age 4–7 (sometimes younger)** Younger children can set the table, hand you a pan, stir in ingredients, knead dough, sprinkle cheese onto food, form meatballs, sift flour, butter pans, pour liquids, crack eggs (the first few times, show your child how to crack the egg *over* the bowl, so nothing is lost if the cracking turns out to be too vigorous), butter bread, brush sauce onto meat or vegetables, assemble sandwiches, use measuring spoons, grate vegetables or cheese, operate the blender, and operate the microwave.

☀ **Age 7–10** Seven- to ten-year-olds can open cans, push garlic through a garlic press, cut cheese, and pour batter onto a griddle.

☀ **Over 10** Older children can chop vegetables, use the stove, and follow a simple recipe.

Many of the recipes throughout this book offer ways for you and your child to share the cooking. Here are a few general tips:

MESS MANAGEMENT Expect a certain amount of mess when kids cook with you. Practice—and maturing coordination—will lessen the mess in a few years. Meanwhile, designate a "floor-wiper sponge," and keep it handy. For particularly messy meals or more extensive cooking projects, lay a cheap, thin plastic drop cloth on the kitchen floor before beginning, then roll it up and toss it out afterward. To protect your child's clothes even better than an apron would, have her wear an old adult-size T-shirt over her outfit. In addition, point out to your child that cleanup is simply part of the job of cooking and the fun of eating.

KID-LEVEL WORKSPACES You can either raise your child up to counter level or bring the work surface down to your child's level. One way to do the former is to push a step stool against the counter so your child can climb up a step or two as needed (make sure it has a broad base). Equally practical for a young child is to bring a little play table into the kitchen where your child can sit or stand and work safely and easily. You'll have to squat from time to time in order to supervise, but you will be offering your child the independence of his own work table.

LEARN THE VOCABULARY OF FOOD As you prepare the meal, talk with your child about the special food words for what you're doing. Show what it means to stir, grind, knead, dice, or mold something; demonstrate how much a dash, a pinch, and a drop are.

ONE HUNDRED CHEERIOS While you're busy cooking dinner, keep your child occupied by introducing the concept of estimating. Fill a bowl with Cheerios or other dry cereal, then ask your child to guess how many pieces of cereal are in the bowl. Once she's guessed, have her count them. (Show her how to separate the pieces into piles of ten or twenty to be added up later; otherwise it's too easy to lose count.) If her estimate is way off the first time, suggest that she count out a handful of cereal and then estimate how many handfuls will fit in the bowl. You can also do this with a quarter cup of rice or a half cup of dried beans.

RECIPES FOR FUN: SIDE-BY-SIDE SUPPERS

Recipes like these offer tasks for both parent and child.

CHICKEN ENCHILADAS
Yield: 4 servings

Assembling enchiladas is just the sort of job children enjoy.

Enchilada Sauce
15-ounce can diced tomatoes
2 tablespoons tomato paste
3 tablespoons chopped fresh cilantro
½ teaspoon salt
1 to 2 teaspoons chili powder

Enchiladas
1 tablespoon oil
1 teaspoon cumin
1 teaspoon chili powder
¾ pound boneless, skinless chicken breast, diced
1 onion, finely chopped
1 sweet red pepper, finely chopped
4-ounce can chopped green chilies
2 garlic cloves, finely chopped
1 tablespoon all-purpose flour
1 cup sour cream
Salt to taste
12 six-inch flour tortillas
1 cup shredded Monterey Jack cheese

This is a kid-friendly dish with strong, but not overly hot, seasoning. Add more or less chili powder according to your taste.

1. To make the sauce, combine all the ingredients in a blender and process until smooth. Set aside.
2. Heat the oil in a large skillet. Add the cumin, chili powder, and chicken. Sauté until the chicken is mostly white and firm, about 3 to 5 minutes. Add the onion, sweet pepper, chopped green chilies, and garlic. Continue to sauté for another 3 minutes.
3. Stir the flour into the sour cream. Stir the sour cream into the chicken mixture. Taste and add salt or other seasoning, if needed.
4. Preheat the oven to 350°. Spoon a small amount of sauce into the bottom of a 9 x 13-inch baking pan.
5. Heat the tortillas all at once in a microwave, according to the package directions. Or heat them one at a time on a dry skillet. Fill the tortillas with a few tablespoons of the chicken mixture, roll up, and place seam-side down in the baking dish. Continue until all the tortillas are filled. Cover with the remaining sauce. Sprinkle the cheese on top.
6. Cover with foil and bake for 30 minutes. Uncover and bake for 5 minutes more. Serve hot.

MEATBALL SUBS SUPREME
Yield: 4 to 6 servings

This makes a casual supper that children enjoy making and eating. And because subs are hip, older children can even eat them with friends without being embarrassed by what's for dinner! With a combination of reduced-fat turkey meatballs and roasted vegetables, these submarines are healthy, too.

Older children can probably prepare this dish on their own, with little or no supervision. Younger children will be able to make the meatballs and/or assemble the sub. If younger children are assembling the sub, though, you may want to give the meatballs and vegetables a chance to cool a bit before they are handled.

If submarine sandwiches are not enjoyed in your house, use the recipe to make meatballs in sauce for a spaghetti topping.

34

Meatballs

2 garlic cloves
½ onion
¾ pound ground turkey
1 slice bread
1 egg white
1 teaspoon salt
1 teaspoon Italian seasoning
½ teaspoon dried oregano

Roasted Vegetables

½ onion, slivered (cut in half, then thinly sliced along the grain)
½ green pepper, julienned (cut in ⅜ x 1-inch matchsticks)
1 small zucchini, thinly sliced
1 tablespoon extra-virgin olive oil
1 teaspoon minced garlic
½ teaspoon dried basil
Salt and pepper to taste

Sub

18-inch French bread (baguette)
1½ cups homemade or bottled well-seasoned spaghetti sauce
¼ pound mozzarella, shredded (about 1 cup)
¼ pound provolone, shredded (about 1 cup)

1. Preheat the oven to 425°.
2. To make the meatballs, chop the garlic and onion in a food processor fitted with a steel blade. Add the turkey. Wet the bread under running water, squeeze out the excess water, and add to the food processor along with the remaining meatball ingredients. Process briefly until well combined.
3. Lightly coat a baking sheet with nonstick cooking spray. Shape the meat mixture into flattened balls and place on the baking sheet. (Keep a bowl of warm water handy; if you keep your hands wet, the meatball mixture won't stick.) Bake for 20 minutes, turning once halfway through the baking time.

4. While the children make the meatballs, prepare the vegetables. In a shallow pan, toss the vegetables with the olive oil, garlic, basil, and salt and pepper. Roast in the preheated oven along with the meatballs for about 20 minutes, until lightly browned.

5. Remove the meatballs and vegetables from the oven and reduce the oven temperature to 300°. To assemble the sub, slice the bread in half horizontally. Remove some of the soft white bread filling. Brush the inside top and bottom slices with sauce. Place the meatballs on the bottom slice. Arrange the vegetables on top. Sprinkle with the cheeses. Fit the top slice on. Wrap in aluminum foil. Bake for about 15 minutes, until heated through. Serve warm.

SETTING THE SCENE

When everyone's in a hurry to get on to the next activity, it's easy to get in the habit of tossing food on the counter to grab and eat on the run. Instead, make dinner into a regular event by setting the table. A few tiny touches—a napkin here, a flower there—can add a sense of festivity.

WHERE-DOES-IT-GO? PLACE MAT Lay out a place setting on an inexpensive plain cloth place mat. A preschooler can trace around the dishes and silverware, first with pencil, then with permanent colored markers. After she decorates the tracing of the plate as colorfully as she likes, she'll have a personal place mat that shows how to set the table.

PLACE MAT OF THE DAY Using construction paper, your child can whip up a one-use place mat while you prepare dinner. Get out the crayons or markers and suggest a theme related to the events of the day.

THE CENTER OF ATTENTION A centerpiece doesn't have to be a vase of flowers. Once a week take turns being responsible for designing an original centerpiece that will be a conversation piece during dinner. Use a small tray as the base to define the shape and space of the centerpiece. Perhaps your child would like to make a scene with small toys or clay. Someone may want to put out a selection of souvenirs from a recent beach trip, such as pebbles, feathers, and driftwood. Holidays and personal landmarks are possible themes for the week. For instance, on the last week of school, the centerpiece might contain a rolled-up and beribboned page of math homework inside a small sand pail, symbolizing the start of summer. Often children bring crafts home from school that can become centerpieces, putting them at the center of the family's attention.

PLACE CARD PERSONALITIES This activity works best if there are going to be three or more people at the dinner table. Your child designs place cards out of folded 3 x 5 index cards. Instead of names, though, he identifies each person with a symbol or drawing—a rattle or pull toy for a little brother, for example. Before sitting down to eat, everyone helps figure out which place card represents each person.

NAPKIN RING ROUNDUP You don't have to use cloth napkins to enjoy using napkin rings. The simplest kind of ring can be made by cutting inch-wide circles from the cardboard tube inside a roll of paper towels. Your child then decorates the rings with paint, colored markers, or crayons. She might like to personalize the rings with the names of family members.

A LITTLE MOOD LIGHTING Nothing softens a scene as much as candlelight does. Older children can take turns lighting the candle or candles under adult supervision, and younger ones will vie to blow them out.

A CHANGE OF SCENERY Family dinners don't have to happen in the same place every night. Convene somewhere different for a change. Here are some options:

- ☀ Everyone sits on the floor around the living room coffee table.

- ☀ Use tray tables in the living room.

- ☀ Eat on the patio.

- ☀ Set up a table in a child's room.

☀ Spread a blanket on the grass in the backyard.

☀ If you have a dining room normally reserved for company or holiday meals, serve an everyday meal there once in a while.

TIME TO EAT!

RING THE DINNER BELL Keep a small bell in the kitchen to ring when dinner's ready. If there are more than two of you in the family, it can be your child's job to announce the start of dinner by ringing the bell. If your child is learning a musical instrument, it can be fun for her to play a short "come to dinner" tune each evening.

REFLECT BEFORE EATING Whether or not your family likes to say a religious blessing before meals, you may choose to take turns saying *something* meaningful before everyone eats. One family makes it a ritual to thank the cook for her or his efforts. In a family that lives on the beach, a child announces the times of high and low tides (facts he saves from the morning newspaper to share that evening). The family says this reminds them of their place in the cycle of nature as they begin to eat the evening meal.

A mother in Omaha missed the regular blessings of her childhood and decided to read a couple of lines of poetry to her family at the start of dinner. Not only did these poetic fragments make her family slow down and think before they dug into their meals, but they often started an interesting conversation as each person talked about the poem and its meanings.

Some families set aside a moment of silence; some hold hands briefly around the table; some hit a meditation gong and listen quietly while the sound fades away; some say the same religious blessing each night or take turns saying a brief original prayer.

One family in which the parents are of different religions wanted to institute the habit of saying a simple grace at meals when their children were young. So they hit upon singing grace to the tune of "Yankee Doodle"—"We thank you Lord for this our food ..." This nontraditional way of appreciating the food put a smile in everyone's day.

Whatever the ritual, a few moments spent each night observing it before eating will go a long way toward building a family dinnertime.

TABLE TALK

The thing that makes sitting down to dinner so important is not really the food but the opportunity for conversation. You want to keep things pleasant and calm (which may be tricky if you have little ones).

Inevitably, one child will complain about a sibling, or someone will find the food "icky," or the conversation will take a negative turn. While it's certainly appropriate for your kids to vent their feelings and concerns at this time, when everyone's finally together, use your instincts to decide when the conversation isn't being productive anymore. Don't overreact. Instead, bring up a new subject, something funny that happened to you today or a dream you had, or talk about what the family is going to do on the weekend. Or try one of the word games suggested here or in the section on quiet games. If you sense that your child has some leftover negative feelings, take him aside after dinner and talk privately with him.

Family mealtimes are not a good time to discipline children. Reprimands and constant reminders about manners depress everyone's appetite and mood. If your child doesn't clean his plate, that's okay. Pushing your child to eat beyond his appetite just leads to confusing him about what real hunger is, which contributes to obesity and eating disorders. Just be sure to limit after-dinner snacking to only healthy foods.

Another common problem is phone interruptions. Some families put their answering machines on during dinner. Others answer the phone but tell callers the person wanted is eating and can't talk now. While children do learn to accept this restriction, some prefer to be allowed instead to keep their conversations with school friends very short—perhaps using an egg timer to remind themselves of the limit—rather than not have the contact at all. However, if their friends make a habit of interrupting your dinner regularly, it might be best to talk with your children about some way of heading off the distraction.

You may find that just getting caught up on school, work, and other activities takes you happily through the dinner hour. But if your family, because of age or temperament, often answers questions in words of one syllable, you can easily spark the conversation with one of these activities.

TALK BASKET Keep a basket on the kitchen table during the day. Any member of the family can add newspaper clippings or notes to the basket. Perhaps something interesting came in the mail—a birth announcement or a brochure describing the upcoming plays at the theater. During dinner, dip into the Talk Basket for discussion topics. The person who placed the clipping there should sum it up and open the discussion.

FEEL-GOOD FRIDAYS A family in North Hollywood, California, found a way to emphasize the positive in all their lives. At the start of dinner each Friday evening, they go around the table responding to the question, "What did you do that made you feel good this week?" An alternate question is, "What good thing happened this week?"

TELL A JOKE As soon as everyone's settled at the dinner table, it's nightly joke time. Each member of the family is responsible for telling a single joke. Earlier in the day, or immediately before dinner, help the younger children, especially preschoolers, find a suitable, easy-to-tell joke. Check your local bookstore or library for collections of knock-knock jokes or other humor that appeals to youngsters.

PURSUE SOME TRIVIA Some coffeehouses keep a basket of trivia cards on the table for their customers' amusement as they eat and drink. You can do something similar at home by using either the cards that come with trivia games or a trivia book. Each night at the start of dinner, someone chooses a card or a page from a book and presents a trivia question to the family. What's the longest river in the world? When did women get the vote? How many legs does a spider have? If, after discussion, no one can answer the question, read the answer aloud.

FOOD TRIVIA

1. Name everything that's in the refrigerator right now. (After everyone names all the items they can think of, send someone who's finished eating to see what was missed.)

2. How many sections does an orange usually have? (Then have oranges for dessert, and find out.)

3. How much of your body is water? (The answer is about two-thirds.)

4. What vegetable is most often used to make pickles? (Cucumbers, of course.)

5. How many kernels are on a corncob? (It depends on the length of the cob, but usually six to seven hundred for an eight-inch cob.)

6. If you spend an hour eating, how many calories will you use up? (About 100, the same number of calories in an egg, an apple, a banana, or nine potato chips.)

BECOME AWARE OF YOUR FOOD Help your children become conscious of that hamburger or potato they're eating. Every so often at the dinner table, talk about where the food you're eating comes from. Does it grow on a tree? Was it an animal? Was it frozen on its way to the market? Did it come from a can or a cardboard box? Research the questions that no one can answer by looking up that food in a general encyclopedia. For instance, if you looked up *banana,* you'd find that a banana plant grows as tall as thirty feet, that there are also small red bananas, and that the fibers of the leaves of the banana plant are used to build roofs for houses.

A IS FOR APPLES While you're eating, play an alphabet game. One person starts by saying, "I'm on a diet and I can only eat *apples.*" The next chooses a food word that starts with B, such as, "I am on a diet and I can only eat *bread.*" To turn this into a memory game, have each person add his word to all those that went before, such as, "I am on a diet and I can only eat apples, bread, and cereal." Keep going around the table until you run out of letters, ideas, or interest.

FUN TIME, FAMILY TIME

SOMETHING SILLY NIGHT One morning a week, draw the name of a family member from a jar. Keep the chosen name a secret if possible. That person then secretly decides what to do at the dinner table that the others will find amusing or outright wacky. The silly person tries to keep a straight face while the others guess who's being silly—it shouldn't be difficult! Here are some ideas to get started: wear a silly nose-and-glasses mask, use makeup to draw a mustache on yourself, wear a funny hat, wear the baby's bib, turn your chair sideways, hang a pot holder from your ear, tell an unbelievable story.

42

LEARN A NEW WORD Every night, present a new word to be learned. A parent can be in charge of coming up with the word, or you can keep a large dictionary near the table and take turns randomly opening it to find a new word. Someone reads the word and its definition. Then go around the table, giving each person a chance to use the new word in a silly sentence.

TV DURING DINNER?

Every expert advises against letting your family get in the habit of staring at the television set during dinner. If this is the one time you're all together during the day, make the most of it and talk to each other. Years from now, your children will have long forgotten the details of the programs they watched while they ate, but children who grew up in families that talked over dinner recall those meals with special warmth and fondness.

Some families like to make an exception for the news, whether on television or radio. If you have young children, you might consider that much of what they'll be hearing is troubling and won't be conducive to happy eating. However, if you do *occasionally* watch or listen to the news at dinnertime with your older children, make it a learning experience by taping a world map on a nearby wall so your children can quickly find the countries mentioned. And leave enough time to discuss what they've heard or seen.

WHAT'S FOR DINNER?

A mother in Los Angeles felt guilty when her childless neighbor teased her one evening, "It's Thursday. Must be spaghetti night." She wondered if there was something wrong with the predictability of her family's dinner menus. In fact, young children love and crave routine. So if you find it a daily struggle to decide what to feed your family, consider making a list of your family's favorite meals. Then parcel them out on a weekly or biweekly calendar. Monday might be spaghetti night, Tuesday chicken night, Wednesday soup and sandwich night, and so on.

Although routines may work for you day in and day out, there are times when you'll want to shake things up. Here are some ideas that will make dinner into an occasion.

BREAKFAST AT NIGHT If your mornings are always too rushed for a complicated breakfast, even on weekends, your family may enjoy a "Breakfast at Night" supper every so often. Pancakes, crêpes, omelets, and French toast are real kid-pleasers.

FOOD THEME WEEK It can be an eye-opening experience for a child to realize how many different forms a single food can take. Occasionally, designate a week where a familiar food will be explored in all its manifestations. For example, during Apple Week, each dinner should use apples in a different way, such as in salad, applesauce, apple pie, apple juice, apple cider, apple jelly, dried apple, baked apple, or apple butter.

Or have a Potato Week in which you, with the help of your child, prepare homemade French fries, baked potatoes with lots of toppings, potato latkes, potato kugel, and good old mashed potatoes. Beans offer lots of possibilities, too.

SPICE UP THE MEAL Place a selection of spices in their original jars on a small tray on the dinner table. As the food is served, family members can read the jars to see which ones might enhance the flavors of that particular kind of food. You'll have to supervise preschoolers so that they don't dump too much spice over everything. This is a healthful, fun way for kids to learn to reduce their use of salt while helping their palates (and their vocabularies) grow more sophisticated.

TOPSY-TURVY DINNER Try serving dinner in the reverse order once in a while. Most kids will delight in being offered dessert first. Serve an appetizer last. What else can your children imagine doing backwards at the dinner table? They can try eating with their "wrong" hand; they can crumple their napkins into a ball at the beginning of the meal, then smooth them out perfectly at the end; and they can work at saying a complete sentence backwards, such as "Today school at test a had I."

MAKE-YOUR-OWN-PIZZA NIGHT Pizza is the all-time favorite of many kids. Use frozen pizza dough, or make the recipe below. Put out bowls of toppings on the kitchen table. Everyone tops the part of the pizza he wants to eat. Or you can have everyone add to a super-deluxe pizza with everything.

RECIPE FOR FUN: HOMEMADE PIZZA

PIZZA
Yield: Two 8-slice pizzas

Homemade pizza baked in a hot oven is far superior to any frozen pizza. Making the dough is an easy job that can be shared with children, though little ones might best enjoy sprinkling on the toppings.

The recipe makes two 10-inch round pizzas (which can't fit in most ovens at the same time) or two 15-inch rectangular pizzas (which can). It should make enough for dinner and leftovers.

Dough
2 cups warm (110°F) water
1 tablespoon baker's yeast
¼ cup olive oil
1 tablespoon salt
5½ to 6 cups all-purpose flour

Topping
2 cups seasoned tomato sauce (homemade or bottled)
4 cups grated cheese (a mix of mozzarella, provolone, and cheddar is delicious)
Optional toppings: raw sliced onion, green pepper, mushrooms; cooked sausage; sliced pepperoni; etc.

1. To make the dough, combine the water and yeast in a medium mixing bowl. Stir until the yeast is dissolved.
2. Add the oil, salt, and 2 cups of the flour, and stir until you have a smooth batter. Continue adding the flour ½ cup at a time until you can no longer stir the dough. Add ½ cup flour to your work surface, and turn the dough out of the

bowl. Knead the dough, adding just enough flour to make a soft, smooth dough. Do not add too much flour, or the crust will be tough. Knead for about 8 minutes.

3. Return the dough to a lightly oiled bowl. Cover, place in a warm place, and let rise for 30 to 40 minutes, or until doubled in bulk. Punch down. Divide the dough in half.

4. Preheat the oven to 500°. Lightly oil two 10-inch round or 15-inch rectangular baking sheets.

5. Carefully stretch the dough to fit the baking sheets, forming a slight ridge around the edges. If the dough will not stretch to fit the entire pan, let it rest for 5 minutes, then finish stretching.

6. Smooth the sauce over the dough. Sprinkle the cheese over the sauce. Sprinkle the additional toppings over the cheese.

7. Bake until the cheese is golden and the crust is lightly browned, about 10 minutes. Let cool for about 5 minutes before slicing.

TASTE TESTS This is a way to introduce your child to the fun of new flavors. When you shop, purchase a variety of the same item—for example, several different melons, such as watermelon, cantaloupe, honeydew, papaya, and crenshaw. Cut them up and enjoy. When your child is confident that he can recognize each of the different flavors of melon, blindfold him so he can see how accurate his taste buds are. Try this for fruits (apples, bananas, peaches, pineapple, grapes, strawberries), for vegetables (tomatoes, carrots, peas, celery, cauliflower, spinach), and for cheese (cheddar, Swiss, Jack, Roquefort).

FOODS OF MANY CULTURES Introduce your family to other cultures by serving an ethnic meal. There are many cookbooks that focus on particular cuisines. A parent or child might start by looking up the country in an encyclopedia to find out a few facts to share over dinner. Your child might like to copy and color the country's flag on a piece of paper. To use the flag as a simple centerpiece, attach it to a small stick and poke it into a lump of modeling clay. This can be especially meaningful if you plan a meal or series of meals exploring the foods of your family's ethnic background.

CRAZY FOOD NIGHT This occasional activity can be masterminded by either a parent or a child. The object is to serve something crazy for dinner. Even if the parents are to be in charge, you can still ask for suggestions from the kids ahead of time. If you're adventurous, suggest that your kids make up the menu themselves. They will also choose the ingredients when you go shopping, cook the meal, serve it, and clean up. Your task is to pay expenses and help out when necessary.

For example, color foods differently. How about blue cottage cheese? One mother offered her delighted kids fruit dipped in "green slime," which was actually yogurt with food coloring. Out-of-the-ordinary sandwiches can be created by combining two slices of fruit with a filling of cheese, peanut butter, or honey. Or combine two foods your child likes that aren't normally served together, such as cherries and potato salad.

When the kids are in charge, be prepared to eat some very odd concoctions, such as fried peanut butter sandwiches. You might feel obligated to set a *few* rules, such as limiting junk food or making sure the meal includes something from each food group.

MAKE YOUR DESSERT AND EAT IT TOO Right after you've shared dinner cleanup duties, make dessert with your child. You can bake a cake, cupcakes, or cookies, or make pudding. Once the dessert is ready to eat, you can call the family back together for dessert.

ENDING THE MEAL

Teach your children to ask to be excused when they're through eating. It's an easy habit to learn, looks wonderfully well mannered, and it gives kids the freedom to decide when they've eaten enough. Even a preschooler can learn that it's his responsibility to move his plate and silverware from the table to the sink area. Young children who have eaten all they want of the main course can be allowed the option of excusing themselves and returning to the table a little while later to rejoin the conversation and enjoy dessert.

CHAPTER 3

TURNING WORK INTO PLAY

A mother in Sacramento was astonished when her nine-year-old daughter's new friend, visiting after school, asked for a sponge so she could clean the bathroom sink. And she cleaned it with gusto! Somehow, this child had learned that cleaning sinks is fun.

In fact, there are elements of fun in all kinds of routine household chores. Dusting, doing the laundry, picking up the clutter, even bill paying and grocery shopping can become games, especially if the family works together.

Homemaking isn't always fun and games, of course, but it can be sometimes, and once everybody gets in the habit of pitching in, parents will have more time and energy for *other* kinds of family fun.

Kids who get involved with the work of keeping the household running smoothly will reap even more benefits than their parents. Working within the family enhances a child's self-esteem and confidence. Also, when the family works side by side, children get to spend more time with their parents, which many find to be the greatest reward of all.

BEGIN EARLY

Parents often underestimate how much their children are capable of doing around the house. One man playfully suggested that all infants ought to have dust rags tied to their diapers so that they'd be cleaning the floor while they crawled around. Though a baby isn't likely to get much benefit out of such a "chore," children as young as three can and *should* join in the family's work. So that your children end up feeling good about themselves, pick tasks that are in line with their developmental abilities.

It also helps to be as specific as you can. Kids won't notice the jobs that need doing, and their timelines probably won't resemble yours. Announce that cleanup time is every day before dinner, for example, or that beds will be straightened before breakfast. But your saying "clean up" isn't enough for a young child. "I'll put away your books while you put all your dolls back on the shelf," works better. Once your child is school-age, it may be useful to write up a list of what you mean by "a clean room" and call the list a "job description."

Although having tiny tots put away their own toys sounds like the natural starting point, for some reason most kids resist this task. Keep your expectations for a clean room reasonable, and step in and help when the job seems overwhelming.

Here are general guidelines for the kind of help you can reasonably expect from children at various ages. An older child can be expected, of course, to do any of the tasks listed for a younger one. Experiment a little to find out what jobs your child can do, and add your family's special chores to the list.

☀ **Age 3-5** Set the table, sort clothes, clean the tub after their bath, tear lettuce for salad, carry own plate to sink after eating, mop up spills, rinse dishes, take out trash, put toys away, dress themselves, water plants, pull weeds.

☀ **Age 6-8** Change sheets, dust, vacuum, load dishwasher, fold and put away own laundry, mix juice, help pack lunches, sweep the driveway, sort grocery coupons, feed pet.

☀ **Age 9-11** Do laundry, make bed, unpack groceries, wash floor, help cook dinner, wash car.

☀ **Age 12-up** Babysit, prepare own breakfast, pack school lunch, cook some dinners, mow lawn, remove cobwebs, change lightbulbs, iron.

FUN WAYS TO DIVIDE UP THE WORK

A good way to start dividing up the work is to hold a family meeting and make a master list of everything that has to be done each week.

When you divide up tasks, consider family members' preferences. Some people daydream their way through ironing, while others grit their teeth with every hiss of the steam iron. If you like the task, you'll go at it with more relish. So on the master list, note everyone's favorite and most hated chores. For example, if you hate ironing, put an H next to your name on the list. Place an OK next to those tasks you don't mind doing. You might make it a rule that no one can put an H unless they've actually done that chore at least two times. Now you can start divvying up the chores. As preferences change over time, change the notations on the master list. You will probably need to rotate the chores *no one* likes. In fact, it's a good idea to rotate chores anyway. Routine tasks seem novel when you haven't done them for awhile. One of the elements of fun in household chores consists of doing something different than usual. Even if your family comprises you and one small child, you can switch off every so often.

If you don't stereotype chores by gender, your child will grow up knowing that it's not necessary to have ovaries in order to handle a dust cloth or dishrag, and that you don't need to be a man to wash a car, mow a lawn, or fix something. Mix and match household duties so that no one, including the adults in the family, gets stuck repeatedly with the same traditional chores.

When you've divided up the chores, your child can design and draw a chart to hang on the refrigerator.

Here are some fun ways to mix things up.

JOB ROULETTE Make a job wheel from a large circle of cardboard. Divide the circle into twelve segments or so. Make a spinner by attaching a thin strip of cardboard to the center of the circle with a small metal fastener (the kind meant to fasten loose-leaf paper). At chore-assigning time, each member of the family spins for his or her allotment of tasks.

Another approach is to have twelve batches of chores (a batch might be "dusting" or "clean the bathroom"). Then roll dice to see which batches are yours for the week or month.

CHORE TRAIL Cut footprint shapes from heavy paper or cardboard. On each one, list a household task. On Saturday, or whenever there's an extended period of time available for chores, lay the footprints about the house so that your child can begin the "chore trail." As he steps on a footprint, then completes that chore, he gets to pick up that footprint. He then resumes his walk where he left off. The final footprint—to be picked up only when all the others have been finished—contains instructions for something fun.

TASK HUNT First hide several slips of paper around a room or around the house, each listing a chore that can be completed in a short time. Set the timer for a half hour or an hour, and have your child see how many slips he can find and how many chores he can complete in that time.

A child who has managed to keep his bedroom clean for a certain period of time might be allowed to choose a new wall poster. Or you can tell her that as soon as she gets the dining room table cleared off, she can begin setting up a toy city there.

Private time with a parent is a very motivating incentive. Explain to your child that the more he helps with cleanup, the faster the work will get done, and the more time you will have for her. To make this work, the parent has to agree to do whatever is reasonable and affordable within the time allotted.

53

PICKING UP THE STUFF

Try some of these games and activities, which just happen to get all that stuff put away.

ENCHANTED CLUTTER Capture your child's imagination by having the messy stuff do the reminding. If dropped towels in the bathroom are the problem, say to your child in a raspy voice, "I'm so sad when you drop me on the floor. I never get a chance to dry, and I'm afraid some icky mold will grow on me. Then I'll smell yucky." Pretend to be a dropped shoe and say, "Oh my, I'm lonely out here in the living room. I feel so much more at home in my own little closet. And what if someone trips on me? What if they sue me? Oh, my!" Soon you and your child will be laughing.

PUT THE PLANES IN THE HANGAR Sometimes kids have trouble cleaning up their rooms because there's no set place for all their things. The solution is to designate places. If you can also give the places amusing names, chances are they'll be remembered. Toys can go onto shelves that are "airports" or "garages" or "homes."

Sometimes it works to label drawers with pictures of what's inside. When your child gets a new toy, cut out the picture on the carton and tape the picture on the side of the bin or box where the toy will be stored. One day, the mother of a ten-year-old boy not formerly known for his neatness discovered that he had pasted small labels on his drawers marked *underwear*, *shirts*, and *toys*. He'd found a system of his own.

RACE AGAINST TIME Set a timer for ten minutes (use an egg timer for a quickie chore). Can your child put all her art materials away and still beat the timer? Choose chores that don't require a lot of finesse, or your child may rush through them or do an incomplete job.

You may want to designate a time every day as the official pick-up time—perhaps before dinner or before the bedtime routine starts. Set a timer for fifteen minutes. When the timer goes off, a parent goes around the house and confiscates anything that is out of place (to be fair, this should apply to the parents' stuff also). If you like, you can limit the pick-up to the "public" areas of the house—kitchen, living room, bathroom—excluding the child's room. In order to get back something that's been impounded and put into the "Jail Box," the owner of the item has to do an extra chore.

GAMES FOR THE CLEAN TEAM

Some household tasks have fun built right into them, if you only know where to look. When your child is raking leaves, for instance, ask her how high a pile she can make. Draw pictures in the dust on the piano, and then erase them. One woman says that when she suggested that her son make sculptures out of the dog's canned food, he eagerly became the pet's regular feeder. Substitute a squirt toy for the usual watering can, and your child will delight in her plant watering assignment (limit this to outdoor or patio plants unless your child is old enough to contain the mess).

Here are some other ways to find that element of fun.

WAYS TO DO IT ALL WRONG While dusting or pulling weeds together, brainstorm a list of alternative approaches. You'll both end up laughing as you come up with instructions such as, "Use a porcupine to dust" or "use the lawn mower to weed the garden."

BET ON IT Children love a challenge. "Bet you can't collect all the garbage from the four wastebaskets around the house, dump them in the can outside, and bring the can up to the curb before I get these dishes done!" And the race is on.

55

ROLE-PLAYING Children love to pretend, so incorporate role-playing into daily routines whenever you can. A child clearing the table can pretend to be a waiter or waitress, asking, "Are you finished, sir?" When feeding a pet, your child might like to be a veterinarian. "Here is your scientifically correct meal, Ms. Dog." She can keep a notebook on her pet's eating behavior—does the animal prefer moist meals or dry? Does it eat quickly or slowly, drink before or after?

TOOLS FOR SMALL HANDS

Purchase an extra set of real, but manageable, cleanup tools for the kids. In fact, let them pick out their own sponges, brand of spray cleaner, and so forth on your next trip to the store.

MEASURE FOR MEASURE Give your child a twenty-five- or fifty-foot children's tape measure so he can measure the length and width of the rooms he is about to vacuum. He might then enjoy figuring the square footage (length times width). At dinner, he can announce, "Today I vacuumed a thousand square feet!" Or "I dusted fifty feet of bookshelves."

Another useful measuring tool is a scale, whether a bathroom scale or a large postal scale that weighs up to about twenty-five pounds. Garbage day? Have your child weigh herself, then weigh herself holding the garbage. Suggest that she keep track of how many pounds of trash your family tosses in a week. A family project might be reducing that poundage by more careful buying and recycling.

WORK TO THE BEAT Take turns choosing a popular tune. Chopin's "Minute Waltz" is a lively piece that tends to make people want to move quickly, or try Raffi or rock, depending on your child's age and tastes. Then begin the chore, either working together on the same job or separately on two different chores. Try to beat the music by finishing the task before the tune ends.

WHISTLE WHILE YOU WORK Teach your kids how to whistle, and they'll see that it really does make them feel happy to whistle while they work. At least, there will be lots of giggles while they're learning. It may be enough to show your child how to purse her lips, place her tongue behind her bottom teeth, and blow gently until she can make a sound. Be encouraging; this is an advanced skill for many kids.

FIND-THE-MONEY DUST GAME Hide a dollar's worth of pennies in the dustiest places in your home. Put the biggest bounty under lamps or in other places often overlooked by kids who are dusting in a hurry. Now set the gang loose (even if it's a gang of one). The duster gets to keep what she's found—and is encouraged to go back and find (and dust) what she missed. The next time you play this game, change most (but not all) of your hiding places. Though most adults wouldn't do all that bending to earn a buck, the challenge of finding the hidden coins, and of outsmarting the person who hid them, can be very motivating.

Don't do this game if you have children under five in the house. A forgotten penny could be a choking hazard for a very young child.

PLAY WORD GAMES Any task that you and a child are doing together—washing and drying the dishes, dusting, or weeding—will go much more quickly if you play a word game like Twenty Questions while you work. In that game, all questions have to be answerable by a yes or a no. Example:

Mom: I'm thinking of something in the house.
Kid: Is it bigger than a breadbox?
Mom: Yes.
Kid: Does it make noise?
Mom: Yes.
Kid: Is it expensive?
Mom: Yes.
Kid: Is it old?
Mom: No.
Kid: Is it in this room?
Mom: Yes.
Kid: So it's big, noisy, expensive, new, and in this room. Is it the refrigerator?
Mom: No.
Kid: Then I give up.
Mom: It's you!

Check out the indoor games chapter for other games that can be played while doing household tasks.

CHANGE THE ACTION BY REMOTE CONTROL This game sends the television generation into giggles. If your child is dawdling while putting her stuff away, aim the remote control at her and tell her you're pressing fast forward. If she's dusting so quickly that you suspect she isn't doing a careful job, aim the control at her and tell her you're pressing slow. For fun, press reverse (while announcing it) so that your kids try to do everything backward for a minute or two. (Use this one judiciously, or you'll find the freshly folded laundry all wrinkled up and tossed on the floor again.)

SEND A MEMO When your voice alone has lost its ability to motivate your kids, try writing them notes. This unemotional and impersonal method often galvanizes kids to action when repeated requests have failed. Be gentle but firm in your written requests, and use humor when you can.

For instance, say you're expecting company and it's especially important to you that your child straighten her room. A child who finds the following note on her desk when she gets home from school is more likely to get started right away:

Miss Jones:

A company inspection team is due to arrive this evening to check on whether we are complying with the government rules regarding orderliness. I am counting on you to come through by making sure your work space and the room around it are clean and clear. Please check off the following items when they are completed:

Desk is neat.
No clothing is on floor.
Surfaces are dusted.
Bed is made.

Thank you for your cooperation.

BE INVENTORS When your child does the dishes, let her fill the sink as high as she can and add an extra portion of bubbly dish soap. Ask her if she can wash the dishes entirely underwater. Or say, "Setting the table the usual way is getting dull. I wonder if anyone's ever come up with a better way?"

CHILD IN CHARGE As soon as your child gets the hang of some chore you do together, give her a chance to be in charge. Say, "Tell me which rag to use and which rooms you want me to dust." She gets to divide the work in half any way she wants to (but if she gives you two-thirds, don't argue). When the job is finished, she gets to tell you what you've left out, instead of the other way around.

GAMES FOR LAUNDRY, DIRTY CARS, EVEN BILLS

LAUNDRY GAMES Announce to the kids, "From now on, we'll deal with the laundry in a new way. Suzie, you gather the clothes and towels; James, you take the sheets off the bed; I'll put all of these things into the washer. When the wash cycle is done, Suzie's job is to put them in the dryer and call us all together. While the clothes are drying, I'll read as many stories as I can to you."

Once the clothes are dry, enlist a child to pair the socks. Show her how to fold two socks together into a ball. Demonstrate how two people can fold a sheet easier and neater than one person alone. Once the laundry basket's empty, use it for a tossing game: have your child step back ten feet and see how many paired socks she can get into the basket.

CAR WASH FUN It can be great fun to wash the car, especially on a hot day. If the car is dusty enough, start by drawing pictures on it with a finger. How about drawing a bull's-eye and letting the kids squirt spray bottles of water at the target? Older kids might enjoy playing a word game together while scrubbing and rubbing.

THE GROWN-UP GAME OF BILL-PAYING Though sending away a huge proportion of your income every month to cover necessary bills isn't innately pleasurable, the task of bill-paying itself can be satisfying. By the age of nine or ten, most children are able to get involved. Begin by piling up the bills that must be paid. Have your child count them and count out an equal number of checks. Your child can then date that many checks. After you show her how once or twice, you may be able to trust her with the job of filling out the checks, leaving you to read over them and sign them. (Individual checks are quite inexpensive, so an error while learning is no big deal.) She could even record the checks in the checkbook, leaving everything for you to examine for accuracy.

Involving your child in bill-paying will make her feel very grown up, and she'll be learning a skill she'll need as an adult. Moreover, the process may help her understand what you mean when you say you can't afford something.

Sooner or later, each of us discovers that if we offer our child something—something we wouldn't have given her otherwise, whether it be a snack, a toy, or something intangible, like lots of praise—she will do things we want her to do. So what's wrong with that?

The down side of rewards is that they achieve only temporary compliance. Numerous psychological studies have demonstrated that the quality of a person's work goes down over time when you motivate him with rewards. Rewards don't change people's behavior in the long run. Eventually you may have to come up with a bigger treat to get your child to cooperate. Even praise eventually loses its power to motivate once your child catches on that you're only praising him to get him to do what you want.

Think about what you really want for your child. Do you want a child who does the right thing because it's the right thing, or do you want a child who only does the right thing when someone is watching, or when he is sure he's going to get something for doing it?

Because many household jobs aren't all that intrinsically rewarding, remind your kids of the things *you* do for them simply because you love them and they're part of the family. Children need to learn that it's the right and fair thing to do to take care of their own space, though you'll get better results if you let them set their own priorities and timeline.

Is it wrong, then, to pay a child to do tasks around the house? Some experts believe that children should do a fair share without payment, and that an allowance shouldn't be tied to performance. But since incentives *do* work in the short run, many parents find it helpful to list a set of *extra* chores their children can choose to do for extra money.

ADVENTURES IN SUPERMARKET SHOPPING

Yes, you can build family bonds and add to your family's storehouse of sweet memories even on trips to the *supermarket*. The trick is planning ahead and giving it some thought.

60

All of the games that follow will work better if everyone involved isn't too tired and if you aren't in a big hurry. If most of your shopping stops take place when you're on your way home from your five-year-old's afternoon play date, beware. When you decide on the spur of the moment to stop at the grocery store, assuring your tired child you'll only get "three things," keep your promise and get those three things. If you rush around picking up seven other things you suddenly realize you need also, your child will sense your tension and become irritable himself.

Also, be consistent and clear about the fact that your child has to follow the basic rules of common decency in the supermarket or else she'll lose any privileges you've decided on in advance, such as being allowed to choose one thing of her own to buy. The rules? She must stay within touching distance of you or your cart, she mustn't argue with you, she has to use her best public manners (no running or yelling), and she's not to touch the merchandise without your permission.

The following activities will help you turn shopping expeditions into adventures. Many of these activities can easily be adapted for department or discount store outings.

THE JOY OF LISTS The fun can start back home. A child who can write can help make out the weekly grocery list. You can poke around the fridge and your cookbooks to dictate the list to your child.

COUPON BOSS Assign a school-age child the regular job of organizing your grocery coupons. Buy either a coupon file with compartments or a 3 x 5 file box. Your child cuts out a week's worth of newspaper coupons, then sorts them into useful categories. For starters, try cereals, drinks, personal care products, miscellaneous food, and coupons for free items. You might want a section for "Use now— about to expire!" or "No expiration date."

The next time you shop, the coupon organizer will be kept quite busy being in charge of the file while you walk up and down the aisles. "Do we have one for Raisin Bran?" "Here, it's forty cents off."

Consider allotting the amount you've saved toward either a special treat for your helper or a special family fun outing, such as an amusement park, which might otherwise be too expensive.

CHOOSE ONE THING A study found that preschoolers ask their mothers for something more than once per minute during a shopping trip. Interestingly, mothers who give in are besieged by exactly as many repeat requests as those who don't.

It helps to emphasize the positive ("You get to choose *one* item at the grocery store") rather than the negative ("No, I said you can only have one thing, not two").

Decide in advance how much you want to spend on the one thing your child gets to choose—with the final decision made by your child in the checkout line. Allow her to change her mind any time before that; this should keep her happily occupied. A variation for an older child is a two-dollar allowance that can be spent during the outing.

TOOTHPICK TREATS Look for supermarkets that sample new foods one or two days a week. Many kids will try all sorts of odd foods when they're on a toothpick or in a tiny cup—maybe your kid will discover a new food that he likes. The snacks, as well as talking to the servers, make the shopping fun.

SUPERMARKET HUNT Involve a preschooler in the quest for the *yellow* bananas, the *green* peppers, the *red* can of beans. Ask her to point to a cereal box with an O in its name. Say "Let's find the *fuzzy* fruit or the *longest* salami."

WORD HUNTS A shopping expedition is an excellent way to practice new reading skills. Most food labels are in large capital letters. "Find me the cereal that has the word *natural* in its name." You might bring a pad and write the word *natural* on a sheet of paper and then set your child searching in the aisle where you are.

GROCERY BINGO Before you shop, make out a list of items likely to be found where you're going, such as a spatula, whipped cream, melon, and pepper. Give it to your child, saying, "Show me each time you find one of these." She can then check off that item. If your child can't read, cut out pictures of foods from magazines or newspapers and paste them on 3 x 5 cards. Again, each gets a check mark when found.

Or you can place the ingredients you'll need for a particular dish on a separate grocery list and have your child point them out to you as she locates them.

FIND THE BIGGEST AND SMALLEST Ask your child to find the biggest box of cereal. Is it the heaviest? Read the weight statement. Find the smallest bar of soap. Now check how many ounces it contains.

SPECIAL STOPS Preschoolers love familiar routines and will delight in making certain stops at the market. Make a point of visiting the funny Jell-O salads, the trout tank, the birthday cakes at the bakery counter, and so on.

WEIGHING IN Make a game of weighing fruits and vegetables. First let your child estimate the weight. For instance, say you've filled a plastic bag with grapes, which cost fifty-nine cents a pound. Say, "Are these over or under a pound? What do you think?" "I bet they're a pound and a half," says one child. If you have more than one child along, each can take a guess. Then weigh the grapes so your kids can see the answer on the scale. Let them guess how many grapes they have to take out to make the rest equal a pound. If you get two pounds, what will it cost?

You needn't do this for every purchase, but if you do it a couple of times per shopping excursion, your kids will be learning to estimate and multiply. You can also advise them to note whether the scale at the checkout counter registers the same weight as the scale at the produce counter. Once you've paid, they can then check your sales slip to see how it reflects *their* transaction.

IN ROUND NUMBERS If your child is over nine, teach him how to round off numbers. Then as you walk around the market, ask him to round off your purchases to the nearest five cents, nearest half dollar, or the nearest dollar. Let's say a cereal costs $3.29 a box. That can be rounded up to $3.30, or up to $3.50, or down to $3.00.

BE CALCULATING Many children enjoy making the rounds of the supermarket with a calculator in hand. As you pick up an item and put it in the basket, announce its price. Your child then enters this into the calculator. You can ask for a subtotal as you approach your spending limit or the end of your list.

BEEP-BEEP! An older child, say nine or so, may enjoy taking charge of the grocery cart. Let him know that his job is to have the cart in the right spot when you need to put something into it. Between times, he can be permitted to practice driving it in your vicinity, as long as he's always careful not to interfere with other "drivers." Avoid crowded shopping times the first few times you turn over the driving to your child.

LET THE CONSUMER BEWARE Use shopping time to turn your child into a wise consumer. Point out the kinds of tricks and gimmicks companies use to get shoppers to buy their products. Then suggest that your child point them out. Notice bold graphics, lines that shout, "Big, new, improved!," long lists of artificial ingredients in impossibly tiny print (find the tiniest print), blurbs for "no cholesterol" in products that have never contained cholesterol, bulky packaging for a tiny amount of product, and foods that have very high amounts of sodium added.

SNACK TIME Kids, especially preschoolers, enjoy shopping more when they can munch their way through the store. Decide ahead of time on an appropriate snack, and head for that department first. For example, a bagel from the bakery makes good hand food.

A BUNCH OF STUFF While you shop with your child, see how many terms for quantities you see—a bunch of grapes, a head of lettuce, a quart of milk, a pint of ice cream. Point out that a quart of milk is always the same size, while a head of lettuce isn't. Make a game of inventing terms for foods that don't have any, such as a herd of pumpkins, a nest of napkins, and so on.

JUNIOR PSYCHOLOGIST When your child is old enough, perhaps nine or so, introduce the idea of purposive people-watching. For this activity, it helps to shop when there are plenty of other shoppers around, particularly parents with children (which is probably when you shop anyway). Explain to your child that he is to be on the lookout for examples of human behavior. He can either point these out to you on the spot, if that isn't too distracting to you, or he can jot his findings in a small notebook to report to you on the way home. Point out to your child that it's not polite to talk about other people in front of them.

Here are some types of behavior he may find: a parent speaking harshly under her breath at a child; a child having a tantrum; a child begging for candy or a sugared cereal; a man and woman who seem to be shopping together for a special meal; someone who is buying small portions of many foods, probably because he lives alone; the family with a large number of kids in tow; parents who speak to their young child as though he were an adult; siblings fighting; and so on.

LOAD 'EM UP AND MOVE 'EM OUT Preschoolers love to help load the groceries from the cart onto the conveyer belt. Older children can take over that job completely, freeing you to sort through your coupons or begin writing your check. Make a point of having one bag packed lightly enough so that your preschooler can carry it outside, and later into the house. A child who can easily reach the kitchen counter is old enough to be in charge of emptying the grocery bags onto the counter while you put everything away.

IT'S IN THE BAG On a day when there are no frozen foods on your grocery list, add as the last item, "Trip to the park." Then, while you're at the market, your child can have the job of filling a bag with peanuts for feeding the pigeons later.

TEACHING THE GAME OF LIFE

Everyone knows about the first three Rs. Yet without the fourth *R*—reality—your children will have a hard time getting along in life. You can easily enrich their education by sharing certain vital life skills with them. This is another way to turn work into play.

Some of the simplest skills, which one person takes for granted, can be exciting challenges for another. Children delight in the sense of independence that comes from mastering a once-mysterious task.

Start by thinking about the everyday skills used in running a household. Hold a family conference to decide which skills will be tackled first. Some skills may even tie in with your child's schoolwork.

Whoever knows how to do something can teach it to someone else; this includes an older sibling teaching a younger one. Many children really enjoy "playing school." Learning life skills can be like "playing trade school."

To help you compile your own family's list of life skills, here are some suggestions:

☼ Learn how to cook simple but nutritious meals. Even cracking and scrambling an egg requires a certain know-how.

☼ Learn how to operate a washer and dryer and do general housecleaning. Even the youngest child can dust.

☼ Learn how to plan and use a budget, and how to keep records. Open the family books and explain why you record certain things and why you keep receipts. Show how to write a check and read a monthly bank statement. Help your child set up a simple budget to use his allowance.

☼ Learn how to do simple repairs, such as installing a faucet washer, changing a lightbulb, or stopping a toilet from running. Teach the location of main shutdown switches for water and gas.

☼ Learn how to pack a suitcase. Practice with a couple of drawers of clothing when no one's in a hurry.

☀ Learn what to do in case of fire or earthquake, and how to use the phone in an emergency. You can see whether your children have learned these lessons by putting them in charge of periodic family drills.

☀ Learn basic first aid, including the Heimlich maneuver for aiding a choking victim. Consider taking a first aid course all together, and one in CPR with your older children.

☀ Learn how to sew on buttons and make hems. These two tailoring tasks will come in handy time and again.

☀ Learn how to read a map, a catalog, a phone book, and a utility bill. Next time you take a family trip, assign your child navigation duties.

CHAPTER 4

··

CELEBRATING YOU, ME, AND US

Does someone in your family excel in an activity that requires precision, from stacking blocks to baking the perfect triple-decker cake? Does someone tell great jokes? Can someone fix almost anything that breaks? Does someone always have an empathetic ear? Each member of your family has unique abilities and gifts.

Sometimes we all forget to tell family members just how much we appreciate their talents and skills. However, even in the middle of our busy lives, every day can offer an opportunity for celebration and love. Browse through these original ways to honor all kinds of achievements, and pick a few for your own family.

You can also celebrate the specialness of your family as a whole by choosing some ways to record its one-of-a-kind history as it develops over the years.

STAR OF THE DAY

A simple ritual marking achievements great and small can become one of the most significant parts of your family life. Here are some traditions that other families have started for their honorees.

HONORARY FOODS When someone in the family earns any kind of honor, rename one of that evening's dinner foods in tribute. If your daughter does well in that day's handball championship at recess, announce at dinner, "This is Shelley's Spaghetti, to honor Shelley's handball skill." When Dad manages to clean up the entire garden in a single day, serve "Benito's Burritos." Make "Rod's Roast" to celebrate Rod's getting a poem in his school newspaper.

RED PLATE SPECIAL One family keeps a bright red plate in the cupboard. Whenever there's something to celebrate, the honoree gets to eat off the red plate. For instance, the red plate comes out when it's someone's birthday, or if a child has completed kindergarten, or if a parent has landed a business contract, or if a child has finally learned to play a long-practiced song on the piano. An effort is made to recognize even the tiniest accomplishments so that everyone has a chance to use the red plate.

GIVE OUT STAR AWARDS Show your child that it doesn't require a special occasion for you to regard him as special. Turn blank, colored, 4 x 6-inch cards into Star Awards by writing something like this on them: "Johnny Gomez is hereby awarded this Star Award for…" (changing his baby brother's diaper without being asked while Mom was getting ready for work in the morning, singing such a lovely song during car pool, learning how to express his upset feelings without hurting other people's feelings, and so on). Use colored markers to make the Star Awards more festive. Your child will surely treasure his collection of awards for a long time to come.

SHOW THE WORLD A family with three daughters allowed each one to wear a treasured family heirloom necklace to school on a day following an unusual achievement or honor. The older girl got to wear the necklace when she completed a term paper that had taken her two months to write. The youngest daughter had her turn when she donated her entire month's allowance to her school's holiday fund drive without being asked. Rather than compete for the honor, the girls learned to cooperate with each other in deciding whose turn it was to wear the necklace. Your family might like to purchase a necklace or pin that is worn by a child only on star days.

HEAD OF THE TABLE In most families, everyone sits at the same place at the dinner table night after night. For a change, designate one chair as "head of the table," and seat the star of the day there.

RECIPE FOR FUN: STAR DESSERT

Start a tradition of marking a special accomplishment with a star-shaped dessert—like a tart. Another possibility is star-shaped sugar cookies.

STAR TART
Yield: 6 servings

The combination of a no-cook filling and a crust that requires no rolling makes this tart very easy to make. Choose whatever fruit your star likes best. For a particularly stunning presentation, arrange overlapping slices of fruit or berries in a large star pattern in the center of the tart. Cover the rest of the tart filling with fruit of a contrasting color. Or arrange overlapping slices of star fruit (carambola) over the tart in concentric circles. Whichever pattern you choose, don't allow any of the filling to show.

Crust

1 cup all-purpose unbleached flour
1 tablespoon sugar
Pinch salt
5 tablespoons butter
1 egg yolk
1 to 2 tablespoons water (optional)

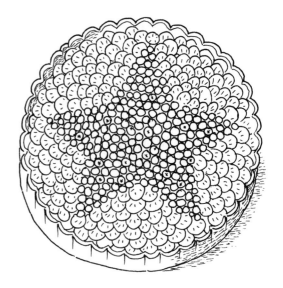

Cream Cheese Filling

4 ounces cream cheese, at room temperature
1 teaspoon grated lemon zest
1 tablespoon fresh lemon juice
4 tablespoons powdered sugar

Fruit Topping

⅓ cup currant or apple jelly
2 to 3 cups berries, sliced fresh or canned peaches or pears, sliced apples, bananas,
  nectarines, oranges, star fruit, or kiwifruit—or any combination of these
1 to 2 tablespoons lemon juice (optional)

1. Preheat the oven to 400°.
2. To make the crust, combine the flour, sugar, and salt in a food processor fitted with a steel blade. Cut the butter in slices, add it to the processor, and pulse until the mixture is crumbly. With the motor running, add the egg yolk and process until the dough is well mixed. You should be able to gather the dough into a ball. If it is too dry, add up to 2 tablespoons of water, 1 tablespoon at a time.
3. Pat the dough into a 9-inch or 10-inch tart pan. Make the top edge of the crust level with the rim of the pan. Bake for 10 minutes. Reduce the heat to 350° and prick the crust with a fork to deflate any bubbles that have formed. Bake for another 15 minutes until the crust is golden brown. Set aside to cool.
4. To make the filling, combine the cream cheese, lemon zest, lemon juice, and powdered sugar in a food processor fitted with a steel blade. Process until well mixed.

5. Heat the jelly over low heat in a heavy saucepan or in the microwave for 1 to 1¼ minutes. Brush the tart crust with the jelly to seal it. Spoon the cream cheese topping into the shell and smooth the top.

6. Thinly slice the fruit, leaving berries whole or slicing them in half. Toss apples, pears, peaches, or bananas with a little lemon juice to prevent browning. Arrange the fruit in a star pattern over the filling, overlapping each slice, if you are using sliced fruit. Arrange a fruit of contrasting color to surround the star and completely cover the filling. Or arrange overlapping concentric circles of sliced star fruit to completely cover the filling.

7. Brush the fruit with the remaining melted jelly. Refrigerate the tart for at least 30 minutes before serving. The tart should be served the day it is made. Keep refrigerated.

SELF-ESTEEM BUILDERS

A person with high self-esteem feels good about who she is. Armed with a healthy sense of herself, she faces the world with confidence in her abilities. She sets high goals for herself and believes she can achieve them. The early years are the time when our self-image is formed; it is important for you to help your child build this foundation before she faces the pressures of early adolescence.

As important as building self-esteem is, it can also be a lot of fun. Here are some enjoyable suggestions that you can use to help your child—and the parents of the family, too—feel good about themselves.

PERSONALITY-PLUS POSTER Hang a current photo of your child on a piece of poster board in his room, leaving space around the photo for handwritten comments. In this space, list everything you can think of that you like about your child, including his skills, attributes, and positive qualities. "Johnny tells funny jokes, puts his stuff away, is gentle with cats, cares enough to recycle," and so on. Add to the list whenever you think of something else. If your child helps you think of some of his good points that you overlooked, include those, too.

"I CAN" BOOK Every day, your child learns new skills, often without realizing it. Bring his maturing abilities to his attention by suggesting that he make a book about himself. On each page, he can write and illustrate something he is now able to do that he couldn't do when he was one year younger. His drawings might show such recent accomplishments as "I can ride a bike," "I can reach the sink without a chair," and "I can cook an egg."

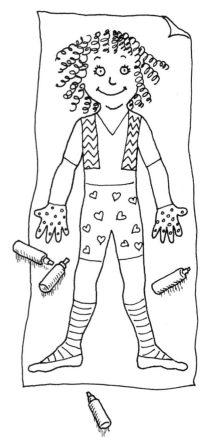

MAKE A LIFE-SIZE BODY DRAWING Buy a roll of blank newsprint (great for many crafts projects) at a stationery store, or tape together sheets of paper until you have a single sheet large enough for your child to lie down on. Trace around your child's body with a colored marker. Now have her complete the drawing any way she wants to, drawing in her face, hair, and clothing, perhaps using the colors she is wearing at the time. An older child may prefer to fill in the large blank outline with words and pictures, either written and drawn, or cut from magazines. She can use the words and pictures to answer the question, Who am I?

"ALL ABOUT MY SISTER" BOOK Children can help others build self-esteem, too. For a wonderfully personal birthday or holiday gift, a child can write a simple book about a sibling or parent. On each page, your child writes or dictates a few descriptive words, then adds a drawing. Here are some ideas for the pages:

☀ What my sister likes to eat.

☀ What my sister does best.

☀ My sister in a silly hat.

☀ A game I like to play with my sister.

☀ A wish for my sister.

DESCRIBE YOURSELF FAIRLY Ask your child to make a list of as many of her qualities as she can—without using judging words. She should include words or phrases that describe her skills, physical appearance, and behavior. Explain that words like *smart, unattractive,* and *clumsy* are judgmental words, but expressions like "gets As in math, has long hair, and knows how to balance on one foot" are nonjudgmental. When she runs out of ideas, you might want to suggest some of your own. Did she think of *straight-toed, animal lover, clarinet player?*

SHOW-AND-TELL AT HOME If your child delights in bringing favorite items to school for show-and-tell, consider instituting a weekly show-and-tell at home. It's a perfect opportunity for your child to show off the latest additions to a collection or a recent craft project. You need only a few minutes per child, perhaps after dinner on a weeknight. Give your full attention to each presenter during that time, expressing interest in what is being shown. Ask questions and make simple comments. ("That leaf is so much larger than the ones you added to your collection last week. Where did you find it?") Of course, a young child isn't going to wait for a special time to share his finds with you, but show-and-tell is when he is guaranteed the stage and the whole family's undivided attention.

CHALLENGE WORD With your older school-age child, decide on a personal quality he wants to cultivate. Write that word on a piece of paper and keep it in view. Talk about instances in which that quality shows up in your child's life. For instance, say you've agreed to focus on courage. Every time you notice your child showing even the slightest bit of bravery or courage, whether in the dentist's office or facing a difficult school assignment or in asking for something when you know it was hard for him to do so, acknowledge this to him.

FRAME IT If you're like most parents, you happily hang your child's artwork on the refrigerator or his bedroom wall. Once in a while, choose a piece you especially like, buy a real frame for it, and hang it in the permanent family art gallery. In one family, an uncle so loved a collage he had been given as a Christmas present that he had it professionally framed in a shadow box. It looked truly impressive.

A CHILD'S MILESTONES

Like all parents, you've no doubt found yourself saying, "They grow up so fast!" Here are some ways to mark and record some of your child's passages.

DRAW A LIFE LINE A life line celebrates key events and changes that led to where you are today. Before your child draws his own life line, he is bound to enjoy seeing you draw yours. Use a large sheet of paper and colored markers. You can start anywhere, using straight lines, circles, even an abstract design. Indicate events of import, such as when you were born, started school, moved, met your spouse, adopted your child, started a business, and so on. Include as much or as little personal material as you like.

Now it's your child's turn. Even a kindergartener has some history to record. Often a child will focus on major landmarks, such as when he lost his first tooth, learned to ride a bike, started school, got his dog. You might be surprised by the more minor events your child considers worthy of inclusion, too, such as the day he lost a favorite toy at nursery school.

MAKE A "NEVER-TOO-LATE BABY BOOK" Many children's baby books are hurriedly put together, with only the major landmarks of the first few years noted. The baby books of all children after the first, in fact, are usually not very detailed, because parents are so short of time. But it's never too late to catch up on those fading memories. Grab a few sheets of paper (or a tape recorder) and record memories like the following:

◎ When you were a baby, your first mobile was made of …

◎ You slept in …

◎ The way we quieted you when you cried was to …

◎ Your first book was …

◎ You used to cry whenever …

◎ Your first smile happened when …

※ The first store I took you to was ... and you ...

※ The object you carried around all the time when you were a toddler was ...

CAPTURE TIME ON A TAPE With a cassette recorder, compile a memory tape that captures your child's life at any given moment. Think of it as a time capsule: Once you've recorded the tape, listen to it, then put it away and wait a year to listen to it again with your child.

On the tape, have your child sing a song (sing along with her if she's shy about singing alone), talk about what she likes to do each day, what she did and ate today, what she learned in school this week, and what she wants to learn to do in the coming year. You might read today's newspaper headlines also. You can either "interview" one child at a time or have one child carry on a conversation with another—whichever feels most comfortable for you and your children.

You might want to start a tradition of adding to the tape each year, perhaps on the child's birthday. If you can, start at the beginning, with coos, cries, and first words.

WATCH ME GROW Make an imprint of your child's hand- and footprints on his birthday date each month (for example, if he was born May 18, take his prints on the 18th of every month). Simply press his hand and then his foot into a plate of washable tempera paint, and press them against a piece of notebook paper. Date each sheet, and add it to a loose-leaf binder for a record of your child's growth. Consider adding a few notes related to that month's activities on each sheet, such as "This month Jamal learned to tie his shoelaces."

FIRST DAY OF SCHOOL The first day of school each year is such a special event in a child's life that it deserves to be marked by a family ritual. Have a special meal or a restaurant celebration that evening. Record the event with photos, too. One possibility is to photograph your child on her first day of school in the same surroundings every year, such as in front of the refrigerator or the sink or against the front door. That way, her growth will be obvious when the photos are compared.

A NOTE FROM THE TOOTH FAIRY When your child loses her baby teeth, you probably exchange each one, which she carefully places under her pillow, for a bit of change. Some parents like to accompany the money with a little note signed by the "Tooth Fairy." By the time she's reached the age of nine, your child will have figured out that the Tooth Fairy is a pleasant figment of the imagination, but there's no need to stop playing the game cold turkey. Just make the notes more and more sophisticated.

For instance, your child might leave a note with her tooth saying, "Sorry this one took so long. It hurt a lot. Give me extra loot." The Tooth Fairy, a.k.a. parent, can then leave some change with a note, perhaps in an altered handwriting, saying, "Thanks for the tooth. Too bad it hurt. You're a brave girl. Here's some money to buy something to remind you how brave you were."

RECORDING FAMILY HISTORY

Keeping records of your family's history is a wonderful way to celebrate your life together. From time to time, you can look back and see how far you've come, which will bring back pleasant memories. And the permanent record you create will be valued by your children and their children as the years pass.

KEEP A FAMILY JOURNAL Your child can decorate a large loose-leaf binder that becomes Our Family Journal, an ongoing record of your family's life. Keep it handy so that anyone in the family can add anything to it at any time. Besides drawings, clippings, and handwritten bits of news about the day ahead or behind, welcome the expression of emotions.

FAMILY BIOGRAPHY Siblings, or a parent and child, can interview each other and put the results into a book. Each person gets a section, or "chapter," in a blank book. Have each person ask the other about the following topics, and then write and illustrate the answers in that person's chapter: his favorite hobby; his favorite school subject; a day he remembers with pleasure; a mistake he made; something he'd like to do or make or buy, a wish he has.

SCHOOL DAYS, SCHOOL DAYS Ask your school-age child to make up a list of questions he might want to ask you about your own school days. You'll find that as you answer these questions, more will come to your child, making it an enriching conversation. Your child can start with the following memory-joggers: What's the earliest school memory you have? What were your teachers' names? How did you get to school? What did you do at recess? What were your most and least favorite subjects? Did you ever get in trouble for talking in class?

FAMILY FICTION AND NONFICTION Gather a batch of family photographs, including snapshots of your child. Ask your child to choose one or more of the photos and compose a story about the people in them. She can either write the story down herself or tell it to you while you write it down. It's fun to see what events related to family life your child either remembers or imagines. Put the stories and photos in an ongoing family storybook.

SHARE THE FAMILY MEMORY PARTY Invite every relative who lives nearby for a special party to share memories. Include long time family friends, too. Ask each person to bring old photos, letters, or handicrafts to talk about with you and your children. Tape each person's presentation of their memories and souvenirs.

Consider asking each guest to bring a one-page essay about such events as the worst trouble he got into as a child or his first job. Your child can compile these essays in a loose-leaf notebook, later asking other guests to add to the book at subsequent family gatherings.

Before the party, your child can begin drawing a family tree. Start with a simple pencil sketch, to be gone over later in ink or colored markers, on a large sheet of paper. Your child, or children, will be at the bottom center of the tree, with branches for parents, grandparents, and all other relatives. Your child can ask the older family members at the party for their help in filling in the family genealogy. Decide on a way to indicate second marriages and half brothers and half sisters, such as lines of another color.

Talk to your child about the ways in which names are often passed along from generation to generation. Where did your child's first and middle names come from?

DESIGN A FAMILY FLAG First, to get a better idea of what kinds of symbols are contained on flags, you might want to gather a selection of pictures of flags of other countries. Or obtain an American flag (or a picture of one), and briefly tell your child what the stars and stripes stand for (the states and the original colonies).

Now discuss what your family flag should express about your family. You might decide to choose symbols to represent how many members your family has, some special event in your family history, or a shared enthusiasm.

You can make the flag itself out of cloth, such as a cut-open pillowcase, some flannel, or a piece of an old sheet. Draw symbols with fabric markers or paints, and staple or sew the flag around a wooden dowel purchased at a hardware store. Or you might decide to make a triangular family pennant instead. For a quickie project, cut the flag out of a large sheet of stiff paper, draw the designs with colored markers, and attach the flag to a dowel or paper towel tube.

Display your family flag at all special occasions, such as holidays, family birthdays and anniversaries, and days when someone graduates or starts a new school term or job. Also, be sure to show it off during children's parties. Just as national flags sometimes undergo changes, your family's flag can be altered with the addition of a new family member, a move to a new city, or whenever the urge hits.

SIGN THE GUEST BOOK Buy a large blank book and place a label on it with the title "Guest Book." Ask everyone who comes into your home to sign and write something in the guest book, from your children's pals to family relatives to the Girl Scout troop. Years from now, you'll laugh together at the happy memories these inscriptions will inspire.

PLAY FAMILY TRIVIA Make an ongoing project out of compiling the Goldberg Family Book of Trivia. In a blank book, inscribe two or three questions and answers on each page concerning the tiny facts and details that make your family unique. For example: How did Mom and Dad meet? What year did you move into your current home? What color were the curtains in the living room before you bought new ones? How much orange juice does your family drink each week? What is the square footage of your living room? How many chairs are there in the house? When is the cat's birthday? What is Mom's favorite number? Stepdad's favorite food? The kids' favorite school subjects? Where did Mom's middle name come from?

Once you have collected a sufficient number of trivia items—at least several dozen—play a simple, noncompetitive game with them. Take turns holding the book and asking each other the questions. Then read the correct answer aloud.

SPORTS RECORDS, FAMILY STYLE The Olympics may be out of reach for most of us, but everyone can break his or her *own* record. The trick is for you and your child to think up some offbeat "sports" categories. Does your child love yo-yoing? See how long he can keep that yo-yo going, and write it down. Then he can try again later. Other fun arenas for personal sports records can be building the most elaborate domino structure or the highest pile of blocks, or the longest time spent jumping rope. Two family members can try to beat their own best record for the length of time playing catch together successfully. Record the current records in a little notebook, or display them on a poster so everyone can see the levels they have to beat.

KEEP A TREASURE BOX Go through the souvenirs and mementos of your own childhood, and gather the most interesting ones in a Treasure Box. Your kids will delight in the chance to poke through your treasures once in a while, especially if you tell them the story behind each item. One woman's Treasure Box contained a plastic pig that had melted when her house burned down, some tiny Cracker Jack toys, a little puzzle she had received as a child, and a date book from the year she started junior high.

MAP YOUR FAMILY'S JOURNEY Even if your family rarely ventures outside the town in which you live, your child will enjoy mapping the places you've visited. Purchase and hang up a detailed map of your entire area. Now, whenever you go on an outing to a park, zoo, museum, or other attraction, have your child highlight the place with a yellow marker. If you hang the map on a bulletin board or cork backing, an older child can use colored pins to mark the places visited. If you're a family that travels a lot, mark a map of the state, the country, or the world each time you take a trip.

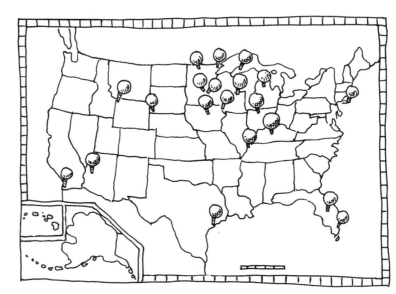

MAKE A FAMILY MUSEUM This family project doesn't have to be elaborate. Simply set aside a tabletop or shelf as your museum and choose a theme—Fun Times, for example. Just as a museum does, you can rotate your exhibits. What will you collect and assemble? Shells picked up on family outings to the beach? Bookmarks, postcards? How about a collection of ink-pad fingerprints (add the impression of everyone who visits)? Other collections that make good family museum exhibits include menus from restaurant adventures (ask before taking), receipts from all kinds of purchases, corks, and keys. Decide how you will collect, organize, and label the exhibits, perhaps appointing one child as curator to keep things in order and to give tours. Nearby, keep a comment book in which visitors can write.

COMPILE A FAMILY DICTIONARY Each family has its own words, expressions, and nicknames that are rarely, if ever, heard in other people's families. Some start with a toddler's first attempts to talk and become part of the family lingo. Start a family dictionary that anyone can add to whenever they notice a special word or phrase. You can begin by listing all the nicknames family members call each other, from "Kev" to "Pookie" to "Honeybunch." Food is another good category—for example, in one family, tortellini are "belly buttons." Other categories could be the body and its functions, games, toys, pets, security blankets and objects, cars and bikes, and neighbors and friends.

EDIT A FAMILY NEWSPAPER When your kids are at loose ends one weekend, suggest they write, edit, and print a one-shot family newspaper. Either share all duties between you and your child, or, if you have more than one child, decide who will write, who will edit, and who will handle the graphics and design of the newspaper. Your newspaper can be a very simple, one-page edition containing the family's news of the week, an interview with a family member, and the editor's favorite joke. Whether handwritten, typed and cut-and-pasted to fit, or desktop-published by computer, such a project not only builds family togetherness but is also educational. And your relatives will love receiving a copy!

Consider including some of the following features in your first issue: an article listing a recent achievement of each family member; an essay about the antics of the family pet; an article about your last or next family vacation; a survey of family members' opinions about a social issue (Should there be more rest rooms at shopping malls? Should schools have free field trips?); a poetry section; a book review; and a classified section in which each family member offers to trade services or used items with other members ("Will make banana split in exchange for washing dishes." "Need skates. Will wash cars in exchange").

CAPTURE TIME IN A BOTTLE An absorbing family project is to make and put away a time capsule containing bits and pieces of your family's everyday life. Several years from now, you and your kids will be amazed and delighted to examine the items you chose to place in the capsule.

Begin with a clean, air tight container, such as a coffee can with a lid or a large plastic food container. The fun begins when you get together with your kids to

83

decide what goes into the capsule. Some suggestions: a movie ticket stub, a clean fast-food wrapper, a homework paper, a receipt from a toy store, a photo of the whole family taken on the day you make up the capsule, a bottle cap, a T-shirt, a pack of bubble gum, a note from a pal, a hair barrette, and so on. To hide your capsule, choose a safe place where it won't be disturbed for as long as you decide, whether that's a year or ten years. Consider burying it in the backyard and putting up a marker so you won't forget where you put it, placing it in a trunk or box, or hiding it in the corner of a basement, attic, or storage closet.

PART TWO

FUN INSIDE AND OUT

CHAPTER 5

···

QUIET PLAY AND SPIRITED GAMES FOR INDOORS

Playing games when you're at home together is a great way for a family to relax and have fun while relieving the tensions of everyday life. In this chapter are both classics you may recall from your own childhood and lots of new inventions. The ideas range from instant activities like a silly sock-pulling game to more elaborate undertakings, such as helping your kids put on a magic show.

Like many parents, you may have wondered if your children are learning any-thing when they're "just playing," but a child's play *is* work. When quiet or spirited play is going on, so is learning. While playing games, a child learns to cooperate, to concentrate on a goal, to use imagination, and to value a sense of humor. In addition, some games teach new words, increase spatial knowledge, or enhance hand-eye coordination. And even when the goal of a particular activity is fun pure and simple, nothing builds family bonds like sharing good times.

If you have more than one child, you know that sibling rivalry is normal. So, of course, when siblings play games together, some conflict is to be expected. Don't pressure an older child to include the younger one in his play all the time; he's more likely to do so when the pressure is off. Guide your children into activities that reward playfulness and originality, so that the younger and less experienced child has a chance to shine, too. This also means that, when you play games together as a whole family, one child is less likely to be pitted directly against another.

Be creative and flexible when introducing activities to children of different ages and abilities. If a child consistently has trouble losing, until she's a bit older guide her toward cooperative games in which there's no winner. Many families prefer noncompetitive games, in any case. You can turn almost any game into a cooperative one by changing the rules. Some of the following games and activities include suggestions for lessening the competition traditionally associated with them.

Teach your children about taking turns and accepting the rules gracefully. Intersperse spirited play with quiet play, so that your young child doesn't become overstimulated. And never pursue a particular game once your child has lost interest. That would take the fun out of it.

Now let's play!

HUNT AND SEARCH GAMES

ABC SEARCH The object is to find and point to items that begin with each letter of the alphabet in order. You may want to limit your hunt to one room of the house. For instance, if you choose the kitchen, you or your child might find the following: aluminum foil, bread, carrots, a dent on a lid cover, and so on. If your child is old enough to find one round of the game too easy, play for two or more rounds of the alphabet, adding the rule that you can't name the same item twice.

TREASURE HUNT Young children love to hunt for "treasure." A treasure hunt can be a very simple, spontaneous activity for which you don't need to prepare a treasure list in advance. If your child is a preschooler, say, "Bring me something blue." When she succeeds in showing you an item that is indeed blue, ask her to find, one at a time, items such as the following: something smooth, a thing that makes noise, a fuzzy thing, a tiny thing, something you can put things on, a writing tool, something you can learn from, a thing you like.

Then ask your child to try to stump you by providing *you* with a series of items to locate.

In a more advanced form of treasure hunt, set the kids to looking for the biggest, smallest, lightest, or longest of a variety of items. If you've asked for the thickest book in the house, the searchers will have to take the time to pull down all the books that appear to come close to meeting that requirement, in order to determine which is actually the thickest. The same goes for the longest measuring tool in the house, the lightest hat (it helps to have both a bathroom scale and a postal scale), the largest piece of paper, and the smallest kitchen utensil.

You can make the searches even more challenging by limiting them to a particular category, such as "red things." Then you can ask your child to locate the largest red item of clothing in the house, the heaviest red book, or the smallest red food.

LETTER HUNT This hunt is ideal for children who are just learning to read. Draw and cut out of cardboard a series of letters about two inches high—perhaps those that spell your child's name. Now have your child wait elsewhere while you hide all the letters around the room. Your child's task is to search out the letters and put them together in the proper order. If she's having trouble finding a hidden letter, say "warmer" and "colder" as she gets closer to, or farther from, a letter.

ART MATERIALS HUNT This is a scavenger hunt with an artistic purpose. Together with your child, make a list of odds and ends commonly found around the house and yard, such as a leaf, feather, piece of cardboard, rubber band, plastic twist tie, flower petal, piece of string, and so on. Once your child has succeeded in finding each of the items, she can make a collage or sculpture that combines them all.

89

FLASHLIGHT HUNT Children love exploring in the dark with a flashlight. Before announcing the start of this nighttime hunt, take a few minutes to hide a selection of items around the house, such as a dictionary, a shoe, a doll, and an apple. Tell your searchers what they're hunting for, turn out the lights, and let them loose.

WORD GAMES

PICTURE TWENTY QUESTIONS To simplify the well-known game of Twenty Questions so that even a preschooler can play, begin by cutting five pictures of objects out of a magazine. Now say, "I'm thinking of one of these pictures. Can you figure out which one?" Explain that she can ask you questions that you will answer with a yes or a no. For example, if you're thinking of the picture of a black kitten, your child may ask, "Is it big?" When you say no, that will eliminate the pictures of big things. With lots of practice, your preschooler will eventually be able to play the game in her imagination, without needing the pictures.

BEAT-THE-CLOCK WORD CATEGORIES See how many words in a single category your child can name in a specified time. Choose a category that will give your child plenty of opportunity to feel successful—for example, animals, foods, movies, or things found in a classroom. As your child gets better at thinking creatively within the bounds of categories, make the categories more difficult, such as vegetables or different ways of saying good-bye.

Preschoolers can be limited to half a minute, older kids to a minute or two, depending on how quick a thinker your child is. Either write down each word your child says, or simply make a mark on a piece of paper for each one. Add up the number of suitable responses when the time is up.

Your child may enjoy coming up with categories for you also. Or decide together on a category, and take turns giving responses until neither of you can think of another one. You might want to hold off saying the more obvious choices so your child can come up with those.

TELEGRAMS Players, who have to be old enough to read and write well, decide on a series of fifteen letters. Each player's object is to compose a "telegram" using the letters, in order, as the first letter of each successive word. For instance, using the letters B, L, M, S, T, O, W, P, the telegram might begin "Bring Louis the mighty stick tomorrow. Oliver will pay" and so on. Periods between sentences are allowed, as are *the* and *and.* If you want to choose a winner, it can be the first player to complete the telegram, or you can simply wait for everyone to finish and then admire each other's creativity.

HEADWORD One person writes any word, known as the "headword," on a piece of paper for the other player or players to see. Then, using only the letters in that word, all players try to list as many words on their own sheets of paper as they can. If the headword is *certainly,* for example, players might list any of the following words: certain, cat, in, at, lie, lay, tin, etc., eat, ate, and so on.

FILL-IN-THE-BLANK STORY Tell your child a story, leaving out words for things or actions. Her task is to act out the missing words. The stories can be either familiar ones ("Jack and Jill———up the hill") or made-up ones ("The littlest bulldozer looked at the big pile of dirt and just knew he could———it").

ASSOCIATIONS One player says a word and the next one says whatever word that one brought to mind. You can specify that the words have to be nouns ("picture words"). Go back and forth, or around the circle if you have more than two players, saying words as quickly as you can. No hesitation is allowed! For instance, if one player says "egg," the next may say "chicken," and the next "coop" or "rooster" or "feed." Keep the game going as long as you want to.

ADVERB MANIA Older kids who understand the concept of adverbs can play this one with you. The first player thinks of an adverb (a word that modifies a verb or an adjective), such as *sneakily* or *noisily.* Then the other player or players ask him to do something, such as eat, sleep, or scratch his head, in the manner of the word. The winner of the round is the one who guesses the adverb first. It's then her turn to be up. If no one guesses the adverb within a certain length of time, the first player reveals it, and someone else gets a turn.

MATCH THE PAIRS This is a word game for parents and older school-age kids who have a pretty good vocabulary. Start by agreeing on a category and the response you'll be aiming for. Take "animals and their babies," for example. One player offers the name for an adult animal, such as deer. The object is to recall the name for the matching baby animal—fawn, in this case. A baby horse is a colt; a baby dog is a puppy; a baby cat is a kitten. Another good category is "objects and their group" name, such as banana and bunch, or card and deck, or fish and school.

SPEAKER OF THE HOUSE This talking game for any number of players helps enhance the imagination, confidence, speaking skills, and quick wits of school-age children. One player acts as the timekeeper, using a stopwatch, a one-minute egg timer, or the second hand of a clock or watch. If two are playing, one makes up a topic title and the other has to speak on that topic for one minute. If more than two are playing, each player can come up with several topics and write them on separate slips of paper. Taking turns, players choose a slip and speak on that topic for a minute.

Topics can be serious or silly, from Why Earthquakes Happen to Current Fashions in Tennis Shoes. The only rules are that the speaker cannot repeat himself and cannot deviate from the topic. Players may challenge the speaker if they believe he has broken a rule.

PHONE BOOK DETECTIVES Spend a half hour with your child letting your fingers do the walking. To get you started, here are some ways to play with the white pages:

☀ Look up your own last name. How many others share your name?

☀ Find the most common names. Try Smith and Chan for starters. In Minnesota, there are pages of Johnsons and Olsons. What names are frequent in your area?

☀ Make up a funny-sounding name. See if you can find one like it in the phone book.

☀ Look for abbreviations used in the book, besides *St.* and *Ave.*

☀ Talk about the resources located in the front of the phone book and how to locate emergency numbers.

In the yellow pages:

- ☼ Notice how many business names begin with the letters A or AA. Why?
- ☼ Design a yellow page ad for an imaginary business, such as Allen Aardvark's Tutoring Service.
- ☼ Have your child hunt for some products or services that aren't listed under obvious heads (such as dishwashers under Appliances).

RECIPES FOR FUN: TIME FOR A SNACK BREAK!

These snacks are as much fun to make together as they are to eat together. For other snack ideas, see the Happy Hour ideas and recipes in chapter 2.

CRUNCHY CARROT BALLS
Yield: 15 carrot balls

There's no cooking involved with these healthy little nuggets, but there are plenty of jobs for little hands, especially pulsing the food processor on and off and rolling the carrot balls in the crunchy cereal coating.

3 carrots
3 ounces Neufchâtel or light cream cheese, at room temperature
¼ cup crunchy peanut butter
3 tablespoons crushed pineapple, well drained
½ cup raisins
⅛ teaspoon cinnamon
¾ cup Grape Nuts cereal

1. Finely chop the carrots in a food processor, pulsing the processor on and off. Do not overprocess. You want little bits of carrots, not carrot puree.
2. By hand, mix the carrots with the Neufchâtel, peanut butter, pineapple, raisins, and cinnamon.
3. Pour the Grape Nuts into a shallow bowl. Form the carrot mixture into balls the size of walnuts. Drop into the Grape Nuts and roll until well coated.
4. Chill for at least an hour before serving. Refrigerate leftovers in an airtight container for up to four days.

BIRD NESTS
Yield: 15 nests

A sweetened peanut butter glue binds these cereal "nests" together and makes a bed for jelly bean "eggs." This is a wonderful treat to make in late winter, when everyone despairs of ever seeing spring again. The nests make wonderful table decorations for a birthday party, too.

Because the peanut butter mixture gets extremely hot, an adult should be responsible for the cooking and pouring steps. Spatters will burn the skin and should be washed off with cold water immediately.

2 cups shredded Shredded Wheat cereal
    (break it up by hand)
1 cup Rice Krispies cereal
1 cup sweetened flaked coconut
⅓ cup light corn syrup
⅓ cup honey
⅔ cup peanut butter
2 teaspoons vanilla extract
Assorted jelly beans

1. Combine the cereals and coconut in a large mixing bowl.
2. Combine the corn syrup, honey, and peanut butter in a heavy-bottomed saucepan and bring to a boil, stirring constantly. Boil for 1 minute.

3. Carefully pour the hot peanut butter mixture into the cereal mixture. Add the vanilla. Mix well. Let cool so it doesn't burn at the touch.
4. Line two baking sheets with waxed paper. Using a ¼-cup measure, scoop the mixture onto the baking sheets. (If the mixture begins to stick in the measuring cup, lightly coat it with butter.) Shape the mixture into nests by making an indentation in the top with a thumb and gently patting the mixture to keep it in a round shape. The mixture will be fragile and loose, but it will come together as it sets.
5. Allow the nests to set for about 30 minutes. Place a few jelly bean "eggs" in each nest.

Eat at once or store in an airtight container.

SNICKSNACKS
Yield: 48 squares, 1 x 1 inch

This recipe has been passed around for a while—probably more from teenager to teenager than from mother to daughter. It definitely doesn't qualify as a "healthy" snack, but once in a while, it's fun to let the kids indulge. A grown-up should be responsible for the cooking and pouring of the brown sugar syrup, taking special care not to let it spatter on anyone, but the kids can handle the rest.

Stored in an airtight tin, these treats will keep for several weeks (if they last that long). They also make good gifts.

Approximately 6 tablespoons smooth peanut butter
Approximately 18 whole (4-part) graham crackers
¾ cup butter
¾ cup light brown sugar
12-ounce package semisweet chocolate chips
¾ cup chopped nuts

1. Lightly oil a baking sheet (with sides), or coat with nonstick cooking spray.
2. Spread peanut butter on each graham cracker and place the crackers on the baking sheet until the surface of the pan is covered.
3. In a heavy-bottomed saucepan, combine the butter and brown sugar and bring

95

to a boil, stirring until the sugar melts. Boil over medium low heat for 5 minutes; do not allow the syrup to scorch.

4. Pour the syrup over the crackers. Immediately sprinkle the chips on, spreading with a spatula to melt the chips into the syrup. Sprinkle the chopped nuts on top.

5. Refrigerate until firm. Then cut into small bars or squares. Store in an airtight container.

ACTIVE INDOOR GAMES

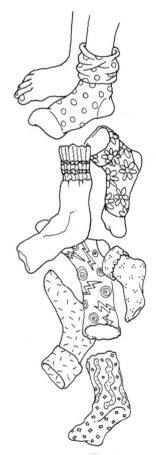

KNOCK MY SOCKS OFF Young children get a real kick out of this active game. Two players with a good sense of balance may be able to play safely on a bed, though a carpeted floor allows more freedom of movement. Wearing socks but no shoes, players crawl around on their hands and knees, trying to pull each other's socks off while preventing the other player or players from pulling *their* socks off. The object is to be the last player left with a sock on. Kicking is not allowed.

Toddlers who are just learning to put their socks *on* may also enjoy a reversal of the game: after everyone's socks are tugged off, they get to put someone else's socks on. You can make a game of this version too: players try to put socks on each other while preventing their own socks from being put on. The last player with a bare foot is the winner here.

SPOON HOCKEY Preschoolers love the simple game of pushing a small ball along the floor with a long-handled wooden kitchen spoon. Any number can play, so why don't you join your child? Use a foam or Ping-Pong ball to avoid marring furniture or walls. Once negotiating a long hallway has been mastered, move the race to the living room, where the challenge is to work around the natural obstacles presented by the furniture. The youngest children can simply learn to maneuver the spoon and ball, while older kids might like to make a race of it.

BALLOON TENNIS   Hang or tape a string across the room to serve as a tennis net. Using ordinary kitchen spoons, two people (or two teams) try to keep a balloon going back and forth over the net as long as possible without allowing the balloon to touch the ground.

GIANT SPIDERWEB   Get a coil of rope or string that is at least a hundred feet long. Together, tie the rope around the furniture to make a room-size "spiderweb."

SIMON SAYS   Get up and around with this "follow the leader" game. "Simon says ... touch your toes." "Simon says ... do one push-up." "Sit down." If your child sits down when you haven't said "Simon says" first, you can follow any rules you've chosen to set. For instance, if a follower accumulates three points doing things Simon didn't tell her to do, it's now her turn to be the leader.

TABLE HOCKEY   Here's a simple version of the popular game of table air hockey for all ages. To begin, make a fence of hardcover books all around a table, leaving a two-inch opening at each end for the hockey goals. The puck can be a wad of paper, a ball of aluminum foil, or a large button. Use popsicle sticks for hockey sticks. Players take turns shoving the puck with their sticks in an effort to get it through the goals at the ends of the table. If there are more than two players, form teams.

A variation is Blow Soccer. Set up the table the same way. Place a Ping-Pong ball in the center of the table. When someone gives the signal, each of the players blows through a drinking straw at the ball, trying to get it through the opposing goal while preventing the ball from going through their own goal. When a goal is scored, the ball is returned to the center of the table. If the ball is blown off the table, the opposing side returns it to the table near where it went off and gets a free blow.

MAKING MAGIC TOGETHER

To perform magic, your child's hands don't have to be quicker than anybody's eyes. Anyone can learn to use showmanship and patter—creative story lines—to entertain and amaze family and friends. Help your child experiment with some of these easy magic tricks.

98 **NOW YOU SEE IT, NOW YOU DON'T** Your child sits at a table across from her audience, her lap hidden from view. She announces, "I am going to make a coin disappear by rubbing it with the bottom of a saltshaker." Covering the shaker tightly with a napkin, she places the coin on the table. She holds the shaker at the base, rubs it over the coin, then moves the shaker toward her quickly, almost to the edge of the table. Meanwhile her other hand covers the coin. "Disappear!" she tells the coin. But the coin is still there. She pretends to be frustrated that the trick didn't work. The second time, she slides the shaker to the edge of the table, dropping it into her lap. She returns the napkin, still held in the shape of the shaker, away from the edge. After the coin doesn't disappear on the third try, she reveals that, instead, the *shaker* has disappeared.

Have her try this vanishing act with other objects. Can she do it with a spoon? A thimble?

GRAVITY STRIKES AGAIN This trick, recommended for beginners, is based on the laws of gravity. If you help your child set it up exactly right, it will always work. Props include a pie tin, three eggs (hard-boiled on your first try), three half-filled wide-topped drinking glasses, three toilet paper tubes, and a broom. Follow the picture to set everything up at the edge of a table. Perch the eggs on top of the tubes (don't wedge them in); place the tubes on the pie tin and *directly* over the glasses. Step on the broom bristles (which then act as a spring), pull the handle back toward you, and then let go. The handle will whomp the pie tin, sending it flying. The eggs should now be floating nicely in the water.

Younger kids can do this trick using only one egg and one glass. Those who are more advanced can try it with four of each. Will it work with long paper towel roll tubes? With toilet paper tubes cut in half? Next, try it with a lemon or a plum. What's the lightest object you can use and still have this trick work?

MIND READING To read minds, all you need is a deck of playing cards, a pencil, and a piece of paper. The magician writes, "You will choose the nine pile" on a piece of paper, then folds it quickly and lays it on the table so that no one can read it. Next, she puts three piles of cards face down on the table (arranged in advance), and asks someone to pick a pile. When the choice is made, the magician opens the paper, proving she knew in advance which pile was going to be chosen.

The trick is in the setup: The first pile has four nines. The second pile has three cards—a five, a three, and an ace, which add up to nine. The last pile consists of nine cards. Thus, each one is "the nine pile."

It works with other combinations of piles and digits too. Try it with only two piles, one containing four sevens (mixed in with other cards), the other containing seven cards. Say, "You will pick the seven pile."

100

1. **Plan it** Help your child choose her best tricks (three for a six-year-old, perhaps five for an eight-year-old). Consider a family show; each of you learns one or two tricks.

2. **Script it** Devise patter, little stories to throw spectators off the track. Your child can describe what she appears to be doing, or she can make up a comedy routine. If she likes, you can add some background music.

3. **Set the stage** Arrange a scarf-topped table in front of chairs or floor pillows. Assemble all props in a box within easy reach.

4. **Practice it** Have your child go over each trick until she performs the motions smoothly. Next, add the patter. A sibling can act as a magician's assistant. Discuss ways to distract the audience: turn her body sideways, point at something else, have her own eyes watching something else (the audience will look where she looks), make quick dramatic movements with one hand while the other one performs the trick quietly.

5. **Invite an audience** Design an invitation, such as: Abracadabra, ala-ka-ZOOM—please APPEAR for a magic show Sunday noon.

6. **Perform it** No matter what fib you say to the audience, say it loudly and with complete conviction, looking them straight in the eye. Act as surprised as your audience when the trick works. Don't forget to take a deep, dramatic bow.

TOSS GAMES

Tossing small objects into, onto, or at larger ones is always entertaining. In the following easy-to-set-up games, you toss pennies or buttons, if your kids are old enough (over three) not to eat them. For the youngest children, make or buy some small beanbags, or simply crumple some aluminum foil into a ball.

KITCHEN TOSS Rummage through the kitchen cabinets for a selection of pots, pans, and plastic storage containers. Write the numbers 2, 5, and 10 on small slips of paper or bits of masking tape, and put one in each receptacle. Now arrange the containers in a group on the floor.

Indicate a line on the floor about five feet from the containers, or closer for a younger child. The game is to toss pennies (or other small objects) into the containers, aiming for the highest score.

RING THE CHAIR Cut out the centers of several paper plates. Tape pennies under each for added weight. Now turn a chair upside down and toss the plate rings onto the chair legs.

BALLOON LANDING Blow up several small balloons. One player holds a large kitchen funnel, and the other tries to toss the balloon so that it lands in the funnel. This is a cooperative game in which the funnel-holder should move the funnel to help the balloon-tosser.

MINI-BASKETBALL Tape a cup, with the bottom cut out, to a wall. Toss marble-sized crumbled aluminum foil.

Or wrap some yarn around a tiny piece of cardboard, then toss that through half a lunchbag that you've taped to the back of a chair or a door.

PITCH AND SINK Fill a large plastic tub or the sink or bathtub about half full of water. Float a variety of light saucers in the water. Step back and toss pennies onto the saucers.

For another version, partially fill a sink or a large bowl with water. Float a single metal pie plate on the water. Provide players with pennies and have them guess how many it will take to sink the plate. Players take turns tossing the pennies until the pie plate sinks.

TARGET PRACTICE Write the numbers 1 through 10 on a large piece of cardboard and place it on the floor. Players begin with ten pennies each and toss them toward the numbers, aiming for the highest ones. After all of a player's ten pennies have been tossed, he adds up his score.

102

COVER IT In this traditional children's game, players take turns tossing coins against a wall. After the first player tosses his coin, he leaves it wherever it comes to rest on the ground. The next player then tosses his coin. If it comes to rest touching the previous player's coin, he picks up both coins. If it doesn't touch another coin, he leaves it, and play continues.

HOW DOES IT WORK?

Some children are always asking, "What's inside?" and "What makes it go?" and "How do they make that?" If you have the kind of child who removes a drawer from the kitchen cabinet to see how the rollers work, you can encourage your young scientist with activities like these.

TINKERING AROUND Collect broken household items and keep them in a box or drawer. Then let your child pry them apart to see what's inside. Include things like broken toys, windup clocks, flashlights, old telephones, transistor radios, a videotape, and an audio cassette tape. (To be safe, first cut off the cord and plug of anything electric.) A very young child will also delight in taking apart such nonmechanical items as an envelope, a flower, and a bell. An elementary-age child will probably need some real tools like screwdrivers and a wire cutter to take apart the more advanced stuff. Explain the safety rules carefully, and always supervise a young child when she's working with real tools.

INVENTOR'S TOOL KIT Shop in a hardware store for inexpensive versions of these materials: a hammer, some nails, a screwdriver set, string, scissors, a tape measure, a magnifying glass, magnets, tape, pipe cleaners, rubber bands, and whatever odd things might become part of an "invention." Ask the clerk for suggestions. Show your child how to hammer safely, and be prepared to supervise tool use.

WHAT DOES IT DO? Explore a cosmetics case with your preschooler. Can she figure out what each item is for and which ones you use the most? Open a toolbox. What might each item's purpose be? (Supervise this so she doesn't touch anything sharp.) Go through the kitchen gadgets, too.

GETTING AROUND WITH MAPS On large sheets of paper, help your child draw detailed maps of her room, the house, and the neighborhood. Suggest that she decide on symbols to represent trees, hydrants, water, power lines, and so on. Get your child a compass and show her how to find north to mark it on her maps. Show her a flat map of the world and compare it with a globe. Talk about scale and explain that an inch can represent a block, or a mile, or fifty miles.

OBSERVATION GAME Scientists and inventors have to be excellent observers, so this game is right up their alley. Repeated play will improve your child's concentration, observation, and memory skills.

Setup is simple: gather a variety of small common objects from around the house. The game will be easier if you stick to a theme, such as kitchen objects, or school-related materials, or baby items. Begin with four objects for a preschooler, and work up to a dozen for older children or adults. Place all the items on a tray and show them to your child. Let her look at them for a minute or so. Now cover the tray with a cloth. Have your child tell you or write down as many items as she can recall.

For a variation, take away one item while she closes her eyes. Can she tell you which one is gone?

SKYDIVE IN THE FAMILY ROOM Your child can find out firsthand how the air trapped under a parachute keeps gravity from pulling it down so quickly. Together, make a toy parachute from a square piece of notebook paper or lightweight cloth. Cut four pieces of string into equal one-foot lengths, and tape them to the corners of the paper or tie them to the corners of the cloth. Tie the other ends of the strings to an object such as a paper clip, cork, or a small toy. Or attach a tiny basket to hold a small doll.

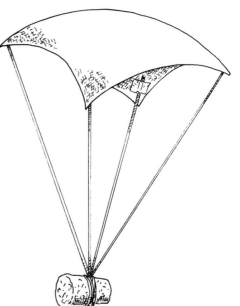

Your child stands on a sturdy chair, lifts his parachute as high as he can, and then drops it. He can also try dropping it from the side of a stairway.

What happens when you use six-inch strings or two-foot strings? Experiment with different objects tied to the bottom of the strings. What happens if you make a small hole in the top of the parachute? A big hole?

You and your child can make and fly this improved version of the traditional "dart" paper airplane, with some additional folds for better flight control.

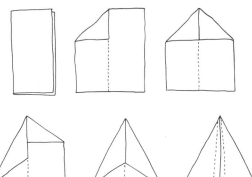

1. Fold an 8½ x 11 sheet of paper in half lengthwise.

2. Now open it and fold the top corners into the center.

105

3. Fold the *new* top corners until they meet in the center.

4. To make wings, first fold the left side of the page toward you, about an inch from the center (along the dotted lines in the illustration).

5. Repeat for the right wing and turn your plane over.

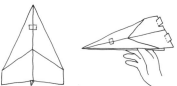

6. Adjust the wings so they are perpendicular or slightly tilted upward, and tape them together on the center crease, near the back of the plane.

7. Your plane should come to a sharp point in the front. Hold it at the back and toss it as far as you can.

Experiment with altering the plane. For instance, create flaps in the back of the wings by making four half-inch long cuts at the rear (see drawing). Your child can turn these upward to keep her plane from diving nose first to the ground. What happens when one flap is turned upward and the other down?

Try making a plane with different kinds of paper, including construction paper or tissue paper, or with a large or tiny piece of paper. What happens when your child adds a paper clip to the plane's nose? To its tail? Two clips?

Make two different planes and have a contest to see which one flies farthest, highest, and most accurately toward a target.

GAMES FOR THREE OR MORE

These activities are good for big families, birthday parties, play groups, and any time the gang is all here.

IT'S ONLY A RUMOR Gather three or more players (the more the better). Sit in a circle. One person starts by whispering a sentence slowly and clearly into his neighbor's ear. The listener then passes the sentence on to *his* neighbor. When the last person hears the sentence, he repeats it out loud. It's great fun to compare what the first person said to what the last person finally heard.

MOTHER GOOSE CHARADES This works best when an adult pairs with a child and acts out the charades in front of at least two other people of any age. Start by writing on 3 x 5-inch cards the names of common Mother Goose rhymes and well-known childhood songs, such as "Old Mother Hubbard," "Jack and Jill," "Old MacDonald Had a Farm," "The Old Woman Who Lived in a Shoe," "Mary Had a Little Lamb," and "Little Miss Muffet." Lay the cards face down. One team picks a card and spends a minute discussing how they will act it out. They then perform their card without talking. The audience tries to guess what rhyme they're acting.

STORY BY COMMITTEE Gather a small group (a family of three is fine). One person begins a story and stops whenever he wants to. The next person continues the story, leaving the plot in midair. Keep going around until everyone has had a few turns. Someone ends the story.

NONCOMPETITIVE MUSICAL CHAIRS You don't have to wait for a party to play this uproarious game. Start by forming a circle with a number of chairs that is one less than the number of children playing, for example, four chairs for five players. The joy of this version of the old favorite is that no one gets left out.

Start some music. While it plays, the children circle the room outside the circle of chairs. When the music stops, everyone sits down. Of course, since there aren't enough chairs, two children will have to sit on one chair. Now, for the next round, remove one chair. Keep playing until all the children are piled on top of each other on the single remaining chair.

CRAB TAG This is a fairly slow form of chase, just right for a small group of restless kids who have to be indoors on a rainy day. First they have to learn to walk like crabs by lying on their backs and using their hands and feet to lift their bodies off the ground. The first crab to be "It" chases the others. A tag occurs whenever the It-crab touches another child with any part of the body. The tagged crab then becomes the It-crab.

You can play a noncompetitive form of crab tag by having anyone who is tagged join the group of It-crabs. The game is then over when everyone has been tagged **107** and is an It-crab.

CHAPTER 6

....

MAKING MASTERPIECES

When children experiment with arts and crafts materials, they're learning about the textures and properties of the world, about how things work, and about the pleasures of self-expression. Join in and celebrate the wonders of art, with your child.

If you happen to independently pursue a particular art, share your enthusiasm and work together on some projects. Avoid the tendency to take over, though, since that can discourage a young child.

In crafts, the best learning comes when children fool around with the materials, enjoying as much freedom and as few adult guidelines as possible. Your role is to be supportive, provide materials, suggest new methods, and appreciate the masterpieces that result. Start by taking your child to a crafts supply shop and letting her choose two or three new materials, perhaps something fuzzy and something shiny.

If two or more youngsters sometimes clamor for your attention just when you need to be doing something else, try setting them up with separate crafts projects. Get the older one started on a project at the table while the younger one has some simple art materials of her own on the floor or at the other end of the table. Be sure to express your interest in their work by making a comment or asking a question every so often, such as "That red really stands out, doesn't it?" or "It looks like you put some effort into getting both sides of your picture balanced." The more specific you are, the more sincere and meaningful your compliments will be for your child.

Some artist's materials can pose a health hazard, so exercise caution when choosing materials for children. Look for the "CP," "AP," or "Health Label" followed by the word "nontoxic" on any product you buy for young children, which indicates that these materials conform to the safety standard of the Art and Craft Materials Institute. To play it safe, children should use water-based inks, talc-free clays, lead-free liquid glazes, and water-based marking pens.

This chapter describes simple everyday craft ideas you can explore with your child. For holiday-related crafts, see chapters 11 and 12.

LOVELY TO LOOK AT

PINHOLE PICTURES Your child draws an outline of a picture on colored construction paper. Now place the picture over a padding of several sheets of newspaper or a scrap of rug and use a pin (pushpin or opened safety pin) to pierce many tiny holes in the drawing. The holes should be as close together as possible without being so close that they blend together and cut out the shape. Alternatively, your child can experiment with different sizes of pins and with spacing the holes in clumps rather than evenly over the entire outline. Hang the finished pinhole picture on a window so sunlight will shine through it.

WIND SOCK Cut out the bottoms of a paper bag, and decorate it. Tape long crepe paper or ribbon streamers to one end. Attach a long string to the other end, and then hang the bag from a porch post or other location where the wind will catch it.

MAKE A SNOW SHAKER You will need an empty baby food jar, glitter, tiny plastic animals or people, circles of felt the size of the jar lids, and waterproof glue. Your child glues one or two figurines to the inside of the jar lid. Put two teaspoons of glitter in the jar and fill the rest with water. Put some glue on the inside edges of the lid and attach it tightly to the jar, then glue the felt circle to the lid, which is now the bottom of the shaker. When the jar is turned over, the glitter will shower down like snow.

BEAUTIFUL BUTTERFLIES Your child folds a sheet of paper in half, then draws a butterfly wing along the fold. She, or you, then cuts along the wing lines, creating a complete butterfly when she opens up the paper. To color the butterfly, your child can paint one wing with thick paint and then close the wings so the paint will be picked up by the other wing.

SWEET SAND ART You'll need a clear jelly jar with lid, and enough white sugar to fill it. Separate the sugar into several small bowls. Your child adds a few drops of food coloring to each bowl, and mixes to distribute the color. Leave one of the bowls white.

With a spoon, your child places a layer of sugar in the jar. Now, with the tip of the spoon, he makes some dents in the sugar, preferably next to the glass. Add some sugar in another color, poke around and make some dents and hills in the sugar, and keep doing this until a pretty design results. Close the jar.

MY ROOM Your child will enjoy turning his bedroom door into a work of art. First, cover the door with a roll of gift wrap or brown mailing paper, taping the ends around the edges of the door. Cut a hole for the doorknob and around the door hinges.

Now your child gets to choose the theme of his decorated door. It might be something simple, such as taping a large ribbon over the door from top to bottom and side to side, adding a large bow in the center. This makes the door look like a giant present. Or he might prefer something more elaborate, like a village scene, with pictures of houses and people cut from magazines and pasted on the door; or he can design a winter or summer scene, complete with seasonal touches; or the door can be turned into a personal "Me" collage, filled with mementos of your child's life and interests.

You'll need to help your child find a safe way to reach the higher section of the door. Or the whole project can be completed on the floor and later attached to the door. If your children share a room, they can each decorate half of the door. It doesn't matter if the two halves don't match. Or one can decorate the front of the door while the other takes the back.

RICE ART   Add a teaspoon of food coloring (or a tablespoon for deeper color) to each of four bowls of uncooked rice, stirring to mix the color evenly. While waiting five minutes for the rice to dry, your child draws a simple design on paper. Then spread a layer of glue over a single part of the design, starting from the top. Sprinkle some of the rice—whichever color seems most appropriate or interesting—over that part of the design. Continue with the rest of the picture, using the other colors of rice.

THING PRINTING   Your child can dip just about anything into paint and make a print. Supply some washable paint, paper or cloth, and any of the following, and see what develops: paper clips, empty thread spools, popsicle sticks, clothespins, keys, pieces of sponge, hair rollers, tiny toy cars to roll into the paint, and treasures from your kitchen junk drawer.

SQUEEZE-BOTTLE DESIGNS   Combine flour, salt, and water in equal parts. Pour the mixture into an old dishwashing detergent bottle, plastic ketchup or mustard bottle, or other squeeze bottle. If you like, you can add some liquid tempera paint. Now your child can squeeze some of this thick mixture out onto cardboard until she has a design that pleases her. It will glisten when it is dry because of the salt.

SUNSHINE WAXWORK   Your child can make a picture or design on a sheet of waxed paper using colored tissue paper and crayon shavings. Cover the design with another piece of wax paper and iron the two sheets together. The light will shine through this masterpiece if you hang it in a window.

CRAFTS USING RECYCLABLES

BINOCULARS Your preschooler can make a pretend pair of binoculars out of two toilet paper tubes. Glue the tubes together, and when the glue is completely dry, decorate the tubes and attach a string.

POSTAGE STAMP ART Begin by collecting every single used postage stamp you and your child can peel or cut off envelopes. Ask your relatives to contribute their used stamps also. At the same time, collect juice cans, notepaper boxes, and other sturdy containers that would benefit from redecoration. Buy glue, a sealer such as varnish, and brushes to apply the varnish.

Your child can either choose the stamps randomly or divide them into groups by predominating color. He applies glue and arranges the stamps on a container in a variety of positions so that all the edges overlap. Let the glue dry for a full day before applying the sealer. Then you can use these decorated containers to hold pencils, notepaper, and assorted small household items.

NUTTY FORTUNES First, crack open a batch of walnuts and save all the perfect shell halves. Your child writes or types a series of fortunes on a sheet of paper, then cuts them into little strips. Place the fortunes in the shells and carefully glue the halves back together. Paint the shells, or attach bits of paper to make them look like animals or people. Offer them to the family at dinnertime, or save for a special occasion.

PAPER PLATE PROJECTS Here are some things to make and do with an ordinary thin paper plate.

☼ Decorate a paper plate as though it were the body of a turtle. Add four feet, a tail, and a head cut from construction paper.

First tape two plates back to back. Decorate one side as a happy clown and the other as a sad clown. Use wool yarn for hair, cut out colored pieces of paper for features, and make funny arms and legs by folding long strips of paper into accordion pleats and attaching with tape to the clown's head. A paper doily can be turned into a collar.

Your child can make a wall holder for important stuff by cutting one paper plate in half and taping it to a whole paper plate. Decorate the plates and hang up with a string.

The same design—a half plate taped to a whole plate—can be turned into a puppet. Your child just draws a funny face on the back of the whole plate, turns it upside down, and places her hand in the pocket between the two plates. Poke a finger through a hole in the face for the puppet's tongue.

SPACE STATION The ingredients for a space station can include shoe boxes, foam meat trays, lightweight pie tins, aluminum foil, cardboard, plastic coffee can lids, round oatmeal cartons, paper towel rolls, and paper cups. Your child can tape the pieces together in any outlandish way he likes, and he can then cover some parts with construction paper, white paper, and aluminum foil. Attach one or more strings to the top and hang the contraption from a tree or ceiling.

YARN BABIES Show your child how to make yarn dolls. Begin by winding some yarn about thirty times lengthwise around a piece of cardboard six inches long. Loosely tie a piece of string around the yarn at one end, then cut the yarn at the other end and remove the cardboard. To make the head, tie a piece of yarn around the bunch near the uncut end. You can remove the loosely tied string now. Separate two clusters of yarn to be the arms; tie these at the wrists with a bit of yarn. Tie a piece of yarn at the waist. Make legs and tie them at the ankles.

EGG CARTON ART Cut apart a cardboard or foam egg carton into individual cups. You can make the cups into flowers by cutting slits in the cups to form flower petals and attaching the cups to pipe cleaners. Make puppets by drawing faces on the cups, using cotton balls or yarn for the hair, and pushing a popsicle stick through the top of the "head" to serve as both a body and a handle for the puppet.

INSTRUMENTS TO MAKE AND PLAY

Music is an art, too, and you can easily help your child whip up a homemade band for making beautiful music. Even toddlers will enjoy banging away; perhaps an older child would like to make an instrument for a younger sibling as a gift.

KAZOO You'll need a cardboard tube from paper towels or toilet paper, a piece of waxed paper (or cellophane, but not plastic wrap), a rubber band, and a sharp pencil. Your child cuts or tears the waxed paper so it fits snugly around the end of the tube. Hold it tight, and secure it with the rubber band. At the same end of the tube, just below the paper, punch a hole into the tube with the pencil. Hum into the open end of the tube.

HORN Your child can simply toot through a paper towel tube. She can decorate the tube first if she wants to.

TAMBOURINE Give your child two foil pie pans and send him to hunt for some small items like pennies or pebbles to place inside. (Because of the small swallowable items, this activity is limited to households with over-threes only.) Tape the ends of the tins together and decorate with some ribbon or crepe paper streamers around the edges. Shake.

Alternatively, a tambourine can be made out of two sturdy paper plates with some bells placed between them. Staple the plates together, decorate them, and shake.

DRUMS Percussion instruments are the easiest to make. All your child needs is an oatmeal box or a coffee can with a plastic lid. Decorate with colorful paper, ribbons, and bright tape. Add something to bang with, such as a spoon or a smooth stick or wooden dowel.

CYMBALS Metal pie plates or pan lids can be smashed together. For a more muted tone, suggest that your child hit a lid with a wooden spoon.

116

WOOD BLOCKS Your child can glue pieces of sandpaper to the flat surfaces of two wooden blocks, hand-sized or larger. Rubbing them together will make an interesting sound.

RATTLES Add a variety of small objects to a lidded metal box to create unusual sound effects. Experiment with rice, paper clips, buttons, bolts, and so on (keep all such swallowable objects out of the hands of children under three).

JINGLE BELLS Sew some small bells onto the fingers of an old glove, a wristband, or the cuff of an old sock. When your child wears this instrument, she'll easily make jingly music.

STRINGED INSTRUMENT Find a shoebox or cigar box and take the cover off. Your child carefully stretches different-sized rubber bands over the box, and then strums the bands for a variety of stringed sounds.

USEFUL THINGS

These crafts create objects that are both attractive and useful. Many of the finished projects complement such activities as reading and writing and may encourage your child to read and write more often. These useful things also make wonderful gifts for relatives at holiday time.

PLAY DESK Your child can make a play desk (or handy bed tray) from a sturdy cardboard carton with the top flaps cut off. Help her by marking and cutting a narrow piece out of each side so that when the box's open side is down, the sides become desk legs. Decorate the desk.

WRITING KIT Your child can make a stationery kit for himself, or for a friend who's moving away, from a shallow box. He can decorate it with stickers and photos or inscribe "My Writing Kit" in bold letters across the top of the box. Fill the box with pens, pencils, and felt-tip pens, as well as writing paper, envelopes, some stickers for letters, and some colorful commemorative postage stamps. You supply a list of names and addresses of all the friends, relatives, and pen pals your child might want to write to.

BOOKPLATES Purchase a box of plain white stickers about 2 x 3½ inches. Either you or your child can write "THIS BOOK BELONGS TO:" on the top half of each one, followed by a line for her to write in her name. Your child illustrates the bottom half of the plate. She can draw the same or a different picture on each bookplate, or she can use a favorite rubber stamp on each one.

BOOKMARKS Your child can make a variety of bookmarks on cardboard, posterboard, or thick paper cut into strips that are anywhere from 1½ x 5 inches up to 2 x 9 inches. She can write her name on the bookmark in fancy script, or glue something on it. She might like to glue a small photo or some recycled stamps to the bookmark and cover it with clear adhesive plastic. She could also cover the bookmark with leftover Con-Tact paper.

To make several pretty bookmarks at once, use a paper clip to scrape crayon shavings onto colored posterboard, then cover the posterboard with a plastic tablecloth or other sheet of vinyl. Place a towel on top of that, then help your child iron the towel with a warm iron. The heat will melt the crayon wax and create pleasing designs. Next, cut the posterboard into bookmark-sized strips. Cut a hole in one end of each bookmark, and thread a piece of colored yarn through it. Tie a knot in the yarn.

PLACE MATS Place mats made by your child for the whole family are a delightful way to make the family dinner hour distinctive. One approach is to make a collage of food can labels. Your child glues them onto a plain plastic place mat. If she likes, she can rub the labels with light brown shoe polish so the composition looks antique. Then she covers the mat and labels with clear adhesive plastic.

Alternatively, place mats can be woven. The first step is to fold a 12 x 14-inch sheet of construction paper in half. Beginning at the fold, cut even parallel slits to within one inch of the end. Now cut lots of strips, 1-inch wide and as long as the place mat, out of paper of another color, such as magazine pages or construction paper. Your child weaves them through the slits. Trim all the ends so they're even, and, for protection from food spills, cover both sides of the completed mat with clear adhesive paper.

PENCIL HOLDERS Juice and soup cans that your child has decorated with stickers or fabric scraps make handy holders for pencils, pens, colored markers, or kitchen implements. Other items that can be glued to cans include uncooked rice or macaroni, string, tiny seashells, torn bits of paper, and leaves. Coat the finished product with varnish for a neater look and to protect the items from being rubbed off.

GREETING CARDS Homemade cards are always better than store-bought ones, especially if the recipient is a grandparent or other relative. You can make them for Valentine's Day, for birthdays, or just to say "Hi" and "I miss you."

Fold sheets of paper in half and in half again to make greeting cards. Your child can draw on, write on, and decorate them any way she chooses. She may find it inspiring to use a real object inside. For instance, she can write, "I'm nuts about you" and attach a small metal nut or two from a hardware store to the inside. "I'm crazy about you, so never leaf me" could be illustrated with a leaf stuck to the card. A card with the message "Here's a very small gift" could contain a penny. For another kind of three-dimensional effect, cut out a shape, such as that of a butterfly, fold in half, and paste one half to the card.

Your child may enjoy adding a touch of nature to her homemade greeting cards. First she gathers and presses some flowers and leaves between newspapers, weighted by some heavy books, for a few days until they dry. Then she can glue the dried leaves and flowers to her cards. To finish, brush over the dried items with some watered-down glue or varnish.

STICKERS Buy a roll of wide brown parcel tape (the kind you have to moisten on the back so it will stick). Your child draws pictures or writes short funny sayings on the front of the tape using colorful crayons or felt-tip markers. Now cut the pictures apart to make homemade stickers.

PAPERWEIGHTS Go for a walk—near a stream or lake if one is nearby—so your child can find some wide, flat, smooth stones. Provide tempera paints so he can decorate them. Two stones with flat sides can also be glued together to make a rock animal or person. Felt scraps or yarn can be attached, too. Glue some felt on the bottom of any stone that is going to be used on a desk or table.

PENNY BANK Cover a coffee can (or other can that has a plastic lid) with stickers. Or wrap the can with construction paper and draw bright designs on it with markers. Help your child make a small slit in the plastic lid that is just the right size to drop coins through. Suggest that your child decide what the bank will help her save for.

POSTCARDS Homemade postcards are a way for kids to express themselves to friends and relatives. One side contains a drawing or photo that's meaningful to your child, and the other has room for a brief message. On one side of 4 x 6-inch index cards, your child can draw pictures, or he can glue together a small collage using various media. Then divide the other side of the card into two sections, one for the address and stamp and one for the message.

Another possibility is to glue on a snapshot of one of your child's favorite spots in the neighborhood or a vacation highlight. Include some photos that feature your child.

120 **KEY STICK** Get a paint-stirring stick (paint stores and hardware stores often hand these out). Break off a 6-inch piece, and sand the ends smooth. Paint the wood, glue a piece of felt or cardboard to the back, and screw in cup hooks about an inch apart. Tie strings around both ends to make hangers. Now you can use the key stick to hang up keys or small tools.

DESK ORGANIZER Help your child cut the tops off several milk cartons. Staple several of the cartons together, either side by side or stacked, and decorate them. Use to hold mail, notes, and magazines.

When children draw, paint, take photographs, sculpt with clay, or experiment with any other art form, they're learning to see and to express what they see in their own way.

A child's behavior is most creative when it's not an imitation of something he or she has seen before. You can enhance your child's creativity by encouraging her to look at the familiar in new ways.

Researchers have found that the more you emphasize evaluation and rewards in all areas of endeavor, the less likely your child is to behave in creative ways. In other words, competition for rewards and approval kills a child's desire to create for its own sake. Instead, focus on the sheer joys of learning and creating.

121

MAKING COOL STUFF

MAKE A PUZZLE Help your child remove a colorful, full-page picture from a magazine, then paste it onto a piece of cardboard, making certain the paste covers *all* of the picture. (Choose the thickest piece of cardboard you can easily cut with a pair of scissors; the kind that new shirts are packed on works well.) With a pencil, draw three to ten irregular shapes onto the cardboard-backed picture. Now cut along the lines, separate and scramble the pieces, and let your child put the puzzle back together.

WHEN A CHAIR IS NOT FOR SITTING If you have an old chair you don't want any more, or find one very inexpensively at a garage sale, let your child turn it into something else by decorating it, gluing odd parts onto it, or taking it apart and putting it together in an imaginative way.

ART MAZE Have your child draw a line of glue on a sheet of paper, then lay a piece of string on it. Now she begins another glue and string line where that one left off, then another, making each one more wiggly than the last. If she interweaves and overlaps the strings, their paths will form a maze that will be fun to follow. Suggest that she try a circular maze, or yarn of different colors.

MAKE SPECTACLES Using pipe cleaners or cardboard, your child can fashion a pair of funny glasses for herself. Suggest that she add yarn and feathers. (Make sure the ends of the pipe cleaners are not sharp; you can fold them over to make a rounded end.)

122

SUN PRINTS Here's a new kind of solar power. Get some dark-colored construction paper. Your child gathers objects of varying shapes. Place the objects on the construction paper (hold down lightweight items with circles of tape placed under the objects), and then leave the paper outside on a sunny day. At the end of the day, remove the objects and see what has happened to the paper.

Your child can experiment by cutting her name out of paper and laying that on the construction paper, or by laying out leaves or cutouts of her handprints.

SPIN THE THAUMATROPE Your child can easily experience the thrill of making a "motion picture." A thaumatrope is a round disc with a different picture on each side. When you spin the disc, the two pictures blend into one. The traditional combination of pictures is a birdcage on one side and a bird on the other, but your child can invent her own combinations. After illustrating a 2-inch disc, punch a hole on either side, and thread a string or rubber band through each hole. Holding one end of each rubber band in each hand, twirl the disc.

A variation is to tape, back-to-back on the top of a pencil, two discs with different pictures. Twirl the pencil back and forth quickly so that both pictures seem to blend.

DISPLAYING YOUR CHILD'S MASTERWORKS

Does your child want his pictures hanging in his room, or would it mean more to him to have his work displayed on a wall in the family room, dining room, or living room?

Frames for the artwork can be simple; after all, it's what's inside the frame that counts. Here are some suggestions for framing and display:

- Tape several small pictures on a large sheet of construction paper or colored posterboard.

- Set aside a large bulletin board just for your child's work.

- Hang a long, broad strip of colored ribbon on the wall, and then attach several pictures up and down the length of the ribbon. That way, you avoid lots of tape marks or holes in the wall and you can easily change the display.

- Provide your child with yarn, rickrack, and materials of other textures to add to posterboard frames.

- Frame art projects with a border of wallpaper, newspaper, or wrapping paper.

- To frame a nature project, make a border of twigs. Glue layers onto a cardboard backing, letting the glue dry after each layer is applied. Varnish the whole frame.

- If you can do it without harming the project, crop some rectangular-shaped works into ovals or circles for variety.

- Connect a series of works on a wall with squiggles of yarn or strips of ribbon.

123

STRAW CRAFT Present your child with a box of drinking straws. What can be done with them? She'll discover lots of artistic possibilities, including cutting and stringing them, pasting them together, slipping them through holes in aluminum foil, slitting them open and pasting them flat, or making a sculpture of them (use a piece of clay as a base). Can your child think of a way to combine straws with gummed reinforcement circles, or a way to make a mask out of straws?

124

HOMEMADE DOUGHS AND PAINTS

LONG-LASTING PLAY DOUGH This recipe for play dough is cooked, so your child will need your help.

4 cups flour
4 cups water
1 cup salt
½ cup oil
1 small can cream of tartar
Few drops of food coloring

Mix all the ingredients together by hand (your child can wear plastic gloves so she won't stain her hands). Cook in a saucepan over medium heat (well below the boiling point) until the mass congeals. Knead it a bit yourself while it cools, but make sure it's cool before your child handles it.

This recipe makes a large amount, suitable for two children. Keep it in an airtight plastic container, and it will last for a long time—even longer if kept in the refrigerator.

PEANUT BUTTER PLAY DOUGH Your child can make sculptures out of a handful of peanut butter play dough, then eat them as a nutritious snack. This is an especially good dough for toddlers who love to put things in their mouths. Start with 1 cup of peanut butter. Mix in ½ cup to 1 cup powdered milk, and 2 to 6 tablespoons of honey, a little at a time until you get the consistency you want. The mixture shouldn't be sticky, but it has to stick together so you can mold it. Your kids can make creatures out of the dough and decorate them with chocolate chips, raisins, or coconut sprinkles.

FINGER PAINTS Kids love to mess around with finger painting because it's such a tactile and satisfying form of self-expression. Here are some ways to make finger paints:

125

- ☼ Combine wheat paste with tempera paint.
- ☼ Mix liquid starch with tempera paint.
- ☼ Mix flour and salt with water to paste consistency and add food coloring.

Any large smooth surface can be painted: a sheet of plastic, waxed paper, oilcloth, the glazed surface of shelf paper, or cookie sheets (after your child paints on the sheet, she can make prints by smoothing paper over the freshly painted surface). It helps to dampen whatever surface you use to make the paint flow more smoothly.

RECIPES FOR FUN: FOUR AFTERNOON BAKING PROJECTS

Baking is a craft that allows you to eat the results! These recipes will fill an afternoon with fun, your house with wonderful aromas, and your tummies with goodies. Baking offers lots of magic for kids, from dough rising to the wonder of making real pretzels. Here are recipes for homemade bread or rolls, soft pretzels, a brownie pizza, and decorated sugar cookies.

CRACKED WHEAT BREAD

Yield: 2 loaves or 24 dinner rolls

Baking bread is an enjoyable activity that happens in fits and starts—just right for short attention spans. This recipe is a delectable compromise between the light white bread most children prefer and the hearty whole grain breads that most adults enjoy. But even children who normally refuse breads with a whisper of whole grains will enjoy the fruits of their labor when the bread fresh out of the oven.

2½ cups milk, scalded
2 packages (2 tablespoons) active dry yeast
2 tablespoons sugar or honey
1¾ cups whole wheat flour
¾ cup bulgur or cracked wheat
1½ cups boiling water
2 teaspoons salt
¼ cup canola oil
2 eggs, slightly beaten
4 to 5 cups all-purpose white flour
2 tablespoons melted butter

1. Scald the milk, then let cool to lukewarm (110°). Pour into a large bowl with the yeast and sugar. Stir until the yeast is dissolved. Beat in the whole wheat flour. Cover and let rise in a warm place until double in bulk, 30 to 60 minutes.
2. While the sponge rises, combine the bulgur and boiling water in a small bowl. Stir well, cover, and let stand.
3. When the sponge has doubled in bulk, stir it down. Add bulgur mix. Stir in the salt, oil, and eggs. Stir in 3 cups of the white flour, 1 cup at a time. When you can no longer stir the dough, and it pulls away from the sides of the bowl, flour a work surface with some of the remaining flour. Turn the dough out onto the work surface and knead in as much of the remaining flour as necessary to make a smooth, elastic dough. Use as little of the remaining flour as you can; the less flour, the lighter the loaf. Knead the dough for at least 10 minutes, or more if

the children are helping (they will not be as efficient at kneading as a grown-up; do not worry about overworking the dough at this stage).

4. Return the dough to an oiled bowl, rolling the dough around so it is evenly coated with the oil. Cover and let rise in a warm place until double in bulk, 30 to 60 minutes.

5. Punch down the dough and knead briefly. Divide the dough into two equal parts. The dough may be formed into loaves or dinner rolls.

To shape into a loaf, pat out one piece of the dough to form a rectangle. Roll tightly as if you were rolling up a carpet. Place seam-side down in a buttered loaf pan. To shape into dinner rolls, divide one piece of the dough into twelve equal-size pieces and choose one of these methods:

* Roll pieces of dough into round balls. Roll in melted butter, and place two inches apart in a buttered baking pan.

* Divide each piece of dough into three smaller balls. Place three balls each in buttered muffin cups to make clover leaf rolls.

* Roll pieces of dough into snakes and curl them into spirals or double spirals.

* Roll pieces of dough into snakes and tie them into knots.

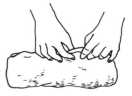

6. Cover the loaves and rolls and let rise in a warm place until double in bulk, about 30 minutes. When the dough is almost double, begin preheating the oven to 375°.

7. Brush the top of the rolls (and loaves, if desired) with melted butter. Bake loaves for about 45 minutes, rolls for 25 to 30 minutes. The loaves will register 190° with an instant-read thermometer placed near the center. All surfaces should be nicely browned and feel firm; the loaves will sound hollow when tapped.

8. Remove from pans and let cool on wire racks.

FUN TIME, FAMILY TIME

HOMEMADE PRETZELS
Yield: 12 pretzels

This recipe makes a soft, chewy pretzel, the kind you might buy from a vendor on the street, with the added nutritional boost of a little whole wheat flour. Some yeast doughs require a light touch, but not pretzel dough. Let the children knead as much as they want.

1 cup warm water
1 package (1 tablespoon) active dry yeast
2 tablespoons butter, at room temperature
½ teaspoon salt
1 tablespoon sugar
1 cup whole wheat flour
   (or substitute all-purpose white flour)
1½ to 1¾ cups all-purpose white flour
6 cups water
2 tablespoons baking soda
2 to 3 teaspoons coarse salt

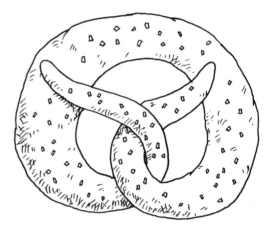

1. In a large mixing bowl, stir together the 1 cup warm water and yeast until the yeast is dissolved. Add the butter, salt, sugar, and 1 cup whole wheat flour. Beat until smooth.
2. Stir in 1 cup of the white flour. Turn onto a floured board and knead in the remaining ½ to ¾ cup flour. Use as much of the remaining flour as you need to make a firm dough. Knead until the dough is firm and not sticky.
3. Place the dough in a lightly oiled bowl, cover, and let rise until double in bulk, 30 to 60 minutes.
4. Punch down and divide the dough into twelve pieces.
5. To shape the pretzels, roll out each piece until it is 12 to 18 inches long and about as thick as a pencil. To make the traditional pretzel shape, loop the ends around each other twice, leaving a tail at least 3 inches long. Bring the left tail over to the right side of the loop, and bring the right tail over to the left side of

the loop. Press the ends firmly against the sides of the loop. Children may prefer to make their own shapes. Place the formed pretzels on a well-oiled baking sheet, keeping the unformed pieces of dough covered with a damp towel.

6. Let the pretzels rise until almost double in bulk, about 30 minutes.

7. While the pretzels rise, preheat the oven to 450°. Combine the 6 cups of water and the baking soda in a large saucepan and bring to a boil. Generously grease two baking sheets.

8. Carefully lower the pretzels into the boiling water and leave for about 1 minute, or until they float to the top. Place them on the well-oiled baking sheets. Sprinkle with the coarse salt.

9. Bake the pretzels for about 10 minutes, until crispy and browned. They are best served immediately, but they can be cooled on wire racks and stored in an air-tight container for up to one week.

BROWNIE PIZZA
Yield: 12 slices

Kids have tremendous fun with this recipe. The brownie batter is spread on a pizza pan instead of the usual square pan. The minute the brownie comes out of the oven, have the children sprinkle it with grated white chocolate to mimic mozzarella. Then let them sprinkle on their favorite candies (in moderation, of course). The heat of the brownie will fuse the candies to its surface. Almost any candy will do, though some work better than others.

3 ounces unsweetened baking chocolate
½ cup butter
1¼ cups sugar
2 eggs
2 teaspoons vanilla extract
1 cup all-purpose flour
2 ounces white chocolate
¼ cup each of two different candies (jelly beans, sliced gum drops, crushed hard candy, sliced licorice, nonpareils) or colored baking bits

1. Preheat the oven to 350°. Butter a 10-inch pizza pan or coat with nonstick cooking spray.
2. Combine the baking chocolate and butter in a medium-size saucepan; melt over low heat. Let cool for a minute, then add the sugar, eggs, vanilla, and flour. Mix well.
3. Pour into the prepared pan and spread with a spatula. Bake for about 18 minutes, or until the top springs back when lightly touched.
4. While the brownie bakes, grate the white chocolate. Measure out the candy toppings.
5. Remove the pizza from the oven and immediately sprinkle on the white chocolate and candies. Cool in the pan on a wire rack for at least 10 minutes. Use a pizza wheel to slice into twelve equal wedges.

DECORATED SUGAR COOKIES
Yield: About sixty 2-inch cookies

Buttery rich sugar cookies are a perennial favorite with children, especially if you have an interesting collection of cookie cutters. Begin your collection with such basic shapes as hearts and stars. Then add to the collection according to your children's interests—dinosaurs, zoo animals, trucks—and the holidays you celebrate—Christmas trees, Hanukkah dreidels, Halloween pumpkins.

For holiday baking, the dough can be made up to two weeks in advance and frozen, or up to four days in advance and refrigerated.

1 cup butter, at room temperature
⅔ cup sugar
½ teaspoon salt
1 egg
1 teaspoon vanilla extract
2½ cups sifted all-purpose flour
Confectioners' sugar
Colored sugar crystals, sprinkles, icing (see decorating box)

1. In a large mixing bowl, cream together the butter and sugar. Add the salt, egg, and vanilla and beat until light and fluffy. Add the flour and mix in.
2. Gather the dough into two balls. Flatten into discs. Wrap in plastic film and refrigerate for 3 to 4 hours before rolling out. The dough may be frozen for up to two weeks at this point.
3. When you are ready to make the cookies, preheat the oven to 350°. Lightly coat cookie sheets with nonstick cooking spray or line with parchment or waxed paper.
4. Lightly dust the work surface and rolling pin with confectioners' sugar. Roll out the dough until ¼ inch thick. Cut with the cookie cutters and place on the baking sheets. Reroll the scraps, using additional confectioners' sugar to prevent sticking. If you are decorating with sprinkles, apply them before baking.
5. If the rolling and cutting (and decorating) take a long time, you may want to chill the cookies briefly before baking; this isn't necessary if you have worked at a normal (grown-up) pace.
6. Bake the cookies for 8 to 10 minutes, just until lightly colored; do not overcook. Remove the cookies to wire racks to cool. Then decorate as desired.

131

Sugar cookies are edible canvases that can be decorated in many different ways. To get a sense of your options, take a slow stroll down the baking aisle of your supermarket. You will see numerous packages of colored sugar crystals, colored sugar sprinkles in various shapes, and candy baking bits. You will also find tubes of frosting, called decorating gel. These easy-to-use frosting gels are sometimes packaged with disposable decorating tips that give you the option of making straight lines, scallops, or stars. Buy large-size tubes; frosting goes fast in the hands of children.

To decorate before baking, simply sprinkle colored sugar crystals, candy sprinkles, chopped nuts, or candy bits on the cookies before they go into the oven.

Pipe on colored frosting gels to create messages and draw pictures.

A simple frosting can be made by mixing confectioners' sugar with a little milk until you have a nice spreading consistency. Tint with food coloring as desired. Apply with new flat paintbrushes or table knives. This icing can be applied thinly and used as a "glue" for sprinkles.

Make your own decorating frosting to pipe on with a pastry bag by combining 1½ tablespoons meringue powder with 2 cups confectioners' sugar and 3 tablespoons warm water in a medium-size mixing bowl. Beat for about 3 minutes. Tint with food coloring as desired. This makes about 1½ cups. Apply the frosting using a pastry bag and decorating tips. If you don't have a pastry bag, you can snip off the corner of a plastic sandwich bag and squeeze out the frosting.

Note: You may be accustomed to making decorating icings with beaten egg whites. Because raw eggs carry a risk of salmonella infection, it is safer to use meringue powder, which can be found at stores and through mail order catalogs that sell cake decorating supplies.

Dip cookies in chocolate glaze—or just dip half the cookie in the glaze, for a dramatic effect. To make the glaze, combine equal parts of semisweet chocolate and butter. Melt together and beat until smooth. While the glaze is still liquid, sprinkle with crushed nuts, if desired.

CHAPTER 7

LET'S PRETEND

Even before children can tie their own shoes, they put on and shed whole personalities with ease. Every time your child talks to a doll, tries on a firefighter's hat, or says to a friend, "You be the mommy," he's playing a role. When you build on your child's interest in pretend play, you will not only encourage his creativity but you will also create a wonderful opportunity to be playful with him.

Pretending to be someone—or something—else is so easy and natural for a child that you can make use of the activities in this chapter any time you want to, often without a moment of preparation. At odds and ends of moments while a meal is cooking, in the car, on rainy weekends, or the next time your child says, "I'm bored," whip out one of these suggestions and presto! The rain and the wait might as well be gone, and all that remains is you, your child, and the wonder of shared imagination.

134 PLAYING THE ROLE

Role-playing is great fun for both you and your child, and it also helps build self-confidence and self-awareness. Your child will learn to see herself from different angles and explore new feelings and ideas in a safe environment. It also helps prepare your child for real situations that may someday occur.

Many preschoolers love to pretend they're keeping house, going to work, flying an airplane, and so on, and they especially love it when you play along.

Once a child reaches eight or so, inhibitions about performing often begin to kick in. So reassure your child that there's no such thing as a mistake in these imaginary interactions.

MIME'S THE WORD Preschoolers love to act out everyday occurrences in mime. Say, "Let's pretend we're baking a cake." Perform every step of the action wordlessly. Don't forget to brush the stray flour off your hands and to blow on the hot cake to cool it off as you very carefully remove it from the oven. Act out putting a baby to sleep, putting on makeup, making an important business call ("blah, blah, blah, blah"), and building a snowman (of course, you'll toss a "snowball" or two in your child's direction, then duck or act surprised when she tosses one toward you).

TRAINS, PLANES, AND AUTOS If your child has a particular interest in airplanes or trains, provide her with plenty of materials to design her own versions of these vehicles. One five-year-old likes to make "airplanes" out of elaborate combinations of large boxes and chairs. Can your child design a cockpit, a pit stop for a race car, or a train station out of furniture, sheets, and odds and ends? Have her pretend to pilot the plane or engineer the train, and go on a "trip" together. Make sure you get your in-flight meal!

DRAMATIC PLAY KITS

Put together several dramatic play kits in large cardboard boxes. For example:

☼ **Costumes** Fill a box with clothing discards or treasures scouted out at thrift shops. Include hats, shawls, scarves, gloves, and shoes and boots of all kinds. Add fresh items regularly.

☼ **Props** In an office or post office kit, for example, include an inked stamp or two, a play telephone, lots of paper and envelopes. A hospital kit might include some tongue depressors, a play hypodermic needle, a clipboard, some files, a flashlight, and a prescription pad. A market kit would contain clean, empty cans and cereal boxes, play or real money, paper sacks, and plastic fruits and vegetables.

135

PIZZA SHOP Preschool and primary-age children enjoy pretending to operate a pizza shop. Provide a large round piece of cardboard and triangular felt pieces to serve as pizza slices. The kids can apply all sorts of "ingredients" to their pizzas, including pieces of yellow yarn (cheese), brown felt circles (pepperoni), green hunks of felt (green pepper), and so on. You and a child can play pizza seller and customer, or several children can divide the roles of order taker, cook, server, cash register operator, and customer.

HOW MANY WAYS CAN YOU SIT? Ask your child to choose any ordinary activity and perform it in as many different ways as possible. Take sitting down, for example. How would he sit down if he had just spent a whole day running a marathon? How would he do it if he had just received some good news? Some bad news? How would he sit if he were waiting for a special telephone call from a friend?

Have your child try out several different ways of falling, the way an actor would. She can do this standing on a bed or on a cushioned carpet. Tell her to fall as though lightning has struck, as though someone has punched her, as though she has suddenly realized she's exhausted, as though she has just won a million dollars, and so on.

Now consider jumping: how differently would your child jump if she were jumping for joy, leaping over a creek, trying to reach the cookie jar, or imitating a kangaroo?

PUPPET PLAY   Keep a selection of puppets, stuffed animals, and dolls in a box. As an alternative to acting out roles herself, your child can put on performances using these props. Your child can add to the puppet collection by making her own: draw a human face or animal body on construction paper, cut it out, and glue it to a popsicle stick. Your child's own fingertips can also double as puppets—use washable paint or nontoxic makeup to draw features on them. For an instant stage, nail or tape a rope across the doorway to an open closet, and throw a lightweight cloth, such as an old tablecloth, over it.

REHEARSING FOR REAL LIFE   When your child is preparing for an unusual or slightly scary situation, act it out together first. Possibilities are an appointment with the dentist, doctor, or school psychologist; the first day at a new school; the first time riding the school bus or going to camp; and so on. Take turns playing the roles.

TRICKY SITUATIONS   Role-play what to do in case someone unexpected comes to the door: a stranger, an adult friend, a salesperson, a neighbor, or a mail carrier. What would your child do if a toilet was about to run over, if there was a fire in the house, if she was stuck in an elevator, or if she was confronted by a bully?

Allow your child to be creative and outlandish in her acting, and only later discuss which behaviors are most appropriate in real life.

NEW HAT, NEW PERSON Gather as many different kinds of hats as you can find around the house, and put them all into a large box. You might even search out headgear at local thrift shops. Try to include the following: cowboy hat, farm hat, stocking cap, beanie, bathing cap, shower cap, feathered hat, sombrero, magician's top hat, hard hat, helmet, painter's work cap, sports cap, nurse's cap, and rain hat. To play, take turns reaching into the box, pulling out a hat, and acting out the behavior of someone who would wear that hat. A variation is to choose a hat and give it to the other person to act out. Change your voice and your gestures to match your new identity.

With an older child, point out that not everyone who wears a particular hat will act in a predictable way. Or make up whole scenarios starting with the hat. For instance, say you've chosen the rain hat. You might be a foreign diplomat caught in the rain while on the way to an important event, or a museum curator visiting London looking for something new for the museum.

DO THE KARAOKE You don't need a karaoke machine to lip-synch to popular songs. In fact, kids often like to pretend they're famous singers by singing along to the words on the radio or their favorite tapes. If you can round up enough kids willing to participate, you can have a lip-synching contest. But even with only you and your child, you can play this game. See how accurately she can lip-synch the words of a very familiar song.

ACTING OUT FEELINGS

Role-playing can help a child express difficult emotions.

DRESS HOW YOU FEEL Provide a varied collection of dress-up clothes and washable makeup and suggest that your child dress up as whoever she wants to be at that moment. Ask her to find a creative way to make her outside match her inside. For instance, if a child is feeling grumpy, she might make herself up as a witch and carry a broom to shoo away bothersome people. If she's feeling proud, she might put on dressy shoes and a long dress and march around as though she's won an Academy Award.

PICTURING EXPRESSIONS Clip magazine pictures that depict all kinds of emotional states and interactions, from laughing to arguing. Have your child imitate the expressions, then talk about what might have caused them. Say, "What do you think happened just before this picture? What do you think will happen next?"

THROW OUT THE GRUMPIES Tell your child she can get rid of a feeling she doesn't want any more by throwing it away. How many ways can she think of to get rid of a grumpy feeling? Did she think of crumpling it up and tossing it into an imaginary wastebasket, stuffing it into an imaginary garbage disposer, flattening it out with a rolling pin and then stomping on it?

THE ART OF EMOTION Play an audiotape, record, or CD, or look through a book of art photos with your child. Talk with your child about how the music or art makes him feel. Now have him act out the emotion. Or ask him to pretend to be the animal that the music reminds him of. Or he can make a drawing that reflects his feelings.

ACT OUT WHAT YOU FEEL What makes your child laugh? What scares him? He can act out scenarios of each feeling and assign roles to you, too. For example, if he finds slipping on a banana peel funny, you might drop an imaginary peel and he can then pretend to slip on it. If he finds monsters scary, he can pretend to be a particularly outrageous monster and make scary faces and gestures at you while you act appropriately alarmed.

PLAYING AN ACTIVE ROLE

High-energy kids and parents will enjoy these active games of imagination.

ADVENTURE WORLD Set up a simple obstacle course in the house or outside. Start with a string on the ground and call it a bridge. Beyond the bridge, place various objects (blocks, boxes, pillows, and so on). Now have your child march across the bridge and describe what she sees. Is this pillow a hayride? Is that pile of rocks a lofty mountain to be climbed? Is this box a store selling magic juice that turns children into whatever they want to be?

MORE THAN ONE WAY TO WIN A RACE Race your child while pretending to be jackrabbits, tortoises, snakes, or some other animals or things.

LEAD THE EXERCISE CLASS Your child is an exercise teacher showing her class how to stretch and relax all parts of the body. How will she describe how to relax an eyebrow? Can she design an exercise for elbows?

MAKE A BODY MACHINE Your child tells you how to arrange your body in connection with hers so that the two of you make a machine. Move arms and legs and make sounds that fit what this machine is supposed to make or do. For example, the doughnut dough goes in here, the hole is punched out here, and when this horn toots, it's ready to fall down through here (a tube made with joined hands).

BE A BUBBLE Pretend that you are both bubbles just blown out of a giant's bubble pipe. First you'll get bigger and bigger. How many different ways can you float to earth? Try waving your arms and wafting gently on a breeze, bumping into another bubble and joining together, plunking heavily against something and bursting wetly, and so on.

GO FISHING Here's the setup for an absorbing and educational "fishing" expedition for young children. Attach a two-foot string to a strong magnet, available at hardware stores; horseshoe magnets are the easiest to attach. Now tie or tape the string to the end of a yardstick or other two- to three-foot pole. Cut several simple fish shapes out of paper or cardboard and attach paper clips to one end of each. (Keep clips out of the hands of toddlers.)

Toss the paper fish around the floor, and your child will easily learn how to fish for them, perhaps perched on the bed. Now embellish the experience. Put some fish under "overhanging weeds" (a chair). Talk about how big the fish you catch are. Pretend that one is fighting to get away. Then get out the pretend pots and pans and cook up your catch for dinner.

ALL IN THE MIND

These cerebral games are useful during quiet times, such as before bedtime or while you're waiting for your food to come in a restaurant. Because they don't require any equipment, you can do them on the spur of the moment to fill a few minutes.

140

MORE THAN THIRTY-ONE FLAVORS Pretend with your child that you're going to hold the grand opening of a new ice cream store. What amazing flavors can you think up? Name them after cartoon characters or famous people or other humorous combinations. How about a Purple Dyno-Scoop? Dollar-Green Ice Cream? Stormcloud Gray Ice Cream? Sunshine-Yellow Sherbet?

TOPSY-TURVY WORLD Ask your child to imagine a mirror in which everything happens in reverse order. When you look in this special mirror, imagine seeing books in which the story is told from the end to the beginning, plants that go from full bloom to seedling, people who grow younger, and newscasters who foretell the news (but weather forecasters who never do). Have your child act out some of these reversals.

USE YOUR SENSES Pick an object—a comb, for instance—and use all your senses to get to know it better. How does it look, feel, smell, sound (if you twang it)? Imagine its history (it was left behind by a creature from another planet) or its future (it will someday find its way to the White House—how?).

FAMILY ROLE REVERSALS

It's enjoyable to exchange family identities for a few minutes at a time. Reversing roles also offers kids a chance to work out some difficult feelings and concerns in a playful way. You may start by suggesting the switch ("I'm going to pretend to be you and you be me"), but before long, your child will be introducing the game and directing the action.

Parents sometimes imitate their children to make a point. By pretending to whine at the texture of your dinner vegetables, you may help your child see his own behavior through your eyes. On the other hand, role reversals in which your child imitates *you* give him an unusual opportunity to gain insight into adult behavior as well as his own.

Toddlers sometimes balk at exchanging roles at first. Being asked to be their own parent may be scary. Try again another time. Most children eventually enjoy role reversals a great deal, and continue to do so for years.

Accept without judgment whatever your child acts out. That way, she'll feel safe to express herself the next time you play. However, keep an eye out for siblings who imitate each other so ruthlessly that feelings get hurt.

Try these role reversals on for size.

SWITCH ROLES AT DINNER Switch roles with your child at the dinner table. What you hear may surprise you. You'll think, "Do I *really* say that?"

MAKE ME FEEL BETTER The day before your child has a test at school or a doctor appointment, pretend to be him and give him a chance to reassure *you*. He'll probably end up feeling better.

YOU FOR A DAY Talk about what would happen if you and your child could switch places—but not identities—for an entire day. Would you put your files in his cubbyhole at school? Would he carry his peanut butter sandwich in your briefcase or purse? How would you feel riding his school bus? What would people think if they saw him driving around town?

MORE ELABORATE PRETENDING GAMES

By playing along with your child's fantasy of being someone else and venturing into another world, you help her expand both her imagination and her coping skills in the real world.

PUT ON A PLAY Two or more children, or a parent and child, can put on a simple play with minimal preparation. Begin by choosing a picture book with lots of dialogue. You may want to photocopy the section you've chosen to act out, so each of you can have a copy from which to read. Or you may prefer memorizing the dialogue, more or less—there's no rule that says your play has to match the book word for word.

Rearrange some of the furniture to set the scene, and use a few toys and household items as props. If several people are involved, one may want to play the role of director, telling the actors where to stand and what expressions to emphasize. Or someone can be both an actor and the director.

After at least one rehearsal, it's show time. Don't forget to invite an audience, even if it's only baby brother, another child, or another parent. If you have access to a video camera, you can record the play and then watch it together.

CAMP OUT AT HOME Have an imaginary campout, spending an hour or two in the living room or backyard (with access to the bathroom allowed). Make a list of foodstuffs and things to play with. Pack up your supplies and trek to your "camping" spot. Do some exploring, making an effort to notice things you never really saw before, such as the fuzziness of your carpet or the peculiar texture of the tree bark in the yard. Enjoy your meal, being careful to leave your camping spot clean when you're finished. Play some games and pack up to go "home."

TEDDY BEAR PICNIC Your child decides which stuffed animals to invite, what they'll "eat," and where the event will take place. Then she can gather her animals and you can help her act out the various roles they are to play. Other possibilities are a teddy bear wedding or a teddy bear family reunion.

PLAN AN IMAGINARY TRIP You can go to any city or country you choose—all in your mind. Begin by gathering a raft of travel brochures from a friendly travel agent's office, or send for the free booklets available from the tourist offices of most countries (check your phone directory or directory assistance for toll-free numbers of agencies such as the Austrian National Tourist Office). You can go into as much detail as you like, depending on the age of your child. For instance, middlegraders might enjoy comparing the cost of a group tour with that of an independent trip and figuring how much money will be left in the budget for souvenirs and other extras after paying for hotels, food, and transportation. Children of any age will enjoy both perusing the brochures in search of attractions to visit and imagining what they will find there.

How far can your child walk in a day? (Take a day beforehand to explore your own neighborhood yourself and figure out the mileage—or the number of blocks—before exhaustion sets in.) Now, looking at a map of another city, imagine what you could manage to see in a single day or week if you were walking. Could you make it from the Eiffel Tower to the Sorbonne, for instance? Use the map scale to determine how far that actually is.

DREAM PARTY Suggest that your child draw up an imaginary guest list of anyone she chooses (TV stars, her favorite children's book authors, cartoon characters), design unusual invitations, plan a menu of impossible foods (blue banana splits, salad à la graham cracker), and arrange a schedule of silly games (Who's got the basketball?, in which guests try to hide a large ball somewhere in their clothing).

If your child is interested, you can carry the imaginary party one step further by having "everyone" sit around an imaginary table and then carrying on a pretend conversation while eating the invisible food.

MOST ELEGANT TEA PARTY You and your child may decide to invite a couple of friends to share in this extra-special event. Plan to have it in the middle to late afternoon. Choose your prettiest tablecloth and adorn the table with a flower-filled vase or a centerpiece of artfully arranged leaves and ferns. Serve a flavored non-caffeinated tea in china teacups.

You'll need some tiny sandwiches and other finger foods to go with your drinks. Tea sandwiches are light, savory snacks, not hearty sandwiches. You can use any thinly sliced, light-textured bread for tea sandwiches, but you and your child will have the most fun with a loaf of unsliced white bread. Slice the bread horizontally and cut the long slices into shapes with cookie cutters. You can use the cookie cutters on regular sliced bread, but there will be more leftover scraps of bread (which you can use as bread crumbs). Whatever bread you use, it is traditional to trim the crusts from the bread—a step that is guaranteed to please most children.

Here are some sandwich suggestions:

- ☀ Lightly butter the bread, then fill with thinly sliced turkey or ham; thinly sliced cucumbers and a sprig of watercress; a tiny spoonful of chutney and a piece of cheese; or chicken, ham, or egg salad.

- ☀ Mix together cream cheese and pimentos, cream cheese and olives, or cream cheese and jam. Spread thinly.

- ☀ Peanut butter and jelly, peanut butter and bacon, or peanut butter and banana slices make delicious fillings, too.

- ☀ To delight very young children, make decorated open-face sandwiches. Spread a piece of bread with peanut butter. Set a heart-shaped cookie cutter on the bread and sprinkle coconut inside the cookie cutter. Remove the cookie cutter, and a white heart remains. Or use cookie cutters to cut out decorative shapes in bologna, salami, or American cheese. Place on bread spread with butter.

RECIPES FOR FUN: AN ELEGANT TEA PARTY

Here are some savories and sweets for a tea party or other fancy occasion.

HAM AND CHEESE TEA BISCUITS
Yield: 18 biscuits

Serve these first, before the sweets, and watch them disappear. The biscuits are so moist and tasty that they don't require additional butter.

Children can help make the biscuit dough. They can cut out the biscuits with a traditional round biscuit cutter or their favorite cookie cutter of comparable size.

2 cups all-purpose flour
2 teaspoons baking powder
½ teaspoon baking soda
½ teaspoon salt
¼ cup chilled butter, cut in thin slivers
3 tablespoons finely chopped ham (1-ounce slice)
3 tablespoons finely chopped Swiss cheese (1-ounce slice)
1 scallion, minced
Approximately ¾ cup buttermilk

1. Preheat the oven to 450°.
2. Sift the flour, baking powder, baking soda, and salt into a medium-size mixing bowl.
3. Add the butter and cut in with a pastry blender or two knives, until the lumps of butter are the size of peas.
4. Mix in the ham, cheese, and scallion.
5. Add the buttermilk, mixing until the dough comes together in a ball. Add more buttermilk if needed.
6. Turn the dough onto a lightly floured board and knead a few times. Pat out the dough into a rectangle about ½ inch thick. Use a biscuit cutter to make rounds, or simply cut the rectangle into about eighteen 3-inch squares. Place the biscuits on an ungreased baking sheet.
7. Bake for 10 to 12 minutes. These biscuits are at their best served hot out of the oven.

CRANBERRY OAT MUFFINS
Yield: 12 muffins

These offer the rustic texture of the scones every tea party needs, in the muffin format most children prefer. These muffins are not too sweet and are lower in fat than most.

1 cup buttermilk
1 cup old-fashioned rolled oats (not quick-cooking)
⅓ cup unsalted butter
1½ cups fresh or frozen cranberries, coarsely chopped
¼ cup sugar
1 cup all-purpose flour
1 teaspoon baking powder
½ teaspoon baking soda
½ teaspoon salt
½ cup firmly packed light brown sugar
1 egg

1. Heat the buttermilk in a small saucepan over medium low heat, just until small bubbles form on the edge. Stir in the oats until completely moistened. Add the butter. Cover and let stand until the butter is melted and the oats have cooled.
2. Meanwhile, combine the cranberries and ¼ cup sugar and set aside.
3. Preheat the oven to 400°. Lightly grease or line with paper liners twelve muffin cups.
4. Sift the flour, baking powder, baking soda, and salt into a medium-size bowl.
5. Add the brown sugar and egg to the oats and beat well.
6. Make a well in the center of the dry ingredients. Add the oat mixture all at once, and stir just until the dry ingredients are moistened. Quickly stir in the cranberries.
7. Spoon the batter into the prepared muffin cups and bake for 20 to 25 minutes, until a toothpick inserted in the center comes out clean. Let cool for about 5 minutes before removing from the pan. Serve warm or at room temperature.

JAM JEWELS

Yield: About 2½ dozen cookies

Only a queen has jewels more beautiful than these glistening, delicious cookies—but real jewels aren't half the fun. The cookies are easy to make. A food processor does the mixing, and the children can form each cookie by hand. A steady (grown-up) hand is required to fill the small centers with jam, or the results will be disappointingly messy.

147

1½ cups all-purpose white flour
¼ cup finely ground almonds
¼ cup sugar
½ teaspoon salt
1 teaspoon grated lemon rind
½ cup butter
1 egg
3 tablespoons cold water
¼ cup sugar
¼ cup jam or jelly

1. Preheat the oven to 375°.
2. In a food processor fitted with a steel blade, combine the flour, almonds, ¼ cup sugar, salt, and lemon rind. Add the butter, cut in slices, and process until the mixture resembles coarse crumbs.
3. Lightly beat the egg with the water. Add to the flour mixture and process until a dough is formed. Gather the dough into a ball.
4. Place the remaining ¼ cup sugar in a bowl. Break off small pieces of dough and form into 1-inch balls. Roll the balls in the sugar and then place on a baking sheet.
5. Bake for 5 minutes. Remove from the oven and press your thumb or a thimble into the center of each cookie to form an indentation. Return to the oven to bake for about 8 minutes more. The cookies will remain light in color; to check for doneness, slide a spatula under a test cookie to see whether it is browned.

6. Remove the cookies from the oven and cool on wire racks.
7. When the cookies are cooled, dab a small amount of jam or jelly into the center of each cookie. Eat at once or store in an airtight tin.

....

CHAPTER 8

GAMES FOR GRASS, PAVEMENT, WATER, AND SNOW

The sun is shining and you have a few minutes or hours to spare. Grab a ball, a piece of chalk, a kid or two, your laughing hat—and go outside to play.

Games are a natural way to teach children about fairness and taking turns. Be creative about deciding who goes first: flip a coin, draw straws (either strips of paper, twigs, or actual straws with one longer than the others), or choose the person who went last the last round you played. Vary the way you play so that everyone has a chance to be a winner. Many games can become cooperative rather than competitive with only a small change.

Here are both traditional and out-of-the-ordinary outdoor games and projects that are all easy to start and fun to finish. Some work best when only a parent and child play, while others are group games—the more the merrier. At the end of the chapter are some events, such as carnivals and pet shows, to cap off a summer of fun in the great outdoors of your own backyard or neighborhood park.

150 GET GRASS-STAINED TOGETHER

FOLLOW THE LEADER The simplest of games, suitable for all ages from toddler to adult, follow the leader can be played anywhere, any time. Any size of group can play, from one parent and one child on up, preferably on a nice grassy area. Choose a leader, and leave enough time so that everyone eventually has a turn being the leader. The only rule is to do whatever the leader does; you're out if you're caught not following the leader's actions exactly. Encourage imaginative leadership: after you've all skipped around the yard while making kissing noises, try yodeling, doing a yoga position, oinking like a pig, or sniffing your own foot. If you're playing right, there should be lots of giggles.

MAGNETIC PERSONALITY Any number can play this silly game, but the more the better. The player who is "It" stands apart from the other players. Everyone else simply wanders around and bumps into each other at random. Then "It" dashes into the rest of the group and yells "Magnetized!" at one of the players. Now everyone else has to immediately cling to the "magnetized" player, either standing and hanging on to him or, if they want to, piling on top of him. Once all the players have attached themselves to the "magnetized" player, they separate and start wandering again. "It" repeats the whole cycle again by choosing another player to magnetize. The only way to change the player who is "It" is for the rest of the players to agree secretly to pile on *him* and make him the "magnetized" one. His turn as "It" is then over.

You can play this game informally within the family, with one family member yelling "I'm a magnet!" and everyone else (even if it's only one other person) attaching themselves to him. Anyone in the family can take a turn whenever they want to.

FOUR TYPES OF TAG

☀ **Backward tag** Everyone must move backward at all times. Players have to freeze in place when they are tagged by "It." Anyone caught moving forward has to freeze in place until released by a touch from a player who isn't "It."

☀ **"Safe" tag** Players agree in advance which material must be touched to keep them "safe" from being tagged, such as wood, plastic, paper, or metal. As long as a player is in contact with the right material, he can't be tagged by "It." Of course, when he isn't being chased by "It," he has to keep moving.

☀ **Carry tag** Players pass a particular object from person to person, and "It" may tag only a person who is carrying the special item. It can be a ball or a potato or a doll, but it must remain in plain sight at all times.

☀ **Ankle tag** The only way to avoid being tagged is to bend down and grab one or both of your own ankles (the group decides whether it will be one or two). Try variations such as elbow tag, two-ear tag, and eyebrow-wiggling tag.

FOLLOW THE TRAIL You need two players and a fairly large area to play this game, preferably one with nooks and crannies for hiding things. A large backyard, a neighborhood park, or even your whole house will do. Cut at least fifty strips of paper, number them, and put them in a bag. One player closes her eyes and counts to a hundred while the other leaves a complicated trail of markers on the ground (or on branches or shelves) as she moves from place to place in the designated area. When the seeker has finished counting, she has to follow the trail exactly, picking up every piece of paper in order as she goes. The seeker will often be able to see the first player ahead of her, but she has to take the time to pick up every scrap. The object of the game is for "It" to get back to the home base before the other player catches up with her and tags her.

NEWSPAPER FIGHT When everyone needs to let off some steam in an appropriate way, have a silly newspaper fight in the backyard. Wad sheets of newspaper into soft balls and toss them at each other (newspaper balls are softer than pillows).

HOMEMADE BUBBLES

It's inexpensive and easy to whip up a big batch of bubble solution. Combine a cup of water with 3 tablespoons of liquid detergent and 3 tablespoons of glycerine (from your drugstore). Pour the solution into a pie pan or other wide container. Lots of things can be homemade bubble blowers:

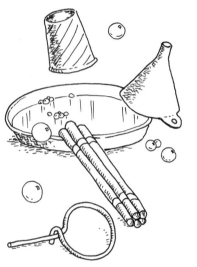

☀ **A plastic funnel** Dip the larger end into the solution and blow through the smaller end.

☀ **Straws** Tape several together in a bunch; dip one end of the clump of straws into the solution, then blow through the other end.

☀ **Wire** Bend one end of a wire into a circle; dip the circle into the solution, then hold the straight end and wave the wire around to make bubbles.

☀ **A paper cup** Poke a hole in the bottom of a cup, dip the larger end into the solution, and blow through the hole.

ON THE BLACKTOP

ME AND MY SHADOW On the next sunny day, take your child outdoors to experiment with her shadow. How tall can she make her shadow? How short? Can she get her shadow to disappear behind her? Can you and she make a giant shadow together? How about a shadow monster combining your body with her arms and legs? Can she do a shadow charade of some activity, which you can guess?

TRACE A SUN PORTRAIT On a sunny day, place a large piece of paper on the ground or tape it to a smooth wall so that the shadow of your child's profile falls on it. Now trace around the shadow of your child's face using a colored marking pen. Switch, and your child traces your shadow. If you like, cut out the silhouette and paste it onto a square of construction paper.

WALK THE LINE With chalk, you or your child draws an elaborate, twisting line on the sidewalk, and the other person tries to walk that line. Every time the walker falls off the line, a point is lost.

CRACK A SMILE Sidewalk chalk can lead to many outdoor games. For a twist, use the flaws in the concrete as part of the picture. For example, make a face with tiny sidewalk holes as eyes, mouths, or nostrils. Zigzag cracks can be turned into smiles, hair, lightning, water, or anything else you can imagine.

CATEGORY HOPSCOTCH As few as two can play this game, and though it's pretty simple, it's not always easy. On the pavement, use chalk to mark a court about 3 x 5 feet (see the drawing). Divide the court into eight rectangles, and write the name of a category in each one. Each player gets to choose some favorite categories. The object is to work your way through the court by bouncing a ball in each rectangle and then naming something that fits into that category.

GAMES	FOODS
COLORS	FLOWERS
BOOKS	SONGS
FRUITS	BIRDS

The first player steps into the first rectangle, bounces the ball there, and, before he catches the bounce, calls out a word in that category. If the category is games, he might call out bowling. Then he moves to the next square, bounces the ball there, and calls out a name that fits that category. If you cannot think of a name quickly enough, you have to start over after the other players have had a turn. Once you go through the entire court, you get to start over. Words cannot be repeated throughout play.

Good categories for young children are foods, books, songs, holidays, and colors. Older children will be more challenged by such categories as fruits, novels, states, automobiles, and birds.

154

RECIPES FOR FUN: COOL SNACKS

Here are some recipes to help you cool off. Make them together ahead of time, and keep them in the freezer until the action heats up outside.

FROSTY STRAWBERRY-LIME POPS
Yield: 6 popsicles

Homemade popsicles can be made with craft sticks and paper cups, but the resulting shape is difficult for most kids to manage, and often the popsicle falls off the stick. Reusable plastic popsicle molds are inexpensive, easy to use, and are likely to inspire you to create your own special frozen treats. Look for them wherever plastic kitchenware is sold.

1 cup sliced fresh or frozen strawberries
¼ cup lime juice
¼ cup white grape juice
¼ cup sugar (or to taste)

1. Combine all the ingredients in the blender and process until smooth. Pour into popsicle molds (or six bathroom size paper cups).
2. Freeze. (If you are using paper cups, insert craft sticks when the mixture has partially frozen, after 30 to 60 minutes.) Freeze for at least 8 hours, or until completely frozen.

FROZEN BANANAS ON STICKS
Yield: 6 servings

There's no tastier summertime snack than a creamy banana smothered in rich chocolate and coated with chopped nuts. You will need six popsicle (craft) sticks for this snack; you'll find them where crafts are sold.

2 ounces semisweet chocolate
1 tablespoon butter
5 tablespoons chopped nuts
3 bananas

1. In a shallow bowl, melt the chocolate and butter in the microwave on high for 2 minutes. (If you do not have a microwave, melt the chocolate and butter in a saucepan over low heat and transfer to a shallow bowl.) Stir until well combined. Place the nuts in a second shallow bowl.
2. Peel the bananas and cut in half. Insert a stick into the cut side of each half. Roll each banana half in the chocolate mixture, using the back of a spoon or a narrow spatula to apply chocolate to any spots that were missed. Holding the coated banana over the second bowl, toss nuts onto the chocolate-coated banana until it is well coated.
3. Place the bananas on a plate that has been covered with waxed paper. Freeze for at least 1 hour before serving. (Or, if desired, chill in the refrigerator until the chocolate is set, about 3 hours.) Cover each banana with plastic wrap. These will keep for about one week in the freezer.

Yield: 12 sandwiches

Assembly is the only tricky part of homemade ice cream sandwiches. The ice cream must be soft enough to handle, but not so soft that it won't hold its shape in the sandwich. Using empty aluminum cans to cut out the cookies and mold the ice cream works like a charm.

156

The best part about making your own ice cream sandwiches is inventing new flavor and color combinations. Anything goes—including low-fat frozen yogurt, if that is your wish. The children can help pack the ice cream into the tin cans, and if they like, they can mix chocolate chips or sprinkles into the ice cream. The children can also help with the cookie making, though the dough is a little stiff and may be difficult for them to roll out.

To make sandwiches, you will need four empty 1-pound aluminum cans and a stand-alone freezer (the freezer compartment of most kitchen refrigerators does not get cold enough).

3 pints ice cream or frozen yogurt, slightly softened
1½ cups all-purpose flour
½ cup unsweetened cocoa powder
¼ teaspoon baking powder
¼ teaspoon salt
½ cup butter, at room temperature
1 cup sugar
1 egg
2 tablespoons milk
1 teaspoon vanilla or almond extract

1. Pack the ice cream into three cleaned 1-pound aluminum cans. Return to the freezer for at least 4 hours.
2. To make the wafer cookie, sift together the flour, cocoa, baking powder, and salt into a medium-size bowl.
3. In a mixing bowl, beat the butter and sugar until light and fluffy. Add the egg, milk,

and vanilla and beat well. Add the flour mixture, beating until well blended. Form the dough into two round discs. Cover and refrigerate for at least 30 minutes.

4. When you are ready to roll out the dough, preheat the oven to 375°. Line two baking sheets with parchment or waxed paper.

5. Dust a work surface with confectioners' sugar (or flour, if you haven't any sugar). Roll out the dough to a thickness of about ⅛ inch. Cut into 3-inch circles using an empty aluminum can. Gather the scraps and roll again, making 3-inch circles from all of the dough. You should have twenty-four cookies. Transfer to the cookie sheets.

6. Bake the cookies for 8 minutes, just until firm.

7. Cool on wire racks.

8. To assemble the sandwiches, remove the ice cream from the freezer, one pint at a time. Use a can opener to remove the bottom of the can. Loosen the ice cream from the sides of the can with a knife and push the ice cream out. Working quickly, slice the ice cream into four slices. Place a slice of ice cream on a cookie, bottom side up. Place a second cookie, right side up, on top. As soon as all four sandwiches are assembled, replace in the freezer and repeat with the next pint of ice cream. Repeat with the final pint.

9. If you are not planning to serve the sandwiches within the next hour, wrap each sandwich in plastic wrap after 1 hour. Serve within two weeks.

THE WONDERS OF WATER

WATER LIMBO Here's a game for the times you have to water your grass. Hold a garden hose out so that its stream of water forms a horizontal line in front of your child. Put on some limbo music (or anything bouncy) and challenge her to wiggle her way under the stream without getting wet. Lower the stream with each round. Keep moving around the yard so everything gets watered.

PAINT THE TOWN WET Give your young child a bucket of water, a broad-bristled brush, and an old paint roller if you have one. It's lots of fun to "paint" everything from the side of the house, to the front walk, to the car.

FIRST RAIN

FIRST RAIN   Celebrate the first rainy day of every winter—or the first rain of spring—by taking a rain walk with your child. Encourage your child to engage all her senses: smell the air, taste the rain, hear how the sound of rain differs when it falls on something squishy and on something metallic, feel the rain's softness, watch how the rain makes everything look clean and shiny. Point out other rainy sights to your child, including rain splashing down rain gutters, puddles filling up, lawns getting soggy, items left on people's lawns becoming rusty, scraps of paper dissolving in the gutter, leaves and twigs sailing down the gutter, and so on.

PUDDLE SCIENCE   After a heavy rain, grab a ruler and a thermometer, put rubber boots on, and explore the puddles. Your child can count the puddles, measure their depth, even check their temperature (use a nonbreakable thermometer). These observations can be recorded in a notebook. Repeat everything the next day and ask your child what's different this time. Have some of the shallow puddles disappeared? Do puddles in shade last longer than puddles in full sun?

If you have a microscope, your child can see what's in puddle water. Can your child find only plant material and dirt, or is there something moving and alive in the puddle sample? If your child shows interest, collect puddle samples from several locations, including some from grassy areas, and put them in marked baby food jars. Check them for changes one day and several days later.

MUSICAL DISHPANS   Perfect for preschoolers, this game is best played outdoors on a hot day. Assemble the same number of dishpans or big plastic containers in a circle as the number of children who will be playing (even one child can play). Fill the containers with water. Now play some music, and the kids march around the dishpans in time to the music. When the music stops, they plop into the pans. Alternatively, fill one pan with water, so that only one child gets soaked in each round.

POOL GAMES

Swimming pool games are unequaled for keeping active kids happily occupied. Make sure an adult is supervising and there's no running or roughhousing on the slippery edge of the pool. If the games are played in shallow water, even kids who aren't good swimmers can participate.

POOL TOSS Throw a bunch of floating objects into the pool and see who can collect the most. For good swimmers, toss items that don't float and let participants dive and collect them.

WHIRLPOOL Several people join hands and move swiftly around in a circle, creating a whirlpool in the water.

ONE IN THE MIDDLE Three players line up in the shallow end of the pool. The two end players toss an inflated ball back and forth while the person in the middle tries to intercept it. When she manages to catch the ball, she gets to replace the person who threw it.

MARCO POLO For this wet game of tag for competent swimmers, "It" closes her eyes and counts to fifty. While she's counting, the rest of the swimmers arrange themselves in other parts of the pool. Eyes still closed, "It" moves around the pool, calling out "Marco" as often as she wishes. All the other players must respond "Polo" from wherever they are, which should make it easier for "It" to locate and tag them, even if they're hiding under water between "Polos." Once you're tagged, you leave the pool. Obviously, the honor system comes into play, since the player who is "It" has to keep her eyes closed throughout the game.

SNOW FUN

If you live in or near an area that gets snow, try some of these ways to play together in all that white stuff. First, dress up everyone in warm, waterproof outerwear. Layers are the trick, but not so many thick layers that your child can't move. Then try the following activities together.

SNOW ANGELS In this old standby, you lie on the snow and move your arms up and down. When you get up, you see the form of a snow angel. Once that's been tried, think up variations. How about a snow butterfly (same arm motions), or a snow archer (move only one arm)? How about two or more people combining their snow angels to form a line of paper dolls?

SNOW TIC-TAC-TOE With a stick, carve a huge tic-tac-toe game in fresh snow. Now play the game with your child, using plastic plates or pie tins for circles and crossed spoons for Xs.

IT WAS <u>THIS</u> DEEP! Keep track of the snowfall in your yard by poking a stick firmly into the snow until it touches the ground. Each morning after it snows, a child can mark the newest snow level with a pencil or marker. Then she can remove the stick and use a ruler or yardstick to measure how deep the new snow was. Your child may want to keep a simple log of snow depths from day to day and year to year.

MAKE A SNOW FAMILY Encourage your child to venture beyond snow men to create snow women, snow babies, and snow pets, too. Raid the house for props like old clothes and hats, wilted vegetables for facial features, and rustproof toys.

SLIDE ON DOWN Store-bought sleds and discs are fun, but a slide you've concocted out of a thick piece of plastic or cardboard can provide even more thrills for your child. Be sure to supervise as he slides down a hill. Check all around the route for rocks and other possible obstructions, and limit your child to small hills.

TARGET PRACTICE Offer your children a snowball target other than little brother. On a fence, low wall, or table, set up a practice range with empty cans and milk cartons, and draw a line in the snow. Then the kids can hurl away at the targets.

SNOWBALL COOKING When it's too cold to be outside for long, fill a bucket with snow and bring it onto a porch or inside (cover the floor with towels to prevent indoor puddles). Gather some large kitchen spoons, ice cream scoops, and pie tins. Make lots of little snowball "cookies" or "cupcakes" and arrange them on the pie tins.

RECIPE FOR FUN: WINTER WARM-UP

After sledding or snowballs, offer a warm mug of hot chocolate. If you have a fireplace, start a fire, and enjoy the glow.

SPICED HOT CHOCOLATE
Yield: 1 serving

Not for kids only, this south-of-the-border style hot chocolate is far richer than any drink made with a store-bought mix. The semisweet chocolate makes it rich, but you can reduce the fat content by making it with skim milk and skipping the whipped cream garnish. If your kids can handle a microwave safely, they can make it themselves without much trouble. The recipe can be multiplied by as many servings as you wish to make.

1 ounce semisweet chocolate
1 teaspoon sugar
1 tablespoon hot water
1 cup milk
⅛ teaspoon cinnamon
⅛ teaspoon vanilla or almond extract
Whipped cream (optional)

1. Combine the chocolate, sugar, and water in a saucepan or microwave-safe container. Heat over low heat or cook in the microwave for about 1 minute until melted. Stir well to blend.
2. In a separate saucepan or microwave-safe container, heat the milk until hot, not boiling.
3. Whisk the milk into the chocolate, stirring until well blended. Whisk in the cinnamon and vanilla.
4. Pour into a mug. Top with a dollop of whipped cream, if desired.

162

EXPLORING YOUR NEIGHBORHOOD

You don't need to stray far from home to find adventure. Encourage your child to look closely at surroundings usually taken for granted. You may both discover surprises that were there all along.

MAP THE NEIGHBORHOOD School-age children enjoy expanding their boundaries by becoming familiar with larger and larger areas of their local territory. To help your child gain confidence, help him map his personal terrain. To start, your child draws a map of your neighborhood on a large sheet of paper, strictly from memory. Ask him to include as many details as he can recall, from shops to street lamps, from unusual houses to memorable landmarks of all kinds. Now go out for a walk or a drive together, so your child can make notes of everything he forgot to include. At home, redo the map more accurately.

Another approach is to take a camera and notepad and tour your neighborhood with your child. Sketch the streets and special "attractions" you pass, and take photos of your child enjoying common activities. For instance, take a photo of your child sliding in the playground, entering the variety store, waving from the gate of her school, and walking up the front path of her best friend's house. Back home, your child draws a large map of the territory on a piece of poster board, leaving spaces for the photos when they're developed. If you have an instant camera, you can complete the project immediately.

EVERYTHING CHANGES Help your child become aware that even the most stable scene changes over time. Adopt an interesting block nearby, and visit it several times during one month to catalog the ways it's changing. Are the flowers or weeds more numerous, taller, grown wilted? Are the same cars parked in the same spots each time you visit? Has something broken or deteriorated since the last time you looked? Now try limiting your examination to a very small part of the area, such as the front of a single house or building. What changes can your child detect from visit to visit? Mail piling up? A forgotten newspaper rotting in a corner? Rust increasing on a railing? Look down, at eye level, and up. Each level offers new things to examine.

BACKYARD SPECIAL EVENTS

For your next block party, or for a big end to summer vacation, your family can work with others to create a special event like a carnival or pet show. Keep your expectations very simple. The children can do most of the work of planning and setting things up—it's often the most enjoyable part of the event.

Planning and putting on a collaborative event is a good way for your kids to become better acquainted with your neighbors' kids. It can also encourage siblings to work together for a common goal.

KID-SIZE PROGRESSIVE PICNIC The parents of three or four neighboring families can help their kids plan a progressive meal just their size. Each child prepares one kid-friendly picnic-style course, which he serves at his own house. Everyone troops together from yard to yard, eating one course after another. Courses can be very simple, such as hot dogs and chips at one house, carrot sticks and lemonade at the second, and cookies at the last. Older kids can be more ambitious (baked chicken, potato salad, etc.).

PET SHOW If you have a cat, dog, or other pet, help your kids take the lead in arranging a neighborhood pet show in your backyard. Invite everyone on your block; those without pets will be the audience. Giggles will abound while kids try to get their pets to walk across the yard to be judged. Give certificates for pets that are the fluffiest, smoothest, friendliest, largest, smallest, cleanest, best-trained, and so on. Leave some certificates blank until the last minute, so everyone has a chance to go home with a winning pet. Have on hand snacks for both people and pets.

BACKYARD OLYMPICS Families don't need Olympic-level sports skills to enjoy a little friendly competition with each other and with neighborhood friends. Make up a list of simple athletic events everyone can do. Decide whether you'll limit participation to the family, the whole block, or your kids' friends from nearby neighborhoods. Announce the event ahead of time so kids have plenty of time to practice.

In this Olympics, everyone gets a gold medal (or certificate with a gold seal) at the end for participating. If you want to recognize special achievement while downplaying the idea of individual winning, divide everyone into teams, and even things out by including older and younger folks on the same team. To give everyone a chance to win, include silly events like slowest walking or shortest broad jump.

Here are some possible events:

- ☼ **Obstacle course** With a combination of old tires, ropes, and large cardboard boxes, set up a course for participants to climb over, creep under, and crawl through. Strings tied between two objects can be jumped over, tires can be hopped in, low beams can be crawled under, and boxes can be opened and made into tunnels to be traversed. Use your imagination to come up with silly additions to the course, such as having to hop on one foot from one box to the next while holding your nose.

- ☼ **Long jump** Choose a soft landing place, such as a rock-free, grassy area. Participants can take only two or three steps to the marked starting line (a running start may result in injury unless you have a sand pit to land in). Measure off distances, and give each participant several chances to better his or her record.

164

- ☼ **Object toss** Who can throw a softball, Frisbee, or plastic garbage can lid the farthest?

- ☼ **Relay races** Suitable for teams comprising people of unequal athletic ability, relay races are the most fun when they include funny features. Pass a doll from runner to runner, or try a three-legged race (tying the left leg of one child to the right leg of another), or have partners or teams help each other fill a can with water using only a teaspoon.

- ☼ **Shoe toss** All players line up, preferably along the crest of a hill, loosen their shoes, and toss them as far as possible. Then each person has to run to the shoes, put the right pair on, tie the laces, and run back to the starting place.

BACKYARD CARNIVAL This can be simple or elaborate, as long as everyone has fun. Start planning early enough before the scheduled date of the carnival so your kids have time to make all the necessary preparations, beginning with posters and flyers to announce the event. Buy or make tickets (though you needn't charge admission—the tickets are just to make the event seem more authentic to the participants). Keep refreshments simple and inexpensive, such as small bags of popcorn and snow cones (crushed ice topped with fruit juice concentrate).

Kids expect a lot of little prizes at a carnival, but the treasures can be *very* little—a piece of hard candy, a new pencil, some of your collection of kids-meal prizes, a sticker. It's best to give everyone a prize for every game, won or not, especially with young children.

Here are some carnival games that are easy to set up:

- ☼ **Sponge squeeze** Two or more players dip a small sponge into a bowl of water and squeeze their sponges into their own cups. The first to fill his or her cup wins.

- ☼ **Cup and paper plate balancing contest** How high can a player pile paper cups and plates, one on top of the other? This can also be tried while two or more players are running (carefully!) back and forth from one spot to another.

Guess the number At the start of the carnival, put out a clear jar filled with corks or marbles or any small objects you have lots of. Have all carnival attendees write down their guesses of how many corks or whatever are in the jar. At the end of the day, award a prize to the one whose guess was closest to the correct number.

Makeup booth Few children can resist the chance to try out makeup. Gather a collection of costume makeup and nontoxic makeup you no longer need. One person, designated as the makeup artist (an adult should always be on hand to supervise), makes up each child in whatever way she chooses. Leave out the eye makeup for safety.

166

Go fish Hang a sheet or blanket on a string between two trees or other upright objects. Hand each child a "fishing pole"—a stick with a string attached to it, with a clothespin attached to the end of the string. When the child tosses the string and clothespin over the sheet into the "pond," a child on the other side attaches a small prize to the clothespin.

Penny pitch Lay out several dishes marked with numbers, indicating twenty-five points for a smaller dish and ten for a larger. Participants take turns pitching pennies into the dishes from a few feet back.

Beanbag throw Hang bags or pails on a string stretched between two objects at the height of most of the participants' shoulders. Pitch beanbags (or corks or any small objects) into the hanging bags.

CHAPTER 9

....

PARKS, BEACHES, CITIES, AND OTHER GREAT ADVENTURES

Some day that school and work aren't in session, take a minivacation together in the great outdoors. Put the chores on hold, and set out for a day of adventure. You don't have to go far, but you do have to *go*. Go to a nearby city, to a lake or ocean beach, to a park to fly a kite or wiggle your toes in the grass.

You'll all have the most fun if you keep your expectations reasonable (impatient kids remain so away from home too). Pace your day by including both active and quiet activities, and involve your kids in the planning. At the end of the chapter are some ways to make the getting there more fun for everyone so the adventure doesn't derail before it even gets started.

URBAN EXPLORING

Put your senses on the alert, and explore an urban environment with your child. There is much more to see than buildings, more to hear than traffic. A world of adventure awaits you in the nearest city or large town. Following are some suggestions.

MAKE CITY RUBBINGS At home, practice making rubbings. Place a piece of paper over the object you have chosen. If you want to rub something soft, such as a fresh leaf, place it on a firm surface first. With the side of a crayon or the tip of a pencil, rub slowly back and forth on the paper over the object. Soon you'll be able to see the pattern of the object on the paper.

Now walk around a city block together, and look together for interesting objects to rub: historical plaques, utility gratings, initials in the pavement, keyholes, and architectural details within reach.

UNDER CONSTRUCTION Stop at a construction site where a house, store, or office building is going up. Repeat visits allow your child to compare the stages of construction. Ask a worker what she's doing and how long the project will take from start to finish. Notice the foundation, the hand tools the workers are using, the large machines and vehicles on the site, the variety of nails and screws lying about. You may see concrete being poured, or bricks being laid, or air conditioning being installed. Perhaps a supervisor will be willing to show your child around the trailer where the blueprints are kept.

WHERE YOUR CHILD CAME INTO THE WORLD Visit the hospital where your child was born. Call ahead to find out what you'll be permitted to see. Perhaps you can join a tour for expectant parents. Describe how your child spent the first day or two of her life at this hospital. What time of day was she born? Did she sleep in your room? What was her reaction to her first sponge bath?

DECODE THE TOMBSTONES Cemeteries are fascinating places to explore. The stones and markers offer many clues to the lives of the people of the past. They're like a series of puzzles to be decoded. Older children might like to discover which first names were popular a long time ago. What might explain many deaths in one period of time? Look for the oldest tombstone and the most recent. Did men used to live longer than women? Notice the variety of symbols carved on the gravestones. Take along paper and a soft pencil, and make rubbings of some interesting old stones.

PEOPLE-WATCHING Cities aren't about buildings, they're about people. Find a place to sit and watch the crowds go by—a restaurant with a sidewalk café or big front windows, for example. The lobby of a big office building is another good place. Using clothing or personal belongings as clues, guess where each passerby is going. Shopping malls are great places for people-watching, too. Visit a mall's eating area and closely observe the crowds around you. See how much you can determine about other people just by looking. Some children will notice concrete details, such as the number of children in a family, who leaves their table full of crumbs and who tidies up after themselves, how many men are present with their families. Other children may notice the irritation in a parent's voice when a toddler dawdles, how long it takes various people to decide on their food order, or who determines where everyone sits.

URBAN ENVIRONMENTALISTS

You don't have to visit the wilderness to explore ways in which people can help protect the environment.

WHERE THE PLANTS ARE Visit a garden center or plant nursery together, and observe the wide variety of plants all around you. Notice the tiniest ones and the largest ones that loom like trees. Point out the stages of plant growth, from seed to seedling to healthy plant to older, dying plant. Does this nursery contain more than one kind of environment for its plants, attempting to duplicate nature in the way air, light, water, and food are provided? Ferns, for instance, prefer a moist environment, while succulents like cactus plants do well with little moisture. Ask an attendant to tell you and your child where the plants come from and how the employees take care of them. Buy a seedling and ask for instructions on how to nurture it.

RECYCLE STUDY Take some recyclables to a local recycling center. Even if your city routinely collects your cans, bottles, and newspapers for recycling, you can take a small load to a nearby collection center on your own. Explain to your child that your trash will be reused instead of wasted. Exchange a bag of aluminum cans for a few cents if you can. Stop on the way home and buy a treat for your child with the money you were paid for your junk.

GREAT JUNK In the phone book, locate a junk dealer who works out of a large yard and who will allow you to bring your child for a visit. Some scrap dealers specialize in car parts. Notice the trucks that come to deliver junk. Discuss the fact that people come in looking for items that others have discarded as useless. Is everything in bad shape, or are some items almost like new? Are machines used to crush any of the scrap? Ask the dealer what happens to the junk that absolutely no one wants.

BE ZOOLOGISTS Make a trip to the zoo an adventure by calling on all your senses. Here's how:

- At every cage or yard, talk about how this animal moves, eats, hears, sees, and protects itself.

- Count how many toes a giraffe has. How about a hippo? A chimp?

- Notice colors. What color is a giraffe's tongue?

- Look at where the animals' eyes, ears, and noses are. Some will be on the top of the head.

- Notice details like skin, fur, teeth, and the shape of animal feet.

- What is the predominant smell at the zoo? How does it smell in the bird cages, in the aquarium?

☀ If there's a petting zoo, have your child compare the way different animal skins feel.

☀ Listen to the voice of each animal. Are some of them silent? How might they communicate?

☀ Choose one animal to "adopt" informally. Spend extra time watching this animal. Take a photo of it every time you visit. Look for changes in its habitat.

ENJOYING NATURE IN FORESTS AND PARKS

Whether your family encounters the great outdoors in a nearby park or in a distant forest, it's fun to explore the natural world together.

Your child may enjoy keeping a naturalist's notebook to record all the new things he discovers. In it, he can make notes about the birds and plants he finds interesting, questions about nature he would like to have answered, details about places he explores. He can include words, drawings, and photographs as well as pressed leaves and other findings.

FOLLOW THAT INSECT Explore until you find a crawling insect on the loose, then observe it for five minutes without disturbing it. Note where it stops, what obstacles it encounters, what friends or enemies it meets, what it stops to smell, and what it eats.

EXPLORE A HABITAT Pick a small place and get to know it—for example, in and around a particular tree, weed, or puddle. Settle down quietly and try to observe everything in the habitat, including insects or butterflies that happen by. What does it smell like here? What sounds can your child hear? She might like to write a paragraph describing her little plot, or she can tell you all about it.

BE A CREEPIE CRAWLIE Young kids love to crawl on the ground, so suggest that yours pretend to be bugs and see what a bug sees. Point out a ten-foot-long trail they should cover, and listen to their running commentary on what they see as they crawl slowly along. For variety, have your child pretend to be a panther slinking along the ground, sniffing out a tasty mouse to eat. What might she see, hear, and smell along the way?

LEARN TO OBSERVE Blindfold your child and take him by the hand. Lead him along for a few minutes, describing everything you pass as you walk together. Tell him about the trees you're passing and the color of the flowers on the ground, and describe any landmarks. Now remove his blindfold and see whether he can show you the same way back. He'll be successful only if he's listened very carefully to your verbal descriptions. Then try it again.

CAMOUFLAGE HIDE-AND-SEEK Take a few of the items you've brought with you, such as a paper napkin, jug, spoon, and book, and hide them in fairly plain sight along a trail. Some of them will be naturally camouflaged. Set your child loose and see how many he can find. (Remember where you put everything, so you don't litter—or leave your good stuff behind.) Talk about how birds, plants, and animals use camouflage to protect themselves.

DAISY CHAINS Collect a bunch of daisies. Use your thumbnail to make a hole in the stem of each one, and then thread the stems through each other to make a chain of daisies. The flowers won't last long, but it's a relaxing natural craft.

KNOW YOUR ROCK Gather at least twice as many rocks as there are people in your group, and pile them up. Everyone chooses a rock and examines it closely until it becomes familiar. What color is your rock? What shape? Does it have any identifying marks? How large and how heavy is it? Now put all the rocks back in the pile. Can you find your rock? How did you do it?

GUESS THE PLANT Sit down with your child in the middle of a natural area that has many plants and flowers around. One of you chooses a plant that is easy to see from where you are, without saying which one it is. Now describe it. Can your child guess which plant you're thinking of? Add more and more details about your plant until she can figure out which one it is. Now it's her turn to pick out and describe a plant for you.

LEAF COLLECTION Make a collection of different kinds of leaves, choosing those that are already on the ground whenever possible. This is an especially intriguing activity with fall leaves that are turning color. Examine the leaves and talk about them. Here's a chance to introduce some new words to your child: *stem, vein, evergreen, ribbed, smooth, rough, soft, fuzzy,* and so on. Which ones are green and which yellow or some other color?

To preserve your child's collection, place firm leaves between pieces of waxed paper. Lay the waxed paper on several thicknesses of newspaper, cover with more newspaper, and then press with a warm iron. Remove the newspaper.

I SEE A DUCKY Look up at the clouds. Are they big, tiny, fluffy, thin, white, gray, or moving? Talk about what you see in the clouds. "That one looks like an ice cream cone. What kind of animals do those look like?" Back home, your child can make a cloud collage with cotton and glue.

RECIPES FOR FUN: FAMILY PICNIC FAVORITES

Outdoor adventures bring out hearty appetites, so pack a big picnic to take along. Here are some recipes for classic picnic fare for the park, the beach, or anywhere else you wander.

LEMON-HERB CHICKEN LEGS
Yield: 12 to 16 chicken legs (4 to 5 servings)

Chicken legs make handy picnic food for families with children. The leg tends to be the part of the chicken children prefer—toddlers will happily munch on one chicken leg for quite a while, while ravenous teenagers may work their way through several at one sitting. The legs are easily packed for a picnic and are ready for eating with your hands.

1 lemon
8 garlic cloves
1 teaspoon fresh or dried rosemary
¼ cup fresh parsley
1 teaspoon soy sauce
1 tablespoon honey
3 to 4 pounds chicken legs

1. Peel the zest (the skin, not including the white part underneath) from half the lemon. Squeeze out all the juice. In a food processor fitted with a steel blade, combine the lemon juice, zest, garlic, rosemary, and parsley. Process until finely minced. Add the soy sauce and honey, and process until well combined.
2. Pour the marinade over the chicken legs and set aside for 30 minutes at room temperature or up to 4 hours in the refrigerator.
3. Preheat the broiler or prepare a fire in the barbecue.
4. Broil or grill for about 35 minutes, turning frequently. Serve hot or cold.

SUMMER PASTA SALAD
Yield: 6 to 8 servings

When local tomatoes are ripe, you can combine them with basil and a little oil and vinegar for a delicious pasta dressing. Peas and canned baby corn, two vegetables that are popular with children, add still more color and flavor, but if you have other vegetables on hand, feel free to substitute them. This salad is easily transported and holds up to the heat of a hot summer day.

Note: To make this salad in advance, combine the dressing ingredients and refrigerate in an airtight container. Combine the cooked pasta with the olive oil, then toss with the vegetables. Refrigerate separately. Combine the salad with the dressing just before serving.

Dressing

2 ripe medium tomatoes, diced
3 scallions, chopped
¼ cup chopped fresh basil
  (or substitute 1 tablespoon dried for less tasty results)
2 garlic cloves, minced
3 tablespoons extra-virgin olive oil
2 tablespoons red wine vinegar

Salad

¾ pound rotini or twists
1 tablespoon extra-virgin olive oil
1 cup fresh or frozen peas
7-ounce can baby corn, drained (from the Oriental foods section)
Salt and pepper to taste

1. In a large bowl, mix together the dressing ingredients. Set aside to allow the flavors to develop.
2. Cook the pasta in plenty of boiling salted water until just tender. Drain. Rinse briefly, then toss with 1 tablespoon olive oil.
3. Toss the pasta with the dressing. Then add the peas and corn. Toss again. Add salt and pepper to taste and serve immediately.

BROCCOLI RICE SALAD
Yield: 6 to 8 servings

A minty mixture of nutty rice and lemon-scented vegetables makes an excellent hot-weather salad. It is easily transported and isn't likely to spoil if it is exposed to the heat. If you aren't serving the salad right away, pack an extra lemon and some salt in the picnic basket to freshen the flavors. This salad will keep in the refrigerator for a few days. An extra tablespoon of fresh mint will also brighten the flavors.

2 medium stalks broccoli with florets, stem finely chopped
1 red pepper, finely chopped
1 carrot, finely chopped
3 scallions, finely chopped
3 cups cooked brown rice
1 cup cooked wild rice
½ cup brine-cured black olives
   (available in the deli department of most supermarkets)

2 tablespoons capers
2 tablespoons chopped fresh mint
½ cup extra-virgin olive oil
⅓ cup lemon juice or more to taste
Salt and pepper to taste

1. Blanch the broccoli in boiling water to cover for about 30 seconds. Drain and plunge into cold water to stop the cooking. Drain well.
2. In a large salad bowl, combine the broccoli, red pepper, carrot, scallions, brown rice, wild rice, olives, capers, and mint. Toss well.
3. Whisk the olive oil into the lemon juice. Pour over the salad. Add salt and pepper to taste. Serve at once or chill before serving.

CLASSIC POTATO SALAD
Yield: 8 servings

This classic potato salad is better the second day than the first. Kids enjoy peeling hard-cooked eggs and using an egg slicer to chop them.

2½ pounds potatoes, peeled and diced
3 hard-cooked eggs, chopped
2 large celery stalks, finely chopped
½ red bell pepper, finely chopped
½ small onion, finely chopped
1 cup boiled salad dressing (such as Miracle Whip)
Salt and pepper to taste

1. Cover the potatoes with salted water. Bring to a boil and boil under tender, 8 to 10 minutes.
2. In a large mixing bowl, combine the potatoes with the remaining ingredients. Chill well. Just before serving, taste and adjust seasonings.

MUFFELATTAS
Yield: 4 to 6 servings

Muffelattas are fantastically delicious sandwiches that were invented in New Orleans at the turn of the century with antipasto ingredients. Even kids who normally turn away from olives and pickles find this irresistible, particularly if they don't see what goes into it first. Those kids who like to snack on the intensely flavored ingredients that make up this sandwich will be happy to help assemble it.

½ cup stuffed green olives, drained
½ cup pitted black olives, drained
½ cup mixed pickled vegetables, drained
½ cup mixed pepper salad, drained
1 celery stalk, sliced
¼ cup chopped red onion
½ teaspoon dried oregano
Juice of ½ lemon
1 tablespoon extra-virgin olive oil
1 round loaf of Italian or French country bread
¼ pound provolone cheese, thinly sliced
¼ pound smoked turkey, thinly sliced
¼ pound Genoa salami, thinly sliced

1. Combine the olives, pickled vegetables, pepper salad, celery, and onion in a food processor fitted with a steel blade. Pulse on and off about ten times to finely chop. Do not overprocess. Mix in the oregano, lemon juice, and olive oil.
2. Slice the bread in half horizontally. Remove the soft insides of the bread, leaving the crust intact.

3. Spread a thin layer of the olive mix on both halves of the bread. On top of the olive mix on the bottom crust, arrange a layer of cheese, more olive mix, the turkey and salami, the remaining olive mix, and the remaining cheese. Place the top layer of bread on top and press together.

4. To serve, cut into wedges. If a heated barbecue grill is handy (or if you wish to eat it warm indoors), you can wrap the sandwich in aluminum foil and heat on the grill or in the oven at 350° for about 15 minutes to melt the cheese.

178

GO FLY A KITE

Buy a colorful kite, or even better, make one yourselves, and take to the skies the next time the breeze is right. Here are instructions for a simple kite, a more complicated one, and takeoff.

CAPUCHIN KITE This simple kite, popular among Algerian children, is named for the North African grasshopper it resembles. First, your child decorates an 8½ x 11 piece of notebook paper with crayons or colored markers. Form a cone by partially overlapping the two upper corners and stapling them (see drawing). At this stapled place, attach a long string for a flying line (you can purchase kite string in 100- to 150-foot lengths, or use a thin string that is 30 to 50 feet long). At the other end of the kite, tape a 5-foot tail made of crepe paper or taped-together strips of paper. Your capuchin is ready to fly!

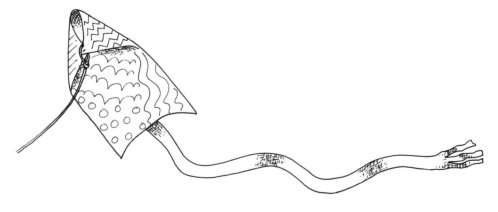

GARBAGE-BAG KITE Turn common kitchen materials into a wind-catching kite. You'll need the following items:

4-gallon plastic trash bag (light-colored so you can decorate it)
five 8-inch plastic drinking straws
clear tape
40-inch string
100-foot string
paper towel tube (optional)
three 3-foot strips of crepe paper or cloth rags

Cut open the trash bag. Following the picture, cut out a six-sided 16 x 20-inch kite. Your child can decorate the kite with colored markers.

Now make a "stick" by pinching the end of one straw so it fits inside another. Cut a third straw in half and insert it into the long straw to make a 16-inch stick. Repeat to make a second stick. Tape the straws as shown, both positioned X to Y.

Put tape on corners A and B to strengthen the plastic, and then punch a hole through them.

Cut a 40-inch piece of string for your kite's bridle (which is one or more strings that connect to a kite, allowing you to control your kite more effectively, just as a horse's bridle allows you to guide a horse). Tie one end of the string to A and the other to B. Now tie a loop in the center of this bridle, which is called the towing point.

Attach your flying line to this loop (either purchase a kite string or wrap 100 feet of thin string around a paper towel tube). At the kite's bottom, tape on three 3-foot tails of crepe paper or strips of cloth torn into narrow pieces. All set!

1. Choose a day with a gentle, steady wind. Hold a handkerchief or a small flag by its corners in your hand. If it extends, there's enough wind.
2. Pick a safe, open place like a treeless hilltop, an uncrowded playground, a field, or a beach.
3. Keep away from power lines, trees, tall buildings, traffic, and thunderstorms.
4. Begin by standing with your back to the wind, facing your kite. You don't need to run (unless you're trying to get a kite to rise on a day without wind). Hold the kite with one hand on the towing point (if there are two strings, this is where they are connected) and hold the reel of line with your other hand. When the wind starts pushing the kite, let out a little line and pull gently as the kite rises. Let out more and more line.
5. If the kite starts to dip, pull in the line until it starts to rise again.
6. To bring in the kite, wind the string slowly and evenly, while you walk toward the kite.

180

AT THE BEACH

It's amazing how much young children can learn within a few feet of a beach blanket at an ocean or a lake, especially if you bring along buckets, shovels, spoons, and funnels for digging and pouring. You can help your youngster enjoy the beach (after taking the proper sun precautions) by sharing some of the activities described here.

FOOTPRINTS IN THE SAND   Get everybody in the family to make footprints in the damp sand along the edge of the water. Compare your prints with your child's. Examine the prints made by dogs and birds. Make funny footprints by hopping, jumping, or combining sliding and walking. Can your child use a stick to make an unusual set of prints?

LISTEN TO THE SEA Ask your child to point out everything she hears, including the sound of breaking waves, seagulls, children laughing, and a dog barking. Can she imitate the sound of a seagull?

BAG IT Do this when you first arrive, and you'll end up with a clean stretch of beach in which to spend the rest of the day. You'll be helping the environment, too. Bring along a bag for each member of the family, and go on a trash hunt. Limit your cleanup activity to a set time, say fifteen minutes. Everyone carefully gathers all cans, bottles, and paper trash and brings them back to your blanket. (Tell children to leave any broken glass in place and report it to you.) One person is put in charge of dumping the garbage in a nearby trash can or putting it in the car to dispose of at home.

Consider giving out *two* bags to each person and having everyone gather trash in one bag, and *Good* stuff, such as shells and pebbles, in the other. Later, you'll come up with lots of uses for the goodies in the second bag.

Bring along wet wipes so everyone can clean their hands after disposing of the trash, or simply use sea or lake water to wash up.

MEMORY GAME FOR THE BEACH Two players each gather ten small shells, stones, or twigs, and then sit back-to-back on the sand. Using their fingers, each player draws in the sand in front of him a game board containing twenty-five squares (six horizontal lines crossed by six vertical lines). The first player arranges his shells or stones in a random way around his board, then for ten seconds lets the other player see and try to memorize his arrangement, before covering it up. Now the second player tries to duplicate the same arrangement of items on his own board. Younger children can place five items and take more than ten seconds, while older children should be able to manage all ten items in only ten seconds.

RACE THE WAVES When the tide is low and calm, you'll all get lots of exercise by running toward the outgoing waves and then trying to outrun the incoming ones as they chase your toes.

WRITTEN IN SAND Firm, damp sand makes an ideal medium in which to sketch letters with a finger or a stick. Write your child's name. Ask her to draw a simple

181

picture. Get together with your child and others and together create a giant message in the damp sand.

A BIGGER GRAIN OF SAND Bring along a magnifying lens. A few grains of sand seen up close take on a whole new appearance, with varying shapes and colors.

SIFT IT With a kitchen sieve, sift through sand and mud to find all sorts of interesting shells, worms, and other life-forms at the water's edge.

WILL IT FLOAT? Toss a leaf, a twig, or a small stone into the waves and see what floats.

SAND MUMMIES AND DADDIES You and any other adults with you lie on your backs in the sand. Now the kids bury you up to the waist.

UNSEASONAL SAND Bundle up your kids and take them to the ocean or your local lake on a winter day. What does your child see, hear, or smell that is different from the way it was in summer? Compare the number of visitors and amount of wildlife.

BUILD A TOY BOAT After asking your child to say "toy boat" three times fast (it's a great tongue twister), set about building one. In case you can't find much on your beach, consider bringing walnut shells from home to serve as the hull of your boat. Or find just about anything that will float, call it a boat, and set sail.

SEARCH FOR BURIED TREASURE Bring an airtight plastic container from home with something fun inside: a lollipop, a special shell, some change. When your child isn't watching, bury the container several inches down in the sand. Now make a treasure map for your child to follow. Keep it simple: "Go ten steps from the top left corner of the blanket, turn right, pass the large piece of driftwood, go five steps past the seaweed, stop and dig at the second pile of pebbles."

SEASIDE ART For art on the spot, round up shells, stones, and sea glass (pieces of glass that have been worn smooth by the waves). Smooth a spot in the sand. Now create a design by pressing the found objects into the sand.

Or bring a clear plastic jar with you to the beach. Collect shells, smooth stones, driftwood, and bird feathers. Then fill the jar with alternating layers of sand, stones, and shells to create a keepable work of art.

BUILD A BETTER SAND CASTLE

All kids—and big people, too—love playing in the sand. Piling up handfuls of the damp stuff seems to come naturally to even the tiniest builder. Any kind of sculpture is possible when the sculptor uses very wet sand that's been stamped down until it's hard. While creations can range anywhere from a dumped-over pail with a feather stuck in the top to an elaborate city, castles are always popular. When your children are ready to improve their castle-building artistry, share with them the information provided here.

Castles are a combination of three structures: towers, walls, and arches. Use this step-by-step guide as a takeoff point for building a simple, but strong, castle.

1. **Gather your tools** Raid the kitchen drawer or workshop for carving implements. Look for a tool with a squared-off edge, such as a narrow putty knife. Your child will use the tip to make windows. Very young children can use a plastic putty knife or ice cream scoop, or melon baller for carving out round shapes. Throw in some muffin tins, cookie cutters, and ice cube trays for variety.

2. **Choose your location** If you have your choice of beaches, choose one where the sand is fairly fine, without coarse grains. The best sand doesn't brush off your leg easily. Set up operations very close to the water line—close enough so you don't have to dig a very deep hole before hitting water, but not so close that your castle will be prematurely wiped out by the tide.

If you live inland, don't rule out castle building on sandy lakefronts. To determine whether the sand will work, take a handful and squeeze it into a ball. If it sticks together, go for it.

If you want to build in your home sandbox, purchase sand that will go through a window screen. That way it will be fine enough to stack up. Wet it and give it the squeeze test to see whether it sticks together. Then simply add water to the sandbox.

3. **Dig a wide, shallow hole,** about half a foot to a foot deep, in the sand. Slowly but surely, the sand at the bottom will become more and more moist. As you dig, put all the sand you've removed into one spot, a foot from the hole. Now have your child stir the sand in the hole with a foot or a hand until it has an even, mudlike consistency. The water in the hole has a tendency to rise to the top, so if you just reach down to grab sand without stirring first, you may get sand that isn't wet enough. It won't work to build using sand that is too dry, as water holds it all together. Sand is just right for building when it oozes between your fingers.

4. **Build towers** Spread out the pile of sand you've taken from the hole—a foot away so it doesn't get sucked back into the hole when you dig and expand the hole—and pat it with the palms of your hands until you have a flat surface on which to build your castle. Once you have a good, solid base, you're going to build two towers so that you can later connect them with a small arch. The beginner will have the best luck building broader towers. To do this, your child pulls big handfuls of very wet sand out of the hole and drops them slowly onto the base. Use two handfuls at a time for one tower, then two handfuls for the second tower. The first few times your child tries this, she should begin building the towers only about two inches from each other. To do this, she drops the sand to form two stacks of round, flat pancake shapes. Have your child put her palms very lightly on top of each dropped handful of sand, pressing gently long enough for the water to settle out of the sand. She shouldn't actually pat the sand down, but rather rest her hand there a moment until each layer settles into a flat shape on top of the one beneath it.

Taper your towers as they get taller by using smaller handfuls as you go up, stopping well before the structure looks precarious. Beginners should aim for a foot-tall tower.

184

5. **Make an arch**   Keep building your two towers upward, dropping each double handful of sand an eighth of an inch closer to the other tower so the two towers lean slightly toward each other. You want them almost to meet at the top. When your towers are a half a foot to a foot high, and only a fraction of an inch apart at the top, put your hand between them and dribble wet sand over the top of that hand. Let the sand settle for three seconds, and then pull your hand away carefully. Use your hand to support the two sides until you put the last dollop of sand right in the middle.

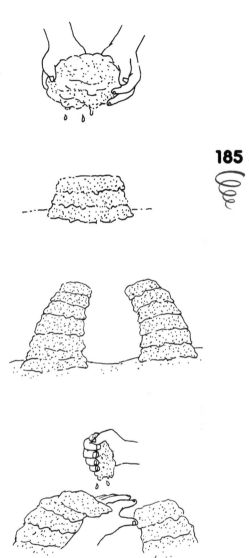

6. **Make walls to connect towers to each other**   Use however much sand fits into two hands and mold it into the form of a brick. Have your child keep her hands around each brick long enough for the water to settle out of it. Then form another one right next to it, then another, until you have a wall. Go from tower to tower or all the way around your base with one layer, then start over to add another layer on top of the first.

7. **Add details** It's easy to tunnel through walls with a putty knife or other long, thin tool. For a two-layer, four-inch-high wall, carve a doorway that's only an inch and a half high. Use the melon baller or ice cream scoop to carve out round windows or add scalloped edges.

   One easy way to add additional structures and variety to the castle is to have your child use a small beach bucket as a form.

   Embellish the castle with flags, seaweed, shells, feathers, and pebbles.

ARE WE THERE YET?

Nothing can destroy the fantasy of a nice family outing more than the reality of bored kids whining in the backseat. Face it—being cooped up in a car or in the limited space of a bus or train is not a child's idea of fun. However, travel time *is* time together, which is the whole point of a family outing. If you plan some interesting activities for this time, *getting* there can leave you with as many pleasant memories as *being* there.

Always keep a travel kit in your car, or keep one ready to take with you on a bus or train trip. Fill a small carrying case with the following: a pad of paper, a pair of safety scissors, a pencil, some colored pens, a deck of cards, pocket checkers and other portable games, a few small construction bricks, and a tiny book or two.

Break up a long car ride with frequent stops. If you have two kids who tend to bicker in close quarters, put a cooler between them in the backseat to double as a play deck. And get their input as to what snacks to bring, in order to avoid snack letdown on the road.

Quiet games suitable for traveling are described in chapter 5. Here are some more activities to keep the most restless youngster engaged. Some of them will involve you, and some are meant for independent play so you can concentrate on driving.

COOL MUNCHIE BAG

Once they were no longer preschoolers, the children in one family were truly embarrassed when their mother continued to carry plastic bags filled with raisins and carrot sticks to school events and family outings. She did this "so the kids would eat healthy" and so the family wouldn't go broke purchasing overpriced snacks in public places. The kids themselves came up with a compromise that made everyone happy. Whenever they passed a health food store, they'd be permitted to purchase a couple of new healthful food items to be added to the Munchie Bag. Now when they had an outing to attend, this interesting bag of goodies would be brought along, instead of the obvious and now embarrassing carrot sticks.

187

COLLECT CAR CARDS Before you leave home, make a set of car cards by cutting out pictures of automobiles from old magazines. Paste these car pictures on a piece of cardboard or heavy paper. On the road, work together to see how many of the pictured cars you can spot. Younger children can match colors instead of makes. You can also do this with pictures of other things you're likely to see on the road, such as farm animals.

REPORTING LIVE FROM THE BACKSEAT Bring along a tape recorder so your kids can talk into it, describing whatever they find significant about the journey so far. Any kind of record-keeping is fun and instructive for kids, though writing in a journal en route may contribute to carsickness.

The tape recorder can also be used to play audiotapes you've prerecorded of your child's favorite stories, plus some new ones.

CLAP IT OUT Slightly more active than most guessing games, this one involves clapping to the rhythms of familiar songs. One player chooses a song and claps it out while the others try to guess what song she's thinking of.

RED LIGHT, GREEN LIGHT This simple game works best in city traffic. The driver can play, too. Whenever the car is stopped at a red light, everyone in the car tries to guess when it will turn to green. The one who says "Change!" the nearest to the actual light change is the winner.

HOW MANY BARNS? Choose an object that you're sure to see lots of as you drive, such as barns, cows, stoplights, wooden gates, bicycles, and so on. Decide on a distance, say five miles. Have each person guess how many of the designated object you'll see in five miles. Now check your odometer and say, "Start counting." Everyone counts together, and the one who guessed closest to the actual number of that particular object is the winner.

SLOGANS School-age children and their parents can have fun with this game, based on the letters seen on the license plates of passing cars. Skip the personalized plates that already spell out words. For the others, make up phrases as quickly as you can. For example, if the letters on a plate are MGP, someone might call out "Mighty George for President," or "My gopher is purple," or "Mean guys pay," or any number of other silly slogans.

CAR COLORS Everyone chooses a primary color—red, yellow, or blue—and gets a point for every car he or she spots of that color. You can get tricky by awarding points for cars whose colors are made up of your color: if your color is red, and you see a pink car, you get a point because pink is made up of red and white. White cars give everyone a point, as white contains all colors. Yellow and blue make green. Red and yellow make orange. Red and blue make purple. Blue and red and yellow make brown or grey. If you want to play this competitively, have players call out the cars they spot, so the first player to claim a two-color car gets the point. It's friendlier, though, to simply allow everyone all the points they spot.

LIPREADING Here's a quiet pastime that will keep school-age children entertained for a while. One player chooses a line, perhaps the first line of a nursery rhyme, and silently mouths it very clearly to the other, who tries to guess what it is. If it's impossible to guess, say one word and mouth the rest, then two, until the guesser figures it out.

LICENSE PLATE COUNT Have your child look for all the numbers in sequence, from 0 to 9, on passing license plates. You might make it a rule that only the last numbers can be used, so that you must first find a plate that ends in 0, then one that ends in 1, then one that ends in 2, and so on.

TRAVEL PICTURE This works best on a bumpy road. Your child puts a pad of paper on his lap and holds the point of a pencil on the paper. The jolts and bumps of the car will cause the pencil to make marks on the paper. After there are enough squiggles, see if your child can see a design in the shapes. If not, can he make something recognizable with only a few additional strokes of the pencil?

189

BRAINSTORM You're almost there, or almost home, and you've run out of ideas for entertaining the kids. The trick is to get them involved. Say, "We have ten minutes. What can we do right here and now?" You and your crew should be able to come up with dozens of possibilities once you let your imaginations go. For instance, plan your next party or your dream party, talk about what you'd do if you won a million dollars, decide what the messiest thing you could do in a car is, think of something new to count (stop signs? bumps in the road?), discuss what the funniest part of this trip was, or begin planning your next trip.

PART THREE

FAMILY HOLIDAYS

CHAPTER 10

· ·

CELEBRATING BIRTHDAYS

A birthday is the one day each year when your child has a right, without hesitation, to be the center of the whole family's attention. Yet there's no need to break the bank or overextend yourself year after year—it's your love and undivided attention your child seeks, not a place in the record books. You can give that special attention not only on party day but also on the days leading up to it, by planning the party together with your child. From picking themes that reflect your child's interests to choosing your child's favorite games, you can plan a party together that says a lot about who your child is.

Following are easy, low-cost ideas for parties that both you and your child will enjoy planning and giving. The first section provides some tips about parties for preschoolers. The suggestions in the next few sections include general party ideas and directions for theme parties for elementary school children. There's a section on slumber parties, recommended for ages nine through the teens. The final sections offer ways to celebrate your child's birthday within the family, and thoughts on creative gifts.

Other activities that can be easily adapted for parties can be found in chapters 5, 6, 7, and 8.

PARTY TIPS FOR PRESCHOOLERS

Don't begin building up a preschooler's excitement until a week to ten days ahead of time, or your child will reach overload before the first guest arrives. Include your child in the planning (see the next section for more specifics), offering some reasonable choices about room arrangements, refreshments, and activities. Limit guests to the age of your child plus one, unless you know your child can respond to a larger group without becoming overstimulated, hyperactive, or cranky. The number you invite may also depend on whether the guests can run off steam outdoors. Line up some help for the party, either another parent or an older child. If the kids are very young, expect their parents to stay the whole time, and have coffee or tea for them.

It's wise to limit a preschooler's party to an hour or an hour and a half at the most. To keep things running smoothly, have an activity in progress as the first guests arrive. Children this age are not very good at group games. Instead of games, provide materials for something they can make and then take home. Play dough and lots of shape-making equipment, such as a variety of cookie cutters, are always popular with this age. Another easy favorite is stringing necklaces from cereal that has holes. Use licorice shoestrings for the strings, and put out lots of bowls of cereal.

Preschoolers also enjoy helping to decorate the birthday cake or concoct ice cream sundaes. You might hire a college student to put on a short magic act, stage a puppet show, or tell stories to the kids. While a clown may sound like fun, many little children find clowns scary.

Consider making the party a brunch, since youngsters are still fresh at this time. Offer them cupcakes so you and your child won't have to deal with cutting a large cake. For a favor, you might give each guest a little plastic bag filled with a lump of play dough and a new cookie cutter. Another idea is to tell the group a story and then give a copy of the storybook to each child to take home.

IT'S ALL IN THE PLANNING

Starting at age five, your child is ready for a more ambitious birthday party. Start by discussing with your child whether the party will have a theme. Themes can acknowledge your child's special interest or hobby, can help pull a party together, and can spark creative ideas, but it's important to keep your plans flexible in any case. Don't feel limited to games and activities that relate to the theme. In other words, if your child has a favorite kind of cake or a game he wants to play with his friends, go with those choices even if they don't fit the stated theme.

Make a list of guests together. Almost everybody breaks the rule of thumb that you should invite only the same number of guests as your child's age plus one, but keep the guideline in the back of your mind and don't go too far beyond it.

Two hours is long enough for a party for five-year-olds. From the age of six on, two to three hours is a good basic guideline. Longer than that, and both you and the kids will be too tired to have fun.

Shop for the invitations together; better yet, make them yourselves (see suggestions below). Decide on the decorations, plan the food, and gather the favors a week or two ahead. Leave plenty of time the day before the party and on the day itself to prepare the food, blow up the balloons, and make a final schedule of games and activities.

Consider avoiding prizes entirely. Make the fun of the game its only object. Be sure every child has a favor or goodie bag to take home, though.

IS IT HERE YET? To help your young child enjoy the anticipation, have him count off the days before the party on a calendar. Or count down with a paper chain (you can buy pre-glued paper strips or make your own). Your child's chain can be as long as his patience. That is, as soon as he starts asking, "How much longer till my birthday?" tell him how many more days and suggest he make the chain that many loops long. Each evening before going to bed, your child rips one more loop off the chain.

 ## INVITATIONS

Your child can help prepare the invitations by filling in the blanks, signing them, or putting on the stamps. Be sure to include who the party is for, that it *is* a birthday party, how old your child will be, location, date, beginning and ending time, what food will be served, and any special instructions: wear play clothes, bring a bathing suit. Ask for your guests to RSVP by a certain date (and you'll probably have to make follow-up calls anyway).

Here are some ways to make your invitations stand out:

FLYING HIGH Write the invitation on a piece of notebook paper and fold it into an airplane shape (see "Build a Better Paper Airplane" in chapter 5 for details). Place the folded plane in an envelope.

INFLATE AND READ Inflate a balloon, hold the end shut (but don't tie it), write your invitation on the inflated balloon with a permanent marker, and then let the air out. Put it in an envelope and mail.

IT'S A WRAP Cut birthday wrapping paper into envelope-size rectangles, or into an unusual shape, and write your invitation on the blank back.

happy birthday

DECORATIONS

To kids, a party isn't a party without lots of balloons and streamers.

THE PARTY IS HERE Tie balloons to the mailbox or front gate. Decorate the front door with Christmas tree lights, no matter what the season, or attach a large poster to the door announcing the party and featuring your child's name. Write your child's name on a trail of construction paper footprints that lead the way from the sidewalk to the door.

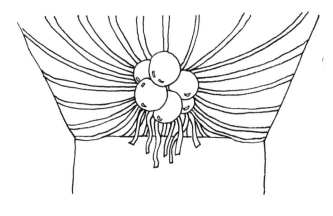

STREAMERS To decorate the ceiling of the party room, first measure the room. Rip some streamers into lengths that are several feet longer than the width of the room. Tape the streamers by their ends to points all around the edge of the ceiling, where the ceiling joins the walls. Now grab hold of two at a time, twist them together, and attach the other ends to the opposite ends of the ceiling. Now gather all the loose middles, push them up, and tape them to the center of the ceiling.

TABLE SETUPS Older kids often have specific ideas about who they want to sit next to. If you think your child's friends would prefer having a place set just for them (or if there are some kids who will be better behaved if they're on opposite sides of the table), there are some creative ways to design place cards. One is to write each child's name on a balloon to tie to the back of each chair. Another is to write the children's names on paper doll cutouts and place them on the plates.

If the party has a theme, you may want to carry it out in the centerpiece. You can make the party table more festive by placing toy trains or cars or trucks on it and filling them with party food. Have your child make a centerpiece with building bricks, then fill cups with building bricks at each place setting for the kids to play with and later take home. One parent extends the theme vertically by always hanging something from the chandelier over the dining room table—tinfoil stars for a space party, little airplanes for an airplane party.

SILLY HATS Does your child want party hats? Here's one way to make them: lay a dinner plate down on a piece of construction paper and trace a circle. Cut out the circle. Cut a slit in it from the edge to the center, and overlap the two flaps to form a pointed cone. Tape the cone together. Now draw with markers on the cone hat, or add stickers, bells, or feathers. Tape two pieces of ribbon to each cone to tie under the chin. If your child thinks it's cute, put party hats on her stuffed animals and spread them around the party room.

FAVORS

Favors of all kinds—anything a guest can take home—are a popular and essential part of most children's parties. Your child can decorate a batch of brown paper lunch bags, then place some goodies in each. Or the kids can decorate them as a party activity, and you can fill them while the group is occupied with another activity. Be sure your birthday child gets the same favor as his guests. If you give the bags out as the children leave, they won't get lost, and they'll help ease disappointment that the party is over. If the children will be collecting favors as they go (as game prizes, or from crackers as described below), make sure each bag has a name on it. At one five-year-old's party, in fact, the biggest hit of the party was the constant checking of the names on the airline luggage tags attached to the handle of each bag—the kids loved to show off their ability to read their names.

FILL THAT BAG Here are some suggestions for favors kids enjoy receiving: colorful shoelaces, hair barrettes, stickers, plastic sunglasses, magic tricks, funny socks, little stuffed animals, tiny dolls, and tiny balls. You can personalize such favors as combs, key rings, and inexpensive cups by writing each child's name with non-toxic acrylic paints.

Craft materials are always popular with both children and their parents. Include pipe cleaners, yarn, ribbon, a tube of glue, a fabric pen, a little notepad, or whatever inexpensive material you can find in a craft or art supply store.

CENTERPIECE SURPRISE Draw some circus animals all around a shoebox or other larger box. Draw "bars" up and down the animals, then cut doors in each side of the box. Put the box in the center of the party table, and put party favors in the box, with a ribbon tied to each, extending outside the box. When each guest chooses a ribbon to pull, out comes a favor.

IOU A PRIZE If you're willing to go the extra kilometer, round up ahead of time a number of gift certificates from the places your child and her friends frequent. Then use them as favors or prizes for party games. Gift certificates can often be purchased for an ice cream cone, a game of bowling, a child's movie admission, or a slice of pizza or a hamburger. This is popular with older kids.

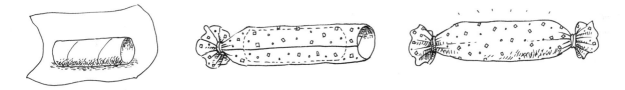

PARTY CRACKERS You and your child can make these party favors, which double as table decorations. Begin collecting toilet paper rolls far in advance of the party. Cover the rolls with pieces cut from sheets of tissue paper extending about three inches beyond the ends of the tube. Tie one end, fill the tube with little goodies, twist the second end, and tie both ends with ribbon. Decorate the crackers with stickers if you like. At party time, guests are told to grab a cracker or two and pull the ends to release their share of the goodies.

RECIPES FOR FUN: MAGICAL BIRTHDAY CAKES

happy birthday

200

Here are four birthday cakes that will serve as commanding centerpieces of any party or family celebration. If your child likes to bake, you can make the cake together the day before.

For young children, the decorations are even more important than what's under the icing. So don't be shy with the sprinkles, the icing tubes, the little plastic animals or figures. Don't forget the candles, of course!

CONFETTI CAKE WITH BUTTERCREAM FROSTING
Yield: 10 to 12 servings

You may remember this fifties classic as a "jimmie cake" or a "sprinkle cake." By any name, this old-fashioned white cake flecked with confetti pastels is guaranteed to win the hearts of young children.

Cake
3½ cups sifted all-purpose flour
5 teaspoons baking powder
1½ teaspoons salt
½ cup butter, at room temperature
½ cup solid white vegetable shortening
1¾ cups sugar
2 teaspoons vanilla extract
6 egg whites, at room temperature
1 teaspoon cream of tartar
1⅓ cups milk
¼ cup mixed sprinkles (do not use colored sugar crystals)

Buttercream Frosting and Filling

½ cup unsalted butter, at room temperature
Pinch salt
1 pound confectioners' sugar, sifted
3 to 4 tablespoons half-and-half, light cream, or milk
1 teaspoon lemon, orange, or vanilla extract
2 to 3 tablespoons raspberry jam
Additional sprinkles for decoration

1. Preheat the oven to 350°. Grease and flour two 9-inch cake pans. Set aside.
2. Into a medium-size mixing bowl, sift together the flour, baking powder, and salt.
3. In a large mixing bowl, cream together the butter, shortening, sugar, and vanilla until light and fluffy. Add the egg whites and cream of tartar, and beat for 1 minute.
4. Add the flour mixture to the butter mixture alternately with the milk. Beat until well blended. Beat for about 2 more minutes. Stir in the sprinkles. Pour into the prepared cake pans and smooth the tops.
5. Bake for 35 to 40 minutes, or until a tester inserted into the center comes out clean. Cool on wire racks for about 10 minutes. Remove from the pans and cool on wire racks.
6. To make the frosting, whip the butter with an electric mixer until light and fluffy. Add the salt and half the sugar and beat to combine. Add the remaining sugar and 3 tablespoons of the half-and-half and the extract. Beat until very smooth, adding more half-and-half as needed to achieve a good spreading consistency.

FUN TIME, FAMILY TIME

7. Spread the raspberry jam between the two cake layers. Then cover the top and sides with the frosting, swirling the frosting to make swirls and peaks. Sprinkle additional sprinkles over the top and sides of the cake.

ORANGE SUNSHINE CAKE
Yield: 12 servings

Budding pastry chefs will have the opportunity to learn how to separate eggs for this orange-infused cake. Be sure they separate the eggs over one bowl, and immediately pour the successfully separated egg whites into a second bowl. Even a drop of yolk in the whites will reduce the volume of this deliciously light cake.

The cake is topped with a luscious chocolate glaze for those who believe that every good cake deserves a little chocolate. The glaze also provides a background for writing a birthday message, if that is appropriate. If you want to skip the glaze, a dusting of powdered sugar or a sprinkling of candied orange zest makes a fine finish.

Cake
2¼ cups all-purpose flour
1½ cups sugar
1 tablespoon baking powder
½ teaspoon salt
½ cup canola oil
5 egg yolks
½ cup freshly squeezed orange juice
½ cup cold water
2 tablespoons grated orange zest
1 tablespoon Grand Marnier or orange liqueur
1 teaspoon vanilla extract
8 egg whites
1 teaspoon cream of tartar

Chocolate Glaze

6 ounces bittersweet or semisweet chocolate
6 tablespoons butter
1 tablespoon light corn syrup

1. Preheat the oven to 325°. Line the bottom of a 10-inch tube pan with waxed paper, cut to fit.
2. Sift the flour, sugar, baking powder, and salt into a large mixing bowl.
3. Make a well in the center and add the oil, egg yolks, orange juice, water, orange zest, Grand Marnier, and vanilla. Beat until smooth.
4. In another large mixing bowl, beat the egg whites until foamy. Add the cream of tartar and continue to beat until stiff peaks form.
5. Add a quarter of the egg whites to the batter and gently fold in. Carefully fold the remaining beaten egg whites into the batter.
6. Spoon the batter into the tube pan and bake for 55 to 65 minutes, or until a cake tester inserted near the center comes out clean and the cake springs back when gently pressed.
7. Invert the pan on a rack and let the cake cool completely before removing from the pan (about 1½ hours).
8. To make the glaze, put the chocolate in the top of a double boiler and melt over simmering water. Beat in the butter, 1 sliver at a time, until blended. Beat in the corn syrup.
9. Brush the crumbs off the cake. Set the cake on a rack over a baking sheet to catch the excess glaze. Evenly pour the glaze over the top of the cake, allowing the excess to flow down the sides. Using a metal frosting spatula, quickly smooth the glaze across the top and along the sides of the cake. Lift the cake from the rack with two pancake turners and set on a cake plate. If possible, allow the cake to set for at least 2 hours at room temperature to firm the glaze.

BROWNIE ICE CREAM CAKE

Yield: 8 to 10 servings

This recipe may look complicated, but it's quite easy. It does require, however, a free-standing freezer (the freezer compartment of most refrigerators just doesn't get cold enough), and it should be made at least one day in advance of serving.

To simplify matters, you can use store-bought brownies for the cake layer (a fudge-type brownie has the most pleasing texture when frozen). If you want to write a birthday message, sweeten heavy cream with confectioners' sugar and beat until stiff. Cover the cake with whipped cream, then use a tube of decorating frosting to pipe out a birthday message.

204

Brownie
6 ounces semisweet chocolate
½ cup butter
2 tablespoons strong coffee
2 eggs
¼ cup sugar
1 teaspoon vanilla extract
¼ cup all-purpose white flour

Crumb Crust
9-ounce package chocolate wafer cookies, crushed into crumbs
5 tablespoons butter, melted

Ice Cream
1½ pints chocolate ice cream or frozen yogurt, slightly softened
1½ pints nut or fruit ice cream or sherbet, slightly softened

Sauce
¼ cup half-and-half
3 tablespoons butter
6 ounces semisweet chocolate
2 tablespoons nut or fruit liqueur

1. To make the brownies, preheat the oven to 375°. Butter an 8-inch baking pan.
2. In a medium-size saucepan, combine the chocolate, butter, and coffee. Heat over low heat until the chocolate and butter melt. Stir well to combine. Remove from the heat.

3. In a small bowl, beat the eggs with the sugar and vanilla until light. Stir into the chocolate mixture. Then add the flour; stir well to combine. Pour into the prepared pan.
4. Bake until the brownies are cracked around the edges, about 25 minutes.
5. Cool on a wire rack. Then chill well, preferably overnight. Chop the brownie into ½-inch pieces.
6. To assemble the cake, coat a 9-inch springform pan with nonstick cooking oil spray. Make the crumb crust: Combine the cookie crumbs with the butter. Pat onto the bottom and sides of the springform pan. Spread the chocolate ice cream in the crust and top with half of the brownie pieces. Place in the freezer while you prepare the sauce.
7. To make the sauce, combine the half-and-half, butter, chocolate, and liqueur in a saucepan. Heat until the butter and chocolate are melted. Whisk until smooth. Stir in the liqueur.
8. Remove the cake from the freezer. Pour ½ cup of the sauce over the brownies and set the rest aside. Spread the fruit or nut ice cream over the sauce. Sprinkle the remaining brownie pieces over the top. Cover with the remaining sauce. Freeze the pie until firm, at least overnight. This will keep in the freezer for up to four days.
9. To serve, remove the cake from the freezer just before serving. Wet a dish towel under hot running water. Wring out the excess water. Then wrap the towel around the sides of the cake and hold for about 30 seconds. Remove the towel and release the springform. The sides of the pan should release from the cake. If not, repeat the towel wrap. Slice with a knife warmed under hot running water.

BIRTHDAY BREAKFAST CAKE
Yield: 6 to 8 servings

Sometimes weekday schedules make it impossible to gather for dinner on someone's birthday. Why not a special birthday breakfast with a birthday cake? This moist pineapple cake with a cream cheese frosting is light enough for breakfast, quick to whip together the night before, and ideal for decorating. Colored gel frostings, available in squeeze tubes in the baking department of the supermarket, are convenient for writing a special birthday greeting on the cake.

Cake

20-ounce can crushed pineapple
2 cups all-purpose white flour
1 teaspoon baking powder
1 teaspoon baking soda
½ teaspoon salt
1 cup light brown sugar
1 egg
¼ cup canola oil
1 cup (8 ounces) lemon or vanilla yogurt
1 teaspoon vanilla extract

Frosting

2 ounces light cream cheese
¾ cup confectioners' sugar, sifted
½ teaspoon vanilla extract

1. Preheat the oven to 350°. Coat a 9-inch round baking pan with nonstick cooking spray.
2. Pour the pineapple into a strainer, saving the juice for another use.
3. Into a medium-size mixing bowl, sift together the flour, baking powder, baking soda, and salt. Stir in the brown sugar, pressing out all lumps.
4. In another mixing bowl, combine the egg, oil, yogurt, and vanilla. Beat by hand until smooth. Stir in the drained pineapple.
5. Make a well in the center of the dry ingredients. Add the wet ingredients and stir just until moistened. The batter will be lumpy. Spoon into the baking pan.
6. Bake for about 45 minutes, until a knife inserted near the center of the cake comes out clean. Cool on a wire rack.
7. To make the frosting, combine the cream cheese, confectioners' sugar, and vanilla. Beat until smooth, by hand, in a mixer, or using a food processor fitted with a steel blade. Smooth over the top of the cooled cake. Decorate as desired.

GAMES AND ACTIVITIES

Always prepare more activities than you think you will need, since a game might be over much more quickly than you expected. Write up a flexible schedule, and have all equipment in a large box. Whether or not your party has a theme, you can use the following pastimes to keep guests busy and happy.

STUFFED ANIMAL SHOW This activity is especially popular with five and six year olds. Ask each guest to bring along a favorite stuffed animal. Before the party, make an award for each guest—construction paper circles with the legend FIRST PLACE printed on the top and a blank below to be filled in later; tape a ribbon to the circle.

Line up the animals so the kids can review the exhibition and agree on what you should write on each award: biggest ears, oldest animal, softest fur, and so on. Stick on each animal's award with double-stick tape.

MAKE A PIÑATA Smashing a piñata is a Mexican birthday party tradition. Usually made of papier-mâché, the piñata is filled with candies, nuts, or small toys. It is hung from the ceiling within striking distance of a blindfolded child, who attacks it with a bat, stick, or broom handle. (Keep all the other kids well out of the way.) When he breaks it open, the kids scramble for the goodies.

You can buy piñatas in some toy stores. Here's an easy way to make your own piñata. Fill a large paper bag with the candy or prizes and tie the opening closed with a long string. Decorate the bag. To ensure that each child gets an equal amount of the goodies, you can place them in small plastic bags; when the piñata breaks, each child can grab only one plastic bag.

MAD HATTERS If your child's friends love to play dress-up and pretending games, this activity will give them a great new prop. Start by combing thrift shops or discount stores for inexpensive straw, cloth, or felt hats. You'll need as many as you have guests. Provide craft materials for decorating the hats, including small items to glue on, cloth scraps to wind around the brim, and bits of lacy material to hang from the brim to act as "veils." Let the guests take their hats home.

208

BURST THE BALLOON Each guest ties a balloon onto his ankle by an eighteen-inch string. The object is to try to stomp on everyone else's balloon while protecting your own. Once your balloon is popped, you leave the playing area. For extended play, provide each player with two balloons, either placing one on each ankle, or allowing a replacement after the first has been popped. The last player with an intact balloon is the winner.

COIN WALK Hand a nickel or quarter to each child to put on top of one shoe. Now the children have to walk a certain distance, either a straight line across a room if they're younger, or around a long demarcated route if they're older. Anyone who makes it to the end with the coin on top of the shoe gets to keep the coin. Or let everyone start over until they *do* make it.

AUTO RACE Form two teams for a tiny-car relay race. Each child pushes his team's car the five feet to the finish line, and the next child pushes it back. But no hands! Have them use only their noses to steer their cars.

BAKE AND DECORATE A CAKE Kids age four and up, both boys and girls, love to bake. You will need an additional adult to supervise the cooking. The kids can sift, separate eggs, mix batter, pour layers, stir the frosting, frost the cake, and apply decorations to the cake.

If you make a sheet cake, you can section it off so each child can decorate a part with individual bowls of icing, food coloring, sprinkles, candies, and icing tubes. Or keep confusion to a minimum by providing each child with two or three cupcakes to decorate.

HUMAN OBSTACLE COURSE For this active game, divide the group in two: half are

Climbers, half are human Obstacles. This game works best on grass or carpet, since the going can get rough. The Obstacles place themselves in any position they choose: bent over, leg raised, on their backs, standing with legs apart in a V position, or however. They may form obstacles in groups of two or three if they wish. The Climbers move around the area, asking how to get across each Obstacle. The Obstacle says what must be done to pass the barrier, such as crawling through its legs, hopping on one foot over an extended leg, or jumping up and down in a circle all around it. There are no losers. Obstacles and Climbers change places midway through the time allotted.

THROW THE DICE This is a simple game for young kids who can add the dots on two dice. Kids take turns rolling the dice, and the high roller is awarded a single piece of cereal (like a Cheerio) each time. The first child to accumulate ten pieces of cereal is the winner. Then play again.

MUMMY Pair the children off two by two. Hand each pair a roll of toilet paper and instruct them to take turns wrapping each other up as mummies. The person who is the mummy has to stand absolutely still to avoid paper breakage. Tuck in the end if it breaks. Once someone is mummified, they can move around stiffly as long as they want to, then break out. Provide a new roll for the next round.

BACKWARDS PARTY

Older children who have had many "regular" parties will especially enjoy helping you brainstorm ways to make their next party fit a particular theme. Following are some suggestions to help get you started.

For a Backwards Party, write the invitations (at least the main sentence) backwards so they have to be held up to a mirror. Note on the invitation that guests are to wear their clothes backwards.

Decorate by hanging some paper lanterns upside down, sticking some balloons underneath tables, and hanging a homemade "Happy Birthday" poster upside down. Turn the present table upside down. Wrap party favors in inside-out paper.

Be sure to say "good-bye" when each guest enters—backing in, of course. Give guests name tags with their names written backwards. Kids should call each other by these backwards names.

For refreshments, serve an upside-down cake, or cookies with decorations on the bottom, and inside-out sandwiches (cheese works best). Be sure to write the birthday child's name backwards on the cake. Serve the meal in reverse order, cake first (keep pieces small). Have the birthday child make a wish, light the candles, then blow them out. Plop some ice cream on a dish and place a cone on top.

Here are some ideas for games and activities for a Backwards Party (remember to hand out a small prize to everyone before play begins, rather than after).

DON'T FOLLOW THE LEADER   Everyone does the opposite of what the designated leader says to do. When commanded to sit, stand. When told to smile, frown.

BACKWARDS TAG   All players must move backwards at all times. Otherwise, Backwards Tag is just like any standard tag game.

MIRROR WRITING   While holding a medium-size mirror perpendicular to a piece of paper on the table, each guest must try to write his name on the paper while looking only at the mirror.

BACKWARDS TOSS   Players try to toss a beanbag or ball over their shoulder into a basket. A variation is to toss something into a box from fifteen feet away using the "wrong" hand (the left hand if right-handed, or vice versa).

BACKWARDS STORIES   Before the party, have your child write some simple sentences on slips of paper. These are the endings to stories. Pass them out at the party and have the guests take turns making up and reading aloud a very short story—a paragraph—that fits the ending they received.

WHAT'S WRONG WITH THIS PICTURE?   In another room of the house, make some backward changes. Later, ask the group to come in and find out what's wrong with the room. Suggestions: turn a wastebasket upside down, turn a book or group of books upside down on a shelf, put a bed pillow on the floor, place a telephone on the stove, and so on.

FUN IN THE DARK PARTY

A Fun in the Dark party takes place after dark and can include a sleepover if the kids are old enough (age nine and up). If it does, state on the invitations that the guests are to bring a sleeping bag and pillow. For decorations, purchase some stars or inexpensive toys that glow in the dark. Hang up paper moons, stars, and black cats.

Here are some games to play. For more, see the section on sleepover parties (page 219).

FIND THE SARDINE In this rousing variation of hide-and-seek that is played in the dark, the person who hides chooses a spot that is large enough for several people to hide in. After the group counts to 100, they go in search of "It." When someone finds "It," he joins him in his hiding place. Eventually, everyone but one player will be hiding in the same spot. That last player will be "It" next time.

ONCE UPON A TIME You don't need a campfire to play this; the kids can gather around a candle set on a low table. Go around the circle, with each child taking a turn to make up a sentence that adds to the group story. Each participant should aim for a scary cliff-hanging ending, such as "and then Jack turned on the lights and saw a huge hand reaching out of the closet ..."

FLASHLIGHT HUNT Show the guests some items. Then, while they are waiting together in one room, hide the items around the house in plain sight. Now turn off the lights and have the kids hunt for the hidden items with flashlights.

NIGHT HIKE Take a short night hike around the house and yard, or around the block. Bring flashlights along, but cover them with red cellophane so everyone's eyes can stay adapted to the dark. While you're walking and exploring, tune in to the silence: how many different sounds can you hear in the dark?

DONKEY IN THE DARK Instead of offering "pin the tail on the donkey" with a blindfold, turn the lights out and have players try to *draw* a tail on a large picture of any animal. Turn each artist around a couple of times to disorient her, then hand her the crayon. Switch the lights back on between turns to see how silly each guest's tail looks.

212 TWIN PARTY

What child hasn't thought at some time that it would be great to have a twin? At this party, the dream comes true. A Twin Party pairs two children for each activity. If you happen to have actual twins, this is an exceptional way to celebrate their joint birthday.

At the start, guests can draw from a hat to choose their twin for the day. Alternatively, twins can be those having birthdays closest to each other, or those who are wearing the same color. Some kids may have a best friend at the party that they simply must be with, and that's just fine.

Write your invitations in duplicate. All the decorations should be in pairs. At favor time, have each child pick a goodie bag out of the pile for her twin. Ideal twin-related favors include Doublemint gum, pairs of colorful shoelaces, or a new pair of scissors. Serve double layer cake, or twin cupcakes (two cupcakes pressed close together and iced as one).

Keep guests involved with the following games and activities.

PARTNER PICTURES Provide art materials so each pair of twins can work on a picture or collage together.

INKBLOT ART WORK Set up an art project in which the children fold a thick piece of paper in half lengthwise and then open it. Then they paint on only one half of the paper. Before the paint dries, they fold the sheet again, then open it to reveal the mirror image of the painting.

THREE-LEGGED RACE All twins line up at one end of the room. Tie the right leg of one to the left leg of the other. At the word "Go!" pairs race to the other end of the room.

BACK-TO-BACK RACE Mark a finish line about thirty feet from the starting point. Each pair of twins sits sideways on the ground, back-to-back, behind the starting line, with their arms folded in front of them. At the word "Go!" they have to stand up together without unfolding their arms and without losing contact with each other's backs. If they manage to get upright, they walk to the finish line, still attached at their backs. Then they have to try to sit down again, still back-to-back. You can either have a winner, or have all pairs trying the feat simultaneously, with plenty of permission to start over each time they fall.

213

SHADOW YOUR PARTNER One twin stands behind the other and tries to copy every motion she makes, whether she is standing still or moving around.

WELCOME TO THE FUTURE PARTY

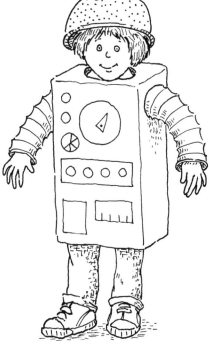

For this futuristic party, state on the invitations that guests should wear something that ties into a science fiction theme (such as an aluminum foil helmet or a futuristic-looking gadget). For decorations, cut some stars out of cardboard, cover them with aluminum foil, and hang them around the room. If your child already likes futuristic things, you probably have some little spaceships or *Star Trek*–type paraphernalia to add to the decorations. If your child wants to, dress him in a robot costume (at least for the first ten minutes of the party). To make one, first buy some dryer hosing from the hardware store, double the length of your child's arm. Cut it into two lengths. Remove the bottom of a cardboard box and make armholes in the sides, slightly smaller than the dryer hosing. Insert hosing into the armholes. Decorate the front of the box with shapes cut out of Con-Tact paper.

Serve something "unreal," such as blue milk (add

a drop of food coloring). Foil wrap the lunch sandwich. Serve a cake with moon-scape icing (craters and peaks).

These activities will keep the group happy:

TIME CAPSULE Ahead of time, your child concocts a time capsule filled with every-day items and hides it in the backyard or in a corner of a closet. Give the guests hints on where to find it, and when they do, have them imagine what each item "must have meant" in the "far distant past" when it was hidden. For example, a bunch of old nuts and bolts could be ancient money, or a scrap of white cloth could be a fragment of the top of a covered wagon that brought a family west.

MOON ROCK HUNT Hide several gaily colored "moon rocks," preferably outdoors, and send the group on a hunt.

ROBOTS Divide the guests into groups of three, each with one human master and two robots (two or four per group will work well, also). All the robots may walk only in a straight line until directed otherwise ("Turn right") by their particular human masters. When a robot runs into a wall or another robot, he has to send out a signal, such as "Beep, beep" or "Zip, zip" or whatever has been agreed upon between each robot and its master. Take turns being master and robot every few minutes.

SPORTS CHALLENGE PARTY

Children love to have a chance to improve their own sports records, whether they're competing with their pals or not. Plan a series of simple events that kids of all abilities can enjoy. Depending on your child's interests, you can choose the "sports team" slant, or the "individual Olympian" slant for this kind of theme party.

For the invitation, cut out a circle and write on it, "Take the Challenge! Come to Carla's Birthday Sports Challenge, an Olympics-style Party. Forget the party duds. Wear clothes and shoes you can run and jump in." Tape two strips of col-ored ribbon to the bottom of the circle to resemble an award ribbon, before you put the invitation in the envelope.

Decorate the party space to carry out the sports theme. Cut out balls of all sizes from cardboard and hang them wherever you can. If your child has old sports uniforms, hang them on hangers and use them as decorations. Cut banners out of felt or colored paper and write winning messages on them ("Happy Birthday," "Go Team!" "You're the Best!" "Go for it!").

Decorate a sheet cake as though it were a playing field, with goals set up at either end (strings strung across candles) and tiny plastic figures acting as players. Use icing to write "You're a winner, Carla!" across the cake. Serve a sports drink.

Favors should be sports related, such as small balls, inexpensive tape measures, chalk, headbands, bandannas, sports cards, and so on. If your emphasis is on teams, you might want to place the favors in baseball caps for the kids to take home.

For games appropriate for a Sports Challenge Party, see the outdoor games in chapter 8, especially the section on having a Backyard Olympics.

COOPERATIVE PARTY

Here's a way to show your child and his or her friends how exciting cooperation can be.

Invitations should be written and illustrated by both you and your child (note at the bottom, "This invitation is a joint project of Joey Smith and Mr. Simon Smith."). Include some banners in your decorations ("Peace is Possible," "Togetherness"). Make cake decorating one of the party activities so it can be a cooperative project. Choose favors that are better when used by more than one person, such as Chinese finger puzzles, jump rope, or marbles.

Here are some noncompetitive games and activities suitable for a cooperative party.

JOINT COLLAGE Lay out a white sheet or create a sheet-size piece of paper by taping together smaller sheets. Provide all kinds of art materials, including colored markers, paints, magazines to cut up, glue, fabric swatches, cotton balls, glue sticks, and any flat odds and ends you can find that would fit into a collage. Have all the guests at the party get down on the floor and work together to create a giant collage in honor of the birthday child. When it's done, hang it on a wall. Take photos of the guests working on the collage and of the finished creation; later, send a print to every guest.

PIGS AND CHIMPS This simple game lends itself to any number of people and to all ages. First decide as a group what two or three animals you'll include (be sure they're animals that make a sound). Say you decide to form two teams, and you choose two animals: pigs and chimps. For a few seconds, everyone thinks about whether they are a pig or a chimp. Keep your decision a secret. Now everyone closes their eyes and hops and moves around the room making the noise of their chosen animal. A parent should watch to see that no one smashes into anything as they move around unseeing. The object is for each player to find his own kind and congregate with them.

TUG FOR PEACE This alternative to the traditional tug-of-war is played by dividing a group of kids into two teams. One team lines up and sits down on one side of a long thick rope, while the other team lines up and sits on the other side, facing the first team. Both sides try to help each other stand up by pulling evenly on the rope.

HUG TAG One way to play this friendly variation on tag is that players cannot be tagged as long as they're hugging another player. While they're not being specifically chased, they must keep moving.

PIN THE DONKEY ON THE TAIL Find or draw a very large picture of a donkey. Cut it up into as many pieces as there are guests at the party. Hang a large sheet of paper on a wall, and pin the tail there. Everyone at the party gets one piece of donkey with a piece of tape attached. Then, everyone simultaneously spins around three times and attempts to immediately place the donkey parts on the paper. This group donkey creation should be good for some laughs.

JAPANESE TEA PARTY

For this party, inspired by the Japanese tea ceremony, write the invitations on pieces of paper and fold them into fans. Include a couple of Japanese words, such as *dozo* (please) and *arigato* (thank-you).

To decorate the room in which you'll be serving tea, purchase inexpensive paper lanterns and fans at an import shop. Buy or make a wind chime and, if the party's indoors, aim a fan at the chimes for a constant Oriental tinkling sound. If you have some straw mats, place them on the floor for guests to sit on. Buy, rent, or borrow a record of some Japanese music to play in the background.

As your child's guests enter, have them remove their shoes and bow to each other. For a craft, you can buy a simple book on origami and supply the guests with colored paper from which to form folded animals.

At tea time, supply hot wet washcloths with which guests can clean their hands. Serve green tea in the smallest cups you have, with cookies or rice cakes. If lunch is to be supplied, serve a stir-fried dish with rice. Supply chopsticks, along with a lesson on how to use them.

217

EIGHT MORE THEMES

PUZZLE PARTY This party works best for children who are at least eight years old. Write out the invitation on an index card, then cut it into six or so pieces and slip them into an envelope. Ask your guests to bring any puzzles or tricks they may have. Gather every puzzle in the house, and purchase some more, including the small metal kind, puzzles made out of cardboard, and books containing puzzles, mazes, and optical illusions. In advance of the party, make a tape of familiar and unusual sounds, then have guests guess what each sound is.

ARTISTS' PARTY All guests are asked on the invitation to bring any rubber stamps they have. Cover a couple of tables with paper or plastic tablecloths. Set up a table with stamps, stamp pads, stamp alphabet set, glue sticks, tape, colored paper, and magazines to cut up. Set up another table with paints and other art supplies. Have available scissors, stickers, stars, felt-tip pens, paper, envelopes, and index cards to be made into postcards.

218

TALENT PARTY Older kids are more likely to enjoy this party at which everyone performs. On the invitation, list some offbeat categories so that even those who think themselves untalented will be able to find a way to participate, such as leading the group in a round, pantomiming, doing a headstand while reciting haiku, telling jokes. Encourage joint acts.

CIRCUS PARTY Decorate all the guests in white clown makeup, rouge, and eyebrow pencil. Supply or make silly hats, and show the kids how to pantomime as clowns do. Encourage spontaneous pantomime. Take photos of everyone.

COSTUME PARTY Consider two variations. Either write on the invitations that guests are to dress up as what they want to be when they grow up, or supply all sorts of dress-up clothes, makeup, hats, and accessories. Then decide as a group which costumes are silliest, most original, fanciest, and so on. Be sure all the children's efforts are acknowledged.

BUBBLE PARTY Supply all kinds of bubble-making equipment. Have the kids fan their bubbles with cardboard to see how far they'll go. See if they can get their bubbles to float across a string tied between two chairs. If the party's in the backyard, fill an inexpensive inflatable pool with bubble solution, and provide oversize bubble-making equipment (try a hula hoop). See "Homemade Bubbles" in chapter 8 for more ideas.

DINOSAUR PARTY Dinosaurs are always a hit with the preschool and primary-age crowd. Use dinosaur stencils to draw dino shapes for the invitation. Group several white balloons in a nest of crumbled newspaper and call them dinosaur eggs. Lay out a trail of dinosaur prints for kids to follow.

Arrange the table so that dinosaurs (plastic or cardboard) gather around a plant, some rocks, and a watering hole made from aluminum foil. Make a dinosaur cave in a corner by covering a table with a blanket. Favors are easy: tiny plastic dinosaurs, dinosaur stamps, or dinosaur bookmarks.

Play Musical Dinosaur Tracks by numbering some large dinosaur footsteps and placing them in a circle. Play some music while the kids march in a circle. When the music stops, each child stands on a numbered footstep and receives the prize that goes with that number.

PLANTING PARTY You don't need a garden for this gardening party; a tarp laid on the kitchen floor will do fine. Note on the invitations that guests are to wear play clothes, as they'll be getting dirty. Buy a flat of flowers, some soil and peat moss, and a selection of six-inch plastic or clay pots. Each child gets to decorate his own pot and transplant a flower into it to take home. Another activity is to have the kids lay a variety of plant materials onto poster board, then carefully press them down under a layer of clear plastic adhesive paper. Decorate the cake with edible flowers or sprigs of rosemary. Attach party favors to long strings ("stems"), and have the guests "follow the stems" to their goodies.

SLEEPOVER PARTIES

Your child may begin clamoring for a slumber party or overnight party at age nine or so. Allow as many friends as you and she or he can handle, though four to six guests keeps things more manageable—at least the first couple of times.

Invitations must be specific so the other families will know what to expect. Say what they should bring (sleeping bag, towel, comb, toothbrush, change of clothes). Clarify what meals will be served, and say whether dinner is included if the party begins later in the evening. Such get-togethers usually conclude at midmorning the next day, after a breakfast bar of cold cereals, milk, juices, and either muffins or bagels and cream cheese.

Discuss bedtime in advance with your child. It's probable that if you have a teen, you won't even try enforcing a bedtime. If possible, have siblings sleep at a friend's house, so your birthday child can best enjoy the special evening.

Leave the decisions about decorations to your child. What was fun at five is embarrassing at ten. As for activities, you might want to begin with an outdoor game (so they'll get tired out and eventually be able to sleep) and follow that by letting them make their own pizzas or their own deli sandwiches, or concoct their own salads from a salad bar, and maybe bake a cake together.

Here are a few game and activity ideas especially suitable to slumber parties:

220

BELLY LAUGHS Each guest has to lie with her head on someone else's stomach and not laugh or talk.

MAKE A MOVIE If you have access to a video camera, an overnight party is a good time for your child and her friends to make a movie. Everyone can provide some talent. Suggest they take turns operating the camera and discussing direction. They might like to write some opening titles on cardboard ("Suzie acts up" or "Danny eats and eats and eats" or "Rose tells a joke").

SHADOW CHARADES Two guests stand on chairs and hold up a large white sheet about six feet away from a wall. Place a bright light close to the wall behind the sheet. Pairs of players stand behind the sheet in such a way that they cast sharp shadows on the sheet. Each pair is given something to act out in shadow, which the others have to guess. Key the scenarios to your child's age: nursery rhymes, proverbs, or everyday scenes such as returning something at a department store, arguing over a television program, or meeting for the first time at a supermarket.

MURDER AT NIGHT Begin by folding up slips of paper, one per player, and placing them in a bowl. All the slips are blank except for one marked with an X and one marked with a D. The player who draws the X is the murderer, while the one who gets the D is the detective. The detective has to leave the room, at which point the lights are turned off.

All the rest of the players now move around the room in the dark. The player who is the murderer chooses someone by putting her hands on the victim's shoulders. The victim screams and falls to the ground. Now the lights are turned back on, and the detective comes back into the room. The detective asks questions of the guests, and only the murderer is permitted to lie. When the detective thinks she knows "who dunnit," she charges the murderer with the crime. If she guessed right, the murderer must confess.

FEELINGS Party guests can't use their sense of sight to win this game, even if the lights are on. Place common household items in paper lunchbags, one item to a bag. Include such things as a spoon, a pen, a funnel, a lipstick, and a comb. Seal the bags with tape, and then number them. Each guest is given a sheet of paper and a pencil. Now the bags are passed around, and players try to guess what's in them by feeling them. They write their guesses by number on their papers, and the one who guesses the most correct items is the winner. For a collaborative version of the game, each person calls out her guess for one of the items, and sees who agrees or disagrees with it. Now open the bag—is the majority correct?

SPECIAL WAYS TO CELEBRATE IN THE FAMILY

Even with all the hoopla of a birthday party, kids love the special attention that comes from "family only" observances. Birthdays are great opportunities to create simple but meaningful traditions for your family. Try out some of the following ideas.

BREAKFAST IN BED Some families serve the birthday child (or parent) breakfast in bed on a tray. If you like, place a small wrapped gift on the birthday tray. Many birthdays fall on school days and work days, so this ritual helps get the day off on the right note. Or gather around the bed to blow out the candles on a Birthday Breakfast Cake (see recipe, page 205).

OUT TO BRUNCH If the birthday party is going to be in the evening, and if you have the party planning under control, consider taking your child out to brunch in the morning. Or one parent can take the child out to brunch while the other completes party preparations. Choose an actual restaurant meal rather than fast food to acknowledge that your child is growing up.

SAVE THE NEWS Save the newspaper for each of your child's birthdays. Wrap them all loosely in plastic. Make it a ritual to unwrap and peruse some of the older ones if your child is currently interested in what happened "when he was little."

DAY OF FREEDOM Make your child's birthday even more special by relieving him of all his regular chores. No criticism is allowed on this day. Your child can also get to stay up late, and he can eat whatever he wants to.

THE HALF-BIRTHDAY If your child is a twin or his birthday coincides with a major holiday, offer him the chance to have a party halfway through the year. Then he can have the truly individual, gigantic celebration he longs for. Even if you only do this once every few years, it will be memorable and much appreciated.

GIANT BIRTHDAY CARD The whole family collaborates on a giant birthday card. Begin making the card by taping together two large pieces of poster paper (available at an art supply or stationery store). Draw and write personal messages to the birthday child, focusing on his or her special qualities.

POSTPARTY POINTERS To avoid birthday-party letdown, make the evening after the party (or the next evening) special by showing home movies of previous birthdays. Plan a family-only outing to a favorite spot the day after the party.

GIFTS THAT LAST

Gifts, of course, are the highlight of birthdays for most kids. When you think about what to give, focus on "real stuff" and toys that open up many possibilities for creative play. Consider a fancy blank book to serve as a diary or journal, a world globe, an ant farm, a fingerprint kit, some bookplates or large blank stickers and markers so your child can make her own bookplates, or several boxes of dominoes so the persistent child can construct elaborate layouts to be knocked down.

Personalized IOUs are enjoyed by older children (so long as they're not the *only* gift). Examples: "IOU $5 worth of photocopying so you can make and duplicate your own magazine," or "IOU five evenings of game playing in the coming month—your choice of games."

Many of the best toys of all are found not in toy stores but in stationery, hardware, drug, or school supply shops. You can put together a kit of real-world tools that reflect your child's interests or may possibly start a new interest. Here are a few of the many possibilities.

BIG-KID KITS FOR PRESCHOOLERS For your tot's next birthday, pack up a hair-care kit (containing mirror, comb, brush, ribbons, barrettes, and a pretty case to keep them all in), a teeth-care kit (child-size toothbrush, small tube of toothpaste, cup for rinsing, small container of floss), or a little helper kit (a colorful plastic pail containing some sponges, a squeegee, an empty spray bottle, and a roll of paper towels).

TOOL KIT Does your school-age child like to get involved in fix-it projects, or do you want to encourage her to be handier than you are? Support her budding confidence by equipping an inexpensive tool kit with a hammer, nails, pliers, a screwdriver, and a basic how-to manual. A half hour in a hardware store will provide you with lots of ideas for inexpensive additions to the kit. Play it safe by providing constant supervision if your child is under ten or is new to working with tools.

KITCHEN KIT Put together a cooking kit in a box. Equip it with a cookie sheet, some unusual cookie cutters, a cookie mix, and a book of recipes. Add a notebook so your child can compile favorite recipes.

SEWING KIT For ages eight and up, a sewing kit can be the beginning of a new hobby. Put everything into an attractive box, bag, or case. Include spools of thread, a set of needles, some pins, an unusual pincushion, some fabric scraps, and a booklet of simple sewing projects.

SCIENCE KIT Even preschoolers (under your watchful eye) will enjoy investigating nature's amazing laws when you fill a kit with one or more magnets, a magnifying glass, a compass, a flashlight, batteries, flashlight bulbs, bell wire, and balloons. Other science-related items you can include are a postage scale, a level, a small pulley, and a metal bucket with which to raise and lower items. At a children's bookstore, you'll find many science books (a great help if your own knowledge of physics is sketchy). These materials are not inexpensive, but they last for years—and as your children mature, they will return to them again and again.

GAME KIT School-age children with board game experience will enjoy making up their own games when you provide them with dice, a sand timer, index cards, colored pens, a large piece of cardboard for a game board, and small plastic animals or other objects to use as markers.

DRAMA AND DRESS-UP KIT Compile an assortment of jewelry, sunglasses, scarves, old nightgowns, makeup, sample perfumes, evening shoes, hats, masks, and purses.

MEDICAL KIT Fill a large purse with adhesive bandages, an elastic bandage, cotton balls, a stethoscope, hand cream, and any other medical supplies you find in the drugstore that are appropriate to your child's age.

SLEEPOVER KIT Make your child's next slumber party or overnight outing more fun by giving her a cosmetics case outfitted with a toothbrush, toothpaste, soap in a plastic case, a comb or brush, and a pack of tissues.

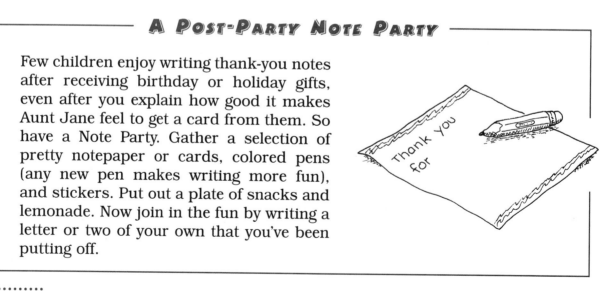

A POST-PARTY NOTE PARTY

Few children enjoy writing thank-you notes after receiving birthday or holiday gifts, even after you explain how good it makes Aunt Jane feel to get a card from them. So have a Note Party. Gather a selection of pretty notepaper or cards, colored pens (any new pen makes writing more fun), and stickers. Put out a plate of snacks and lemonade. Now join in the fun by writing a letter or two of your own that you've been putting off.

. . . .

CHAPTER 11

FAMILY CELEBRATIONS THE YEAR ROUND

From Valentine's Day to Thanksgiving, holiday celebrations are often the highlights of a family's year together. In many families today, though, ethnic or regional traditions have been forgotten. Many people no longer live where they grew up, and older relatives, the keepers of traditions, are far away. Because family members today have busy lives and spend much time away from the rest of the family, new traditions have often not been created.

If you want to adopt, adapt, or invent traditions for your holiday celebrations, try adding an activity or two each time. If something works, you may want to do it again next year. Before you know it, a tradition has been born. Consider your family's heritage, your values and spiritual beliefs, the ages of your children, your childhood memories, and the parts of each holiday that mean the most to you. To get you started, here are some fresh ways to mark holidays throughout the year.

226 SHARING LOVE ON VALENTINE'S DAY

The origin of Valentine's Day is lost in history, though we know it was celebrated as far back as the fifteenth century in England. On this day people exchange tokens of affection. You and your children can use the occasion to remind everyone in the family how much they are loved.

REALLY PERSONALIZED VALENTINES Put out the craft supplies, with lots of tinfoil hearts, and set aside an evening for valentine making. Each card should say something special about the recipient. Help younger children think about what makes each member of the family unique, such as a tinkly laugh, a habit of thinking of others, or the ability to lift a small child way up high.

LOVE COLLAGE The whole family can work together on a collage of images torn from magazines that represent expressions of affection. Don't limit yourselves to hugs and kisses; instead, look for the offbeat ways in which people express love. Everyone should explain why they chose the images they did, as they might be quite personal and not easily grasped by someone else. For instance, a can of chicken soup might mean love to someone, while a bottle of children's cold medicine might remind someone else of being taken care of when he's ill.

VALENTINE TO NATURE If your child is interested in the environmental movement, have her compose a valentine to the earth. She can use her imagination for this; one way is to collect small twigs, leaves, seeds, and grass blades and glue them on a card along with an inspiring earth-loving message.

SPONGE HEARTS Cut a sponge into heart shapes and have your child dip one side of the heart into a thin layer of paint poured into a pie tin. Now she can compose a heart-filled picture, either on a large sheet of paper or on a homemade valentine card.

VALENTINE'S RED DINNER Have an all-red family dinner party. Everyone dresses in red (or pink, if you want to stretch the rule). Use red napkins and candles, serve cranberry juice, radishes, or red peppers, finish with heart-shaped sugar cookies with red icing.

RECIPE FOR FUN: COOKIES THAT SAY "I LOVE YOU"

CHOCOLATE-RASPBERRY CREAM HEARTS
Yield: 12 cookies

Chocolate and raspberry are a combination made in heaven, and these crisp chocolate wafers topped with a raspberry buttercream frosting are heavenly. You can also make these cookies at Christmastime, using Christmas shapes.

Chocolate Hearts
5 tablespoons butter, at room temperature
⅓ cup sugar
1 egg
1 cup plus 1 tablespoon all-purpose white flour
2 tablespoons unsweetened cocoa powder
¼ teaspoon salt
Confectioners' sugar

Raspberry Cream Frosting

1 ounce cream cheese
2 tablespoons butter
2 tablespoons seedless raspberry jam
1 tablespoon confectioners' sugar

1. To make the cookies, beat together the butter and sugar until light and fluffy. Add the egg and continue to beat until smooth.
2. Sift the flour, cocoa, and salt into the bowl with the butter. Work into the butter mixture to form a stiff dough. Form the dough into a disc. Cover with plastic film and refrigerate for about 30 minutes.
3. Preheat the oven to 350°. Lightly butter a baking sheet.
4. Lightly sprinkle a pastry board with confectioners' sugar. Roll out the dough until ¼-inch thick.
5. Cut out into heart shapes, rerolling and using all the scraps. A 3 ¼-inch heart-shaped cookie cutter will yield twelve cookies. Use a spatula to lift the cookies and place them closely together—without touching—on the baking sheet (they will not spread).
6. Bake the cookies until set, about 10 minutes. Cool on wire racks.
7. To make the frosting, combine the cream cheese, butter, jam, and confectioners' sugar in a food processor fitted with a steel blade. Process until smooth. Spread on the cooled cookies.

WELCOMING EASTER AND SPRING

Whether your family celebrates Easter or simply wants to mark the glad return of warm days, you can adopt some springtime traditions that have ancient roots. Many of the activities here center on the egg, a traditional symbol of birth and rebirth. Thousands of years ago, people colored eggs and either ate them or gave them as gifts. The rabbit has also long been a symbol of fertility and spring.

EGG DECORATING Begin with cool, hard-boiled eggs. The basic method is to pour boiling water into little bowls, add a tablespoon of vinegar and a few drops of food coloring to each bowl, and soak the eggs in the dye solution. Remove each egg with a big spoon, and set it in an empty egg carton to dry. Now rest the eggs on a towel for stability, and draw designs on them with crayon. Try these variations:

- Wrap rubber bands around some eggs and paint the areas defined by the rubber bands with different shades of water colors.

- Write on some dry, room-temperature eggs in crayon. Then dip them in egg dye. The writing will show through the dye.

- Cut an old nylon stocking into three-inch bands. Place some small flowers and leaves on the egg and tightly wrap the nylon around the egg over the greenery, tying both ends of the nylon. Dip the egg in dye. When it's dry, remove the nylon to see the outlines of the leaves on the egg.

- After dyeing an egg, use a pointed tool to gently scratch a design into the egg.

GROW A LIVING BASKET Line a small container (such as a small produce basket) with plastic. Fill the basket with vermiculite (from your garden supply shop). Sprinkle some rye grass seeds in the potting soil, and water the seeds daily. Within three days, you'll have the beginnings of a tiny plot of grass. Before long, your living basket will be full of green blades. Place some decorated eggs in the basket and use it as a centerpiece.

HOW MANY EGGS? Have your child draw a picture as complicated and as detailed as possible for his age. Now have him "hide" some eggs in his picture. That is, have him add some oval shapes that will be camouflaged by the details of his picture. See if he can confuse a sibling or a friend about how many eggs are actually hidden.

PLASTIC EGG HUNT Purchase a set of plastic eggs you can open and fill with small goodies. As an alternative, have your kids decorate a series of egg-size rocks. Hide them every year and let your kids try to find them all. If one is missed, no problem—it won't rot before eventually turning up.

BOUNCE THE EGG   Here's how to make an egg bounce: Remove the shell from a hard-boiled egg and place it in half a glass of water. Fill the rest of the glass with vinegar and leave it overnight. The next day you'll be able to bounce the egg gently. Or leave a hard-boiled egg (shell and all) in vinegar for a day or two, and the shell will dissolve, turning the egg quite rubbery.

TOSS THE CASCARONES   Hispanic and Latino children play a traditional Easter game with cascarones, eggshells half filled with confetti. Start by making a dime-size hole in one end of a raw egg to drain the insides (save the insides for scrambled eggs). Now gently wash the inside of the eggshell. When it's dry, make confetti out of recycled paper torn into *tiny* pieces. Half fill the eggshell with confetti. Cover the hole in the egg with a paste made of flour and water, or simply tape it over. The game is simple: Throw the confetti-filled eggs back and forth, or sneak up and break one on a friend's head.

SURPRISE EGG   Here's one more eggy activity: draw a picture or secret message on the bottom (the wide end) of a hard- or soft-boiled egg and serve it to your child in an egg cup, narrow side up. After the egg is eaten, your child can turn the egg over to see the surprise.

RECIPES FOR FUN: EASTER OR SPRING TREATS

MINIATURE BASKETS
Yield: 12 to 14 baskets

Children will enjoy helping you make, decorate, and fill these delightful almond-flavored cookie baskets. These minibaskets can be miniature Easter baskets or bird nests to celebrate spring. Three jelly beans or gum drops fill them up.

1½ cups sifted all-purpose white flour
¼ cup finely ground almonds
¼ cup sugar
½ teaspoon salt
⅛ teaspoon nutmeg
½ cup butter
1 egg, beaten
3 tablespoons cold water
Decorating gel (available in the baking section of the supermarket)
½ cup flaked sweetened coconut
Jelly beans, gum drops, M&Ms, or similar colorful candy

1. Combine the flour, almonds, sugar, salt, and nutmeg. Cut in the butter until the mixture resembles coarse crumbs. Beat together the egg and water and mix into the flour to make a stiff dough. Form into a ball, wrap in plastic, and refrigerate for at least 30 minutes.
2. When you are ready to roll out the dough, preheat the oven to 450°.
3. On a lightly floured surface, roll out the dough until ⅛ inch thick. Cut out 3-inch rounds with a cookie cutter and place over the back of an upside-down muffin tin. Prick each round with a fork in several places.
4. Bake for 10 to 12 minutes, until very lightly colored. Do not overbake; the insides of the baskets may scorch before the outside is fully browned. Set the muffin tin on a wire rack to cool.
5. Carefully remove the cookies from the muffin tin. Turn right-side-up. Decorate the edges of the baskets with the gel. Place about a tablespoon of coconut in each basket. Then fill with candy.

HONEY BUNNIES
Yield: 14 rolls

These sweet rolls are superb for brunch on Easter morning—or any morning. If your children help shape the rolls, some of the bunnies may look like cats, but they'll taste wonderful no matter what form they take.

Be sure to give these bunnies plenty of space on the baking trays.

Sweet Bread Dough

1 cup milk
4 teaspoons active dry yeast
¼ cup vegetable oil
½ cup honey
2 eggs, slightly beaten
1 teaspoon salt
Approximately 4 cups all-purpose white flour

Glaze

3 tablespoons butter
1 tablespoon honey

1. In a saucepan, scald the milk. Set aside to cool to lukewarm (110°).
2. In a large mixing bowl, combine the yeast with the warm milk, stirring well to dissolve the yeast. Stir in the oil, honey, and eggs. Add the salt and 3 cups of the flour. Beat well. Gradually add some of the remaining 1 cup flour, a handful at a time, until you have a dough stiff enough to knead.
3. On a lightly floured surface, knead the dough, adding as much of the remaining flour as needed, until you have a smooth, elastic dough. Place in an oiled bowl, cover, and let rise in a warm place until double in bulk, about 40 minutes.
4. Grease two baking sheets.
5. Divide the dough into two balls and work with one ball at a time. Divide a ball into eight equal pieces. Divide seven of these pieces into two unequal-size pieces, one about three times as big as the other. Form the large one into a ball for the body; form the smaller piece into a ball for the head. With your thumbs, smooth the top of the dough balls and place them *seam-side down* on the baking sheet. Firmly pinch together the heads and bodies. With the eighth piece of dough, pinch off tiny pieces and shape into balls for tails and tiny ovals for ears. Press firmly to attach the tails and ears where they belong.

6. Cover and let the rolls rise until doubled in bulk, about 30 minutes (less if it has taken a long time to form the rolls with the children's help).

7. Preheat the oven to 375°. Melt the butter.

8. Just before baking, brush the rolls with the melted butter. Bake for about 15 minutes, until golden. While the rolls bake, combine the remaining melted butter with the honey. When the rolls are done, remove from the oven and brush with the honey-butter mixture. Cool briefly on wire racks. These are best served fresh and warm. If you must make them ahead, reheat for about 15 minutes at 300° and serve at once.

DISCOVERING PASSOVER TRADITIONS

Passover is a Jewish holiday, celebrated for eight days in March or April, that commemorates the liberation of the Israelites from Egyptian slavery. One of the main symbolic foods is matzo, a flat unleavened bread. It is flat because the Israelites fled from Egypt in a great rush, leaving no time to allow the bread to rise before fleeing. A special dinner, called a seder, is held on the first and/or second night of Passover. During the seder, the Passover story is retold, and special foods are eaten.

For Jewish families, a seder is one of the most important observances of the year, a time when families gather and enjoy a feast.

Here are some activities in the Passover tradition:

PUT ON A PLAY Tell your kids the story of Passover and then have them put on a play in which they act out the scenes you've described. A few families prefer this to the traditional lengthy seder, at which children can become restless.

THE FOUR QUESTIONS During the seder, it's traditional for the youngest child present to ask the Four Questions, which ask, "Why is this night different from all other nights?" During a seder, or at another time during the Passover holiday, ask your child to consider ways in which "this day is different." Think about answers that relate to the weather, the activities of family members, and so on. For instance, "This day is different because we're cleaning up everything for all the relatives who are coming to visit," or "It's different because I just had my birthday and I'm older now," or "It's different because this is the first Saturday since the storm."

Alternatively, have your child come up with a new set of Four Questions that relate to this (or another) holiday.

234 **FEELING FREE** During their sedar, a family of four in North Carolina focuses on the symbolic meaning of freedom. They take turns around the table, with all members of the family talking about a time when they felt imprisoned in some way in the course of the past year, and how they managed to free themselves. For instance, a child may have felt stuck in an uncomfortable situation in school and resolved it by talking to the teacher. Perhaps a parent felt boxed in at work and finally figured out a way to break free of the feeling or the job.

HUNT THE AFIKOMEN Every traditional seder ends with a children's hunt for the afikomen, a hidden piece of matzo. When it is found, the finder gets a reward, and everyone present shares in the eating of the matzo for good luck. In some families, the finder is encouraged to return the afikomen to the adult who offers the best reward. Develop your own ritual for hiding, finding, and returning the hidden matzo.

RECIPES FOR FUN: TRADITIONAL PASSOVER DISHES

On the seder table are the foods that each family associates with this holiday. Common dishes include chicken soup with matzo balls, gefilte fish with horseradish, roast chicken, potato kugel, charoset (see recipe), and desserts made with matzo flour, such as macaroons and cakes, along with lots of matzo, sweet kosher wine, and candies.

CHICKEN SOUP WITH MATZO BALLS

Yield: 4 to 6 servings

Matzo balls—Jewish dumplings—with chicken soup are a traditional Passover treat. They are made from matzo meal, which is nothing more than ground matzo crackers, and eggs. This recipe makes a nice average matzo ball—not too heavy, not too light. To make a lighter matzo ball, add one more egg. To make a heavier one, add more matzo meal.

Children can help mix the batter and shape the matzo balls, provided you aren't too concerned with making each matzo ball of uniform size and texture, and you don't mind cleaning up the inevitable mess. Since the dough contains raw eggs that may contain salmonella, make sure your child doesn't touch his face while shaping the dough, or eat any raw dough. The soup is fine with just the matzo balls, but you can add chopped greens, scallions, celery, or carrots to the soup and heat for about 30 minutes before serving.

Chicken Soup
3 to 4 pounds chicken (necks, wings, gizzards, leg quarters, or whole chicken cut into pieces)
12 cups cold water
4 celery ribs, including green leaves, quartered
2 onions, quartered
2 carrots, quartered
1 bunch parsley
Approximately 3 dill heads, or 3 sprigs fresh dill weed, or 1 tablespoon dill seeds (optional)
Salt to taste

Matzo Balls
2 tablespoons light vegetable oil (canola is recommended)
2 large eggs
2 tablespoons water
1 teaspoon salt
½ cup matzo meal (available where kosher foods are sold)

1. To make the soup, rinse the chicken under running water and remove any visible clumps of fat. Combine the chicken and water in a large soup pot. Bring to a boil, then skim off the gray foam that accumulates on top. Reduce the heat and simmer for about 30 minutes. Then add the vegetables and herbs. Partially cover and simmer for 1 to 2 hours. The soup will be clear if you do not let it boil.

2. Let cool slightly, then strain the soup. Pick the meat off the bones; discard the vegetables, bones, and skin; save the meat for future use. You will have about 8 cups of stock and 3 to 4 cups of meat, if you used a whole chicken or leg quarters.

3. Add salt to taste (the soup will taste flat without it).

4. If possible, refrigerate the soup overnight. Then skim off the hardened fat with a spoon. Or let stand for at least 30 minutes to allow the fat to rise to the top, then skim it off.

5. To make the matzo balls, combine the oil, eggs, water, and salt in a medium-size bowl and beat well. Add the matzo meal and beat to combine. Refrigerate for 15 minutes. Meanwhile, bring a large pot of salted water to a boil.

6. Reduce the heat to keep the water gently boiling. Form the batter into 1-inch balls. Don't make them too big—they blow up when they cook! You will have eight to ten balls. Drop the balls into the water. Cover the pot and gently boil for 30 to 40 minutes. The balls will fluff up and float on the top as they cook. The only way to tell whether a matzo ball is cooked through is to remove it from the water and cut it in half.

7. While the matzo balls cook, heat the soup, adding more salt to taste if necessary.

8. To serve, place 1 to 2 matzo balls in each bowl and add the soup.

CHAROSET

Yield: About 3 cups

One of the ceremonial dishes placed on the traditional seder table is charoset, a fragrant blend of apples, nuts, wine, and cinnamon. The ground mixture is meant to symbolize the mortar that the enslaved Jews used to build vast monuments in Egypt. The exact blend of fruits and nuts varies considerably, though apples and almonds are most commonly used in the United States.

6 apples, peeled and grated
½ cup finely chopped almonds or walnuts
2 tablespoons honey or more to taste
½ teaspoon cinnamon
¼ teaspoon ginger
2 tablespoons sweet red wine or more to taste

1. Combine all the ingredients, mixing together thoroughly. Taste and add more honey, spices, or wine as needed.
2. Chill before serving.

CHOCOLATE MACAROONS
Yield: About 30 macaroons

Moist, chewy macaroons are traditional Passover treats. Because these are so easy to make, having the children help out—or take over—will be no problem. Just be careful not to overbake.

½ cup slivered almonds
3 cups sweetened flaked coconut
6 tablespoons unsweetened cocoa
3 egg whites
1 teaspoon vanilla extract
¾ cup superfine sugar
¼ teaspoon salt

1. Preheat the oven to 325°. Line two baking sheets with parchment or waxed paper.
2. In a food processor fitted with a steel blade, grind the almonds to the consistency of fine bread crumbs. Add the coconut and process until well chopped.

Add the cocoa and process until well mixed. Set aside.

3. In a large bowl, beat the egg whites until foamy. Add the vanilla and salt, then the sugar a little at a time, beating constantly until the mixture stands in soft peaks.

4. Fold the coconut mixture into the egg whites until well combined.

5. Drop from a teaspoon onto the baking sheets.

6. Bake for 15 to 20 minutes. Do not overbake; the cookies should still be slightly soft in the center.

7. Set the pan on a wire rack to cool for 10 minutes. Then remove from the pan with a spatula. Store in an airtight tin.

HONORING MOTHER AND FATHER ON THEIR DAYS

We all like to be reminded that we are valued, especially busy moms and dads who do so much for their children out of love. Encourage your child to express gratitude toward the other parent on Mother's Day or Father's Day. If you're a single parent, take the initiative and let your child know how much it would please you to be remembered on your special day.

If your child isn't comfortable including her stepfather or stepmother in the usual Father's Day or Mother's Day celebrations, encourage her to observe Stepparent's Day on the second Sunday in October. Homemade cards and small gifts are in order.

While your child is very young, help her find ways to be thoughtful. Eventually she will develop a lifelong habit of expressing appreciation when it's due.

IT'S YOUR LIFE We all like to talk about ourselves. Suggest that your child honor you by asking you for an interview. Depending on his age, he can ask you anything from "Where were you born?" to "What was your mother's middle name?" to "What kind of shoes did you wear as a child?"

BREAKFAST IN BED Make a family tradition out of serving breakfast in bed to Mom or Dad. Even a preschooler can concoct something simple with the help of one parent, then help carry it to the "still sleeping" parent on a tray. Look for simple recipes like those you'll find later in this section.

PUT IT IN WORDS Encourage your child to make a card to be given to the other parent on Mother's or Father's Day. It can be placed on the breakfast tray and might include a drawing. A young child should say something simple like "I love you, Mom" or "Love, Sally." An older child can design a card that says *why* her parent is so special to her, such as "You're the best, Mom. You make great brownies and you take care of me when I'm sick and you hug me when I need it." Or, "Happy Father's Day. I'm so glad you're always there for me and hardly ever yell at me, even when I goof up."

TERMITE SPREAD One mom in Chicago loves a particular dark-colored jam that no one else in the family appreciates. Her husband and son have taken to calling it "termite spread." On Mother's Day, her son prepares her toast and "termite spread" in the morning before she wakes up. Do you have a favorite food that you don't often serve to the family? Encourage your child to remember this item on your special day.

PAINTED FLOWERPOT Everyone loves flowers, and flowers that last a long time are surely cherished. An excellent Mother's or Father's Day gift is a houseplant in a hand-painted pot. Either purchase an inexpensive plastic pot and have your child paint it for you (or for the other parent) before planting a seedling in it, or buy a plant already potted in a pretty container. Pothos is one plant that lasts a long time with minimal care and is likely to be around for many Mother's Days and Father's Days to come.

A HANDS-DOWN GREAT GIFT Anything with a handprint on it makes a memorable gift on those May or June holidays, especially from a preschooler or early grader. Have your child dip the palm of her hand in tempera paint and place it gently on a piece of stiff paper. Be sure to have her write her name on the paper and add the date. Alternatively, she can press her hand on a lump of clay and allow that to harden for a keepsake.

240 WAKE-UP SHAKE-UP
Yield: 4 servings

Kids love to make and enjoy blender drinks. This frosty cocktail is so easy to make that even young children may be able to make it without much help. And the drink is so tempting that any parent would be delighted to start the day with it.

2 cups pineapple juice
1 cup canned peaches
1 cup buttermilk
2 tablespoons sugar
4 ice cubes
Optional garnish: nutmeg or orange slice

1. Combine all the ingredients (except the garnish) in a blender. Process until well combined, about 1 minute.
2. Pour into tall glasses. If you like, garnish with a very light dusting of nutmeg or a slice of orange.

BAKED FRENCH TOAST
Yield: 4 servings

Because no hot griddle is required, children can make this savory breakfast dish. They may want to get a head start on the morning by assembling the toast and jam in the baking pan the night before. Then in the morning, all they have to do is whip together the egg mixture, pour it over the toast, and pop the whole thing into the oven. By the time the coffee is made and a tray is set up for breakfast in bed, the special-occasion French toast will be all ready.

12 to 14 slices (about 1 pound) slightly stale French bread, egg bread, or cinnamon swirl bread
3 to 4 tablespoons butter, melted
3 tablespoons strawberry or raspberry jam
3 eggs
1 cup milk
¼ cup pure maple syrup
½ teaspoon vanilla extract
½ teaspoon cinnamon
Garnish: Fresh sliced strawberries or whole raspberries

1. Butter a 9 x 13-inch baking dish. Preheat the oven to 350°.
2. Lightly toast the bread. Brush with the butter on both sides. Spread the jam on half the toast and top with the remaining toast. Arrange the jam sandwiches in the baking pan, slightly overlapping the sandwiches if necessary. (This part can be done the night before; cover tightly and refrigerate overnight.)
3. In a medium-size bowl, combine the eggs, milk, maple syrup, vanilla, and cinnamon, and beat until thoroughly combined. Pour over the toast.
4. Bake until the top is brown, about 25 minutes.
5. Remove from the oven and garnish with the berries. Serve warm.

LIGHT PEAR CRUMB CAKE
Yield: 12 servings

An agreeable way to start the day is with a coffee cake that is low in fat but high in flavor, like this one. The pears keep the cake moist, so the kids can help make the cake a day or more in advance. It's yummy served at room temperature, or it can be briefly reheated and served warm. The children can help with the measuring and mixing or even take it over. Younger children will need supervision and help with peeling and slicing the pears. Even the youngest can help to arrange the pears on top of the batter and sprinkle the streusel topping over the pears.

Cake

2 cups all-purpose flour
1 teaspoon baking powder
1 teaspoon baking soda
¼ teaspoon nutmeg
¼ teaspoon salt
8 tablespoons butter (1 stick), at room temperature
1¼ cups white sugar
1 teaspoon vanilla or almond extract
3 egg whites
1 cup buttermilk
2 large pears, peeled and thinly sliced

Streusel Topping

¼ cup all-purpose flour
¼ cup light brown sugar
¼ cup Grape Nuts cereal
2 tablespoons butter

1. Preheat the oven to 350°. Lightly butter an 8-inch-square pan or coat with non-stick cooking spray.
2. Sift together the flour, baking powder, baking soda, nutmeg, and salt into a medium-size bowl. Set aside.
3. In a medium-size mixing bowl, cream together the butter and sugar. Beat in the vanilla and egg whites. Add the flour mixture alternately with the buttermilk, beating well after each addition.
4. Pour the batter into the prepared pan. Arrange the pears in three overlapping rows over the batter.
5. Mix together all the streusel topping ingredients, working in the butter with your fingertips until the mixture resembles coarse crumbs. Sprinkle over the pears.
6. Bake the cake for about 55 minutes, until a tester inserted in the center of the cake comes out clean. Cool on a wire rack. Serve warm or cooled.

242

TRICK-OR-TREATING TOGETHER

If your children are preschoolers, focus on the surprise aspect of Halloween. This is a time for people in funny costumes to say "Boo!" and for friendly ghosts, face painting, and smiling pumpkins. Older children are more likely to enter into the spirit of scariness and superstition. After all, Halloween is about dead souls wandering the streets. As long as your kids are old enough to know the difference between fantasy and reality, you can have fun joining them in a good pretend **243** fright.

If you go trick-or-treating with children, accompany them on their rounds to friends' homes before darkness falls, and later go home with them for a gathering of family or friends, or to a neighborhood Halloween party. Even older children should be accompanied to every door, and do examine all treats before they are eaten. Unwrapped treats or fruits should be discarded.

RECIPES FOR FUN: BEFORE-THE-TREATS HALLOWEEN SUPPER

If your children won't be trick-or-treating this year, or if you just want them to eat something that's good for them before the candy orgy begins, serve a Halloween supper.

DEVIL'S FINGERS
Yield: 4 servings

Serve this low-fat version of the popular fast-food chicken nuggets with barbecue sauce for dipping (but call it blood sauce).

½ cup all-purpose flour
Salt and pepper
1 egg white
1 teaspoon prepared mustard
¼ cup milk
1 cup bread crumbs
2 teaspoons Italian seasoning

1 to 1¼ pounds boneless chicken breast tendercuts (or boneless, skinless chicken breast cut in 1-inch-wide strips)

1. Preheat the oven to 400°. Lightly coat a baking sheet with nonstick cooking spray or coat lightly with oil.
2. Set three shallow bowls on the counter. Place the flour and salt and pepper in the first bowl. Combine the egg white, mustard, and milk in the second bowl and beat until well combined. Mix together the bread crumbs and Italian seasoning in the third bowl.
3. Dip each piece of chicken in the flour, then in the egg white mixture. Roll in the bread crumbs. Place on the baking sheet.
4. Bake for about 20 minutes. Serve hot, with barbecue sauce on the side for dipping.

MONSTER MASH
Yield: 4 servings

These are spectacularly delicious potatoes—and all the more appealing because they are also low in fat. The secret is cooking the potatoes with chicken broth and garlic.

2½ pounds potatoes, peeled
3 garlic cloves
1 cup chicken broth
1½ cups water
1 tablespoon butter
½ cup buttermilk (milk may be substituted; buttermilk tastes richer)
Salt and white pepper to taste

1. Cut the potatoes into chunks. Place in a saucepan with the garlic. Add the chicken broth and water, adding more water to cover if needed. Bring to a boil and boil until tender, about 10 minutes. Drain well.
2. Mash the potatoes and garlic with the butter. Whip in the buttermilk. Add salt and white pepper to taste. Serve hot.

COBWEB SALAD

Yield: 4 servings

Alfalfa sprouts stand in for cobwebs in this colorful salad. The combination of fruit and a sweetened dressing makes this slaw a real kid pleaser.

Salad
1½ cups shredded purple cabbage
1 carrot, grated
2 scallions, chopped
¼ cup raisins
2 apples, grated
1 tablespoon lemon juice
Salt and pepper to taste
Alfalfa sprouts (to garnish)

Dressing
½ cup buttermilk
2 tablespoons honey
2 tablespoons lemon juice
½ teaspoon cinnamon
¼ teaspoon ginger

1. In a large mixing bowl, combine the cabbage, carrot, scallions, and raisins.
2. Grate apples and toss with 1 tablespoon lemon juice. Add to cabbage mixture.
3. Combine the dressing ingredients and mix well. Pour over the salad. Add salt and pepper to taste.
4. To serve, spoon onto individual salad plates. Garnish with sprouts.

EASY FRIGHT To include "scars" in a scary costume, color patches of moleskin (from the foot care section of your drugstore) with markers or paints. These scars are easy to apply and easy to remove. As a last-minute makeup ploy, you can use washable markers on your child's face and hands.

CANDY SUBSTITUTES Talk with your child about passing out alternatives to candy. Here are a few suggestions: small boxes of raisins, sugarless gum, plastic rings, tiny pads of paper, decorated pencils, stickers, sports cards, or bookmarks.

246

PUMPKIN FARM Make an annual outing to a pumpkin farm and let your child do the picking. Some children enjoy having a whole pumpkin family, including one or more miniature pumpkin "babies."

THE ART OF PUMPKIN DECORATING Cut either the top or the bottom off your pumpkin, and scrape out the seeds and "guts." Your child can draw a face on the pumpkin with a wax marking pencil or crayon. You'll need to do most of the cutting. Many people like to place a candle (a votive candle is the right size) inside the pumpkin (or under it, if you've cut off the bottom).

It can be fun to carve different faces on both sides of your pumpkin. Young kids enjoy using toothpicks to attach pieces of vegetables to a pumpkin to make the face: a cucumber slice makes a good eye, and a piece of apple peel or a line of raisins can serve as a mouth. Use potato chunks for ears and a little carrot for a nose. Add a pair of pipe-cleaner glasses and a cooking pot for a hat.

ROAST PUMPKIN SEEDS When you clean the inside of your pumpkin before carving it, remove the seeds and separate them from the pulp. Wash them and spread them on a cookie sheet. Add salt or a brush of oil if you like. Bake them in a 300° oven for up to thirty minutes, turning them over a couple of times, until they turn toasty brown.

HOW MANY SEEDS? Gather all your dried pumpkin seeds in a jar. Have everyone guess how many there are, then dump them out and count them.

SEEDY PROJECT If you have more seeds than you want to roast, your child can use the extra seeds in a collage or mosaic. Add rice, macaroni, and popcorn, too. Glue everything down inside a box lid for a framed effect.

APPLE CUTUPS You can help your older child carve a miniature jack-o'-lantern out of an apple, potato, or squash. Apples, in fact, are easier to cut than pumpkins.

MAKE A "BOO" MASK When trick-or-treaters call, answer the door wearing a "boo" mask. Write the word *BOO* in thick letters on thick paper or cardboard. Cut the word out with the letters still connected. Cut eye holes out of the two Os. Attach a stick or straw to the B and hold the mask up to your eyes for a funny effect.

THAT'S MY BAG Before trick-or-treating, make and decorate your own goodie bags. Choose a large, heavy-duty paper grocery bag. Fold a cuff around the top edge, and insert a thin strip of cardboard into this cuff. On opposite sides, staple a string or ribbon through the cardboard for a handle. Now decorate the bag with cutouts, pictures, or stickers in a Halloween theme.

HAVE A SKELETON HUNT Purchase and take apart a cardboard skeleton. Hide each of the "bones" in a different spot around the house. One child or several can hunt for the bones until they find enough to put the skeleton back together.

MAKE PUMPKIN FRIES Cut a small fresh pie pumpkin in half and peel it. Cut into "french fry" sticks and toss with two to three tablespoons of oil. Bake on a cookie sheet in a 450° oven until brown and tender, stirring often. If you like, sprinkle the "fries" with cinnamon.

TRICK-OR-TREAT FOR UNICEF Take the greedy commercialism out of Halloween by encouraging your children and a group of their friends to carry UNICEF boxes as they go door to door. Instead of candy, they'll be asking for small change to help the poor children of the world. Often children carry both UNICEF boxes and goodie bags, so they can accumulate some candy too. For a supply of boxes and informational pamphlets, contact the U.S. Committee for UNICEF, 333 East 38th Street, New York, NY 10016.

GIVE A HALLOWEEN PARTY

A frightfully fun party can be a great alternative to trick-or-treating. There are many reasons why a party might be a better choice—your children's ages, safety considerations, cold weather, and of course the mountain of candy that can otherwise come home. A party can also follow trick-or-treating, or it can be held the weekend before the holiday. Here are some suggestions for a great Halloween Party.

☼ **Decorations and atmosphere** Decorate the house with cutouts of scary objects like black cats, ghosts, and goblins. Drape the room with orange and black streamers. Exchange some plain lightbulbs for colored ones. Keep the lights dim. An older child or two can prepare an audiotape of scary sounds—clinking chains, crinkling cellophane, scissors cutting cardboard, howls, moans, and maniacal laughter.

☼ **Refreshments** Serve a cake with orange icing (mix red and yellow food coloring). Use black jelly beans to create a face on the cake. Hang doughnuts from strings in a doorway to eat without using any hands. Then serve cider.

☼ **Activities** Read stories with a Halloween theme to younger kids. Older kids can read scary stories in a darkened nook, storage room, or spooky backyard. Provide a pumpkin for each guest to decorate with cut-up vegetables and toothpicks or construction paper and scissors. Guests can bob for apples in a large tub of water with their hands kept behind their backs. Put on a magic show (see page 100). Begin or end with a costume parade at which everyone oohs and ahs over each other's costume.

☀ **Haunted room** Convert one room into a scary experience for your guests. Line up some large boxes and tables, and add a tent if you have one. Be sure it's very dark in the room. Have your child lead one friend after another through the "tunnel" while making scary sounds, including an occasional scream. Decide on some surprises to inflict on the "victim," such as asking him to dip his hand into a bowl of peeled grape "eyeballs." Freeze some water in a rubber glove for a frigid hand.

GIVING THANKS AS A FAMILY

Thanksgiving is a harvest celebration. Many cultures around the world have ways to give thanks for a bountiful harvest. The Thanksgiving holiday now celebrated in the United States and Canada comes from the Pilgrims' first Thanksgiving feast, although the Native Americans had harvest festivals of their own. In Canada, Thanksgiving is celebrated on the second Monday of October instead of the fourth Thursday of November, because of the shorter growing season there.

On this holiday it has become traditional to give thanks not only for a good growing season but also for everything good that has happened in the past year. Here are some old and new ways to give thanks as a family.

EXPAND THE GUEST LIST You can go a long way toward sharing the deeper meanings of a season of thanksgiving with your children by inviting someone less fortunate to share your feast. Do you have an older friend or distant relative whom you rarely see? Check with your local senior citizen center or retirement home, or your church or synagogue, to see if they can recommend someone who would appreciate joining your family for Thanksgiving dinner.

TREE OF THANKS Cut a big tree trunk out of construction paper and tape it to a piece of posterboard. Also cut out a pile of leaves, each big enough to write a sentence on. Throughout Thanksgiving day, as each person in the family thinks of something he's thankful for, he writes it on a leaf and adds it to the tree. During dinner, talk about what you've each written.

BOOK OF THANKS Begin a family book of things you're thankful for. Add to the book each year, then go back and read what you wrote the previous year. Alternatively, go around the table and have family members speak into a tape recorder about what they're thankful for (or allow people to speak in private if they prefer). Add to the tape year after year.

THANKS FOR THE MEMORY Each member of the family sends a homemade thank-you card to someone they're especially grateful to. It might be a favorite teacher, a music teacher who was unusually patient, a doctor or nurse who helped in a time of need, a friend who moved away (or one who didn't). It could even be another family member.

BRINGING THE HARVEST HOME A visit to a farm during the harvest will help your family gain a greater appreciation for the labor that goes into cultivating the land.

MAKE A SUKKAH The Jewish holiday of Sukkot, which takes place in September or October, is a celebration of the harvest and a commemoration of the period after the Exodus from Egypt when the Jews lived in huts. You might like to help your child make a sukkah of his own. Use a huge box or build one from boards. Leave holes or cracks between slats in the roof so that you can see through it to the sky. Add plastic or real flowers, fruits and vegetables, branches, and leaves to the outside of the box. Your child can eat a meal or two outdoors in his sukkah as observant Jews do on this holiday.

CHAPTER 12

HAPPY HOLIDAYS!

For many centuries, people have celebrated festivals of light at the start of the cold, dark winter. Over time, major religious groups have added their own holidays at this time of year. Sometimes families in which the parents are of different religions choose activities from both traditions. Whatever holidays you grew up with, you can greatly enrich your children's lives by discussing and sharing with them some of the activities and rituals celebrated by other cultures.

In this chapter you'll find a selection of old and new ways to appreciate

Hanukkah, the winter solstice, Christmas, Kwanzaa, and other holidays, followed by suggestions for welcoming in the new year with joy and optimism. Some of the suggestions in particular sections are easily adaptable to other holidays, so skim them all.

MAKING LATKES AND MEMORIES FOR HANUKKAH

Hanukkah is a Jewish holiday that commemorates a victory won by the Jews over the Syrians, who had driven them from their temple. When the Jews won back the temple and purified it, they celebrated. Hanukkah means "dedication." Legend has it that a small amount of oil for the temple's holy lamp, oil that should have lasted only a day, lasted instead for eight days. Thus, Hanukkah, which starts in late November or December, continues for eight days.

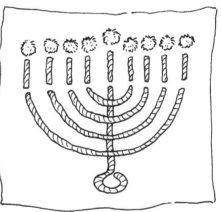

Candles are placed in a menorah, a candlestick with eight branches and a separate holder above or below the others for the head candle, or *shammes*, which is used to light the others. On the first night, first the shammes is lit, then one candle. On the second night, the shammes and two candles are lit. More candles are lighted each night until, by the eighth night, all are lit.

Here are some other Hanukkah activities to share.

DESIGN A MENORAH Glue yarn, straws, or pipe cleaners to paper to form a menorah. Cotton balls dipped in yellow paint make pleasing flames.

PLAY DREIDEL Purchase a dreidel, a toy top with four Hebrew letters on it. You can call a nearby synagogue to find out whether it has a gift shop that sells Jewish items. Card stores in your area may also carry dreidels around the holiday.

Each side of the dreidel has a Hebrew letter on it: *nun, gimel, heh,* and *shin.* These are the first letters of the Hebrew phrase *Nes Gadol Hayah Sham,* "a great

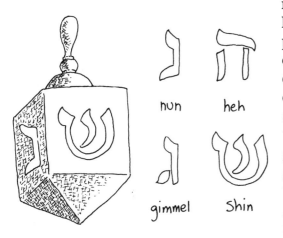

nun   heh

gimmel   shin

miracle happened there," which refers to the legend of the oil burning for eight days. Each person playing gets the same number of counters (pennies, pieces of cereal, candy, or dried beans) to start. Each person puts a counter in the pot. Now the first person spins the dreidel. The letter that ends up on top tells you what to do. If it is *nun*, you don't get anything. If it is *gimel*, you win all the goodies in the pot. If it is *heh*, you are entitled to half. If it lands on *shin*, you have to give back one counter. The player with the most counters at the end of the game wins.

Or make a simple English-language dreidel-like top by cutting a two-inch square from a piece of cardboard. Draw diagonal lines from corner to corner, dividing the square into triangles. Now write a different letter in each triangle—for instance, A, B, C, and D. Poke a hole in the center of the square (the parent should do this part), and place a toothpick through the hole. (For the sake of safety around young children, you can add a dab of clay to the top end of the toothpick.)

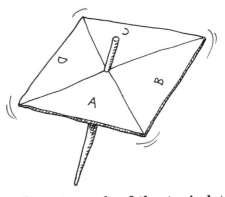

To play an easy spinning game, allot different values to each of the top's letters, such as "all" for A, "zero" for B, "half" for C, and "one" for D. The children sit in a circle with a pile of ten pennies each. Each child puts a penny or two into a bowl in the center of the circle. One child spins the top. If it lands on B, for instance, which signifies "zero," the child gets nothing. When the top lands on D for "one," the child has to put a penny into the bowl. Before each child takes a turn spinning the top, everyone puts another penny or two into the bowl. Keep playing until there are no pennies left in the bowl.

Some kids like to play human dreidel, in which they spin themselves around until they drop.

MAKE STARS Show your child how to make a six-pointed star, the Star of David. Draw a triangle, then draw another triangle upside down on top of that one. Or you can cut out two triangles, and invert one over the other to form a star.

If you have a favorite cookie recipe, make six-pointed-star cookies by cutting the dough into triangles, placing one triangle upside down on top of the other, and pressing them together.

Your youngster can make an attractive wall or window hanging in the shape of a Star of David. You'll need six popsicle sticks, poster paint, and glue. Paint one side of the sticks, let dry, then paint the other side. Glue the sticks together to form two triangles, one inverted on the other. Attach a string to hang.

254

CREATIVE GIFT-GIVING Instead of giving your child a major gift on each of the eight nights of Hanukkah, consider designating each night for a certain *kind* of gift. For example, the first night could be child-gift night, because kids are so impatient. The second night could be the night your child gives one of his parents a gift, and the third night could be the night for a gift for his other parent (or stepparent). You might say that these gifts from your child are to be homemade.

Think of other activities for the rest of the nights, such as Story Night, when the family gets together and shares stories about former Hanukkahs, or the parents read from a book of religious stories if they choose. The last night might be another child-gift night, or it could be the night you give your child his first lesson in sewing, baking, or some other skill he's been asking to learn. Some families dedicate one night to gathering change to give to charity, or to going through their toys and clothes to find items to donate to a local charitable thrift shop.

RECIPES FOR FUN: TRADITIONAL HANUKKAH TREATS

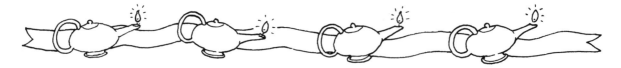

It's a Hanukkah tradition to eat fried foods, commemorating the lamp oil that lasted for eight days.

POTATO LATKES
Yield: 4 to 6 servings (18 pancakes)

Potato pancakes have long been a favorite fried food for Hanukkah. But with today's concern for foods lower in fat, you may want to try a nontraditional way of cooking them. Instead of frying in oil, cook these in a nonstick skillet or cast-iron griddle coated with nonstick cooking spray.

3 pounds potatoes, peeled
1 large onion
2 eggs, lightly beaten
2 teaspoons salt
¼ teaspoon black pepper
Vegetable oil for frying (optional)
Applesauce
Sour cream

1. Coarsely grate the potatoes and onions by hand or in a food processor.
2. Pour into a large bowl filled with acidulated water (1 tablespoon lemon juice or vinegar to 4 cups water). Swish around with your hands for 1 minute. Pour into a strainer and drain well. Place a clean dish towel on the counter. Pour the potatoes onto the towel and pat dry. This step will keep the potatoes from turning an unattractive grey.
3. In a food processor fitted with a steel blade, pulse the potato mixture until finely chopped, but not pureed.
4. In a mixing bowl, combine the potato mixture with the eggs, salt, and pepper. Mix well.
5. Preheat the oven to 250°. Heat 1 inch of oil in a frying pan over medium high heat. Or coat a nonstick skillet or cast-iron griddle with nonstick cooking spray. Drop the potato mixture, ¼ cup at a time, into the pan and fry until golden, then turn and fry on the other side, about 1½ minutes per side. Drain on paper towels.
6. Keep the latkes warm in the oven while cooking the remaining batter. Serve with applesauce and sour cream.

JELLY DOUGHNUTS
Yield: About 15 doughnuts

Sephardic Jews, those whose ancestors lived in Spain and the Middle East, make jelly doughnuts at Hanukkah. These rich, fried pastries are a glorious once-a-year treat.

If you aren't accustomed to deep-fat frying, try this one out on your family before serving to friends. A good frying (or candy) thermometer is essential. If the oil is too hot, the doughnuts will brown too quickly on the outside, leaving the inside gooey and raw. If the temperature is too low, on the other hand, the doughnuts will be greasy.

The children will enjoy helping to mix the dough and cut out the doughnuts. But for everyone's safety, they should stay clear of the stove while you do the frying.

1¼ cups milk
¼ cup solid vegetable shortening
1 tablespoon active dry yeast
Approximately 5 cups sifted all-purpose flour
3 eggs, lightly beaten
1 cup sugar
½ teaspoon salt
Pinch nutmeg
¾ cup strawberry or raspberry jam or jelly
Oil or vegetable shortening for deep frying
Sifted confectioners' sugar

1. In a small saucepan, scald the milk. Add the shortening and cool to lukewarm.
2. Pour the milk mixture into a large bowl. Add the yeast and stir well to dissolve. Add 2½ cups of the flour and beat until smooth. Cover and let rise until double in bulk.
3. Stir down. Add the eggs, sugar, salt, and nutmeg. Add enough of the remaining 2½ cups flour to make a dough that is stiff enough to knead.
4. On a lightly floured board, knead the dough until smooth. Return to a well-oiled bowl. Cover and let rise again until double in bulk.

5. On a lightly floured board, roll out dough to a thickness of about ½ inch. Cut the dough into 2½-inch rounds. Place heaping teaspoons of jelly on half of them and cover with the remaining rounds, pressing the edges together firmly.

6. Let rise, uncovered, for about 1 hour.

7. Heat 4 inches of oil in a deep, heavy pot to a temperature of 360°. Lower the doughnuts into the hot fat, cooking three or four at a time. Turn them when they are brown on one side, and brown the other side. Drain them on paper towels. Liberally dust with confectioners' sugar. They are best served at once, but they will hold for up to 4 hours.

THE WINTER SOLSTICE

Since ancient times, people have celebrated the winter solstice, which takes place on the longest night of the year, following the shortest day. Rituals, especially the lighting of lamps and candles, relate to the coming return of the light and longer days. In recent decades, more and more people have begun celebrating the solstice, which occurs on the evening of December 21, with a variety of old and new customs. If you want to commemorate this turn of the year toward spring and hope, consider a simple ritual to observe together.

FIRST LIGHT When you feel your child is old enough, winter solstice might be the right time to allow him to light candles, under your supervision, for the first time. Most children take such a responsibility quite seriously.

A WREATH TO CIRCLE THE SEASONS Evergreen wreaths are ancient symbols of the solstice, representing the life cycle. Talk about the seasons with your child, and then help her make a wreath of evergreen sprigs to hang on your door.

DANCE IN THE DARK Clear a large space in your living or family room. Turn out all the lights and turn on some slow music. Dance slowly with your family in the dark. If you have a gong (you can make a temporary one out of an aluminum pan), let it represent the sun. Your child can strike it and welcome back the light. Turn on a single lamp or light a candle and continue your slow dance.

FUN TIME, FAMILY TIME

ENJOYING A MERRY AND BRIGHT CHRISTMAS

Christmas is both a religious holiday observed by Christians around the world, and a national and legal holiday in many nations. Families have a wide range of choices for celebrating this holiday season, from focusing on the deeper meanings of Christmas to emphasizing the spirit of play symbolized by Santa Claus. Following are some ideas to inspire you and your family to make the most of the season in whatever way suits you best.

Whatever that way is, you'll all have more fun if you keep things simple. Too often, the Christmas season becomes a time of doing too much and giving too many or too elaborate presents. The extra demands of a full-blown Christmas celebration can put real strains on both parents and children. Consider which elements of the holiday are truly important to your family, and let everything else go. For example, if holiday baking isn't a highlight for you, get your cookies from the bakery instead, then spend the afternoon sledding or taking a walk or relaxing together.

Here are some simple activities that offer opportunities to enjoy being together at this time of the year.

IS IT HERE YET? Children enjoy the Christmas season better when it's more evenly paced, instead of focused totally on the Big Day at the end. You can adopt the traditional Advent calendar to help spread out the fun. Help your child make a one-month calendar, using two sheets of paper taped one over the other. On the bottom sheet, marked off with the month's days, list a simple holiday-related activity, such as the ones given here. Include something for the post Christmas let-down week. In the top sheet of paper, cut windows that fold open to reveal the surprise. Your child opens one window each morning.

DEAR SANTA Many children write (or have their parents help them write) a letter to Santa Claus asking for what they want. If your child believes in Santa, you might want to make a letter-writing ritual part of the countdown to Christmas. Choose a day, say two weeks before Christmas, and help your child compose a pleasant letter. You might include a few words about what your child has done in the past year, especially any outstanding good deeds.

After the letter is written, discuss with your child what gifts he will give to other family members. In that way you help shift the emphasis from getting to giving.

On Christmas Eve, your child can also write a simple note of greeting to Santa to be left with the plate of cookies in the living room.

OUT WITH THE OLD Make a ritual of going through your child's toys, clothes, and "stuff" in the weeks before the holidays. With his agreement, gather a collection of items no longer used and give them to charity. Explain that you're making room for new things by giving away the older things to children who don't have very much.

Or have an annual garage sale of unneeded items and donate a portion of your proceeds to a good holiday cause. Or take your profits and purchase some new toys for your child to place in a Christmas toy collection box for needy children.

BIG BOX OF HOLIDAY CHEER Keep all your holiday decorations, tree ornaments, storybooks, and so on in a large box your child has decorated with holiday-related pictures cut from magazines. Bring it out every year for an instant mood enhancer.

TREE STARS Your family may enjoy a tradition of making a few new tree ornaments each year. Here's one to get you started. Use plain cotton swabs, or, for a more colorful decoration, dip the cotton tips of four swabs into paint. When they're dry, put some glue in the center of each swab and lay them out on top of each other in a star shape. Tie them together at the center with thread, leaving a length of thread for hanging the ornament on your tree. You can also brush glue along the length of the swabs and sprinkle glitter onto the star.

Small Styrofoam balls (from a craft shop) and colored toothpicks (you can buy them that way) can also be used to make stars.

TWINE BALL ORNAMENTS Here's another easy ornament. Gather a ball of thin kite twine, some small round balloons, and liquid laundry starch. Unwind the twine and soak it in the starch. Blow up the balloons to the size you want your final ornaments to be, and tie the ends. Your child wraps the wet twine around the balloons in a lacy design. Now hang the balloons up to dry. Once the twine is completely dry, pop the balloons with a pin and pull them out of the lacework. Hang up your new ornaments on a hook or a string.

PHOTO ORNAMENTS Cut out a square piece of a recent photo of your child's face or whole body. Frame it by gluing toothpicks around the sides. Write your child's age on the back. Tape a wire hook to the back of the photo. Hang the photo on your tree, and add a new one each year.

FOR ALL THE NIGHTS BEFORE CHRISTMAS Start a collection of books that relate to this time of year, and bring them out and read them together each year. Some favorites are *A Child's Christmas in Wales* by Dylan Thomas, *How the Grinch Stole Christmas* by Dr. Seuss, *The Gift of the Magi* by O. Henry, and *The Polar Express* by Chris Van Allsburg.

CELEBRATE WITH SONG Caroling is an old-fashioned custom that is just as much fun today as it was years ago. Invite your children and their friends, or several other families, to come along; the larger the group, the less shy each of you is likely to be. Photocopy the words to some simple familiar holiday songs, and make the rounds of the neighborhood singing as sweetly as you can.

SEE THE LIGHTS Go on an outing to see your neighbors' house decorations. If a nearby neighborhood is known for its elaborate light display, check it out.

HOME SHOPPING If you have a preschooler or young child, consider opening up a "home store." Shop in advance for several small giftable items, price them so they're within the limits of your child's allowance, and place them in a box. Add wrapping paper. Before the holiday, offer your child a chance to spend his allowance in the home store. In that way even a very young child can learn the pleasure of giving gifts to others, along with the sense of responsibility that comes from paying for them.

SECRET SANTAS If you would like to cut back on gifts for your extended family, suggest that each relative have a "secret pal" and buy a nice gift only for that person. This custom provides more surprise at much less expense. If the whole family gets together only once a year, pull out slips of paper to choose secret pals *this* Christmas for *next* year.

KID CARDS Send everyone a Christmas greeting made from one of your child's artworks. Choose a favorite drawing, reduce it on a photocopying machine, and make lots of copies onto the top half of a sheet of paper. If you like, invest in color photocopying. Now all you have to do is fold the sheet over for a ready-made card with a blank space inside for the greeting. Even better, include a photo that shows your child in the process of creating the artwork.

EVERGREEN PAINTINGS A long sprig of evergreen from your tree makes an interesting paintbrush. Try green or red paint on white paper for a delicate look.

MAKE A KISSING BOUGH Bend a metal hanger in a half circle. Tie some evergreen sprigs to the hanger with thread. Attach some mistletoe to a few apples with toothpicks, and hang the apples among the evergreen. Hang up the whole bough with string or wire. Whenever anyone in the family stands beneath the mistletoe kissing bough, they get a kiss.

PAPER-PUNCH TREES You or your child cuts out some tree shapes. Now hand her a paper punch so she can make holes all over the tree. When she places the punctured tree over a piece of paper of another color, the holes will look like ornaments.

CHRISTMAS CANDLE Whether it's in the shape of Frosty the Snowman, Santa, or something more elegant, a big fat candle lit only at dinnertime during the week before Christmas is part of a favorite ritual for some families.

NEW PJ'S With growing kids in the house, you probably have to buy new pajamas at regular intervals. Think about starting a tradition of buying everyone a new set at the holiday season. That way, those annual photos in front of the tree (or the menorah) will have everyone looking their best.

IOU A TRIP TO THE MALL Among the gifts you give your child, include a coupon "good for one post-Christmas shopping expedition to buy a special outfit." Then wait for the post-holiday sales, and buy the outfit and some holiday decorations for next year.

CHRISTMAS SLUMBER PARTY If your kids want to, let them sleep in their sleeping bags under the tree the night after Christmas. Turn the tree lights off once they're asleep.

A MESSAGE FOR NEXT YEAR As you put away the decorations and ornaments at the end of the holiday, each member of the family writes something on a slip of paper to add to the box: an anecdote about the holiday, a prediction, a secret, or something funny. Next year you'll all have fun discovering what each of you wrote.

RECIPES FOR FUN: DELICIOUS HOMEMADE HOLIDAY GIFTS

It's a splendid family tradition to spend an afternoon in the kitchen making food gifts for all the people you want to remember at this time of the year. Teachers, baby-sitters, coworkers, barbers, neighbors, and relatives will of course all welcome these sweet treats.

LITTLE DEVILS
Yield: 4 cups

A child can do all the measuring and mixing and packing into jars. All the grown-up has to do is remove the nuts from the oven. To give the nuts as gifts, pack them into decorative tins or jars. A canning jar filled with nuts and topped with a bow makes a fine package if you don't have anything fancier.

The recipe makes enough to fill two pint jars and requires only a single baking sheet. If you double the recipe, be sure to use two baking sheets. Friends who like their foods spicy and hot will appreciate the optional cayenne. Without the cayenne, the nuts are mildly spiced.

4 tablespoons butter
4 tablespoons hot pepper sauce
1 to 2 teaspoons liquid smoke (optional)
¾ pound mixed nuts
¼ cup sugar
1 teaspoon cinnamon
1 teaspoon allspice
½ teaspoon ground ginger
¼ teaspoon salt
¼ to ½ teaspoon cayenne (optional)

1. Preheat the oven to 275°.
2. Melt the butter in a microwave or over very low heat on top of the stove. In a medium bowl, combine the butter with the hot pepper sauce and liquid smoke, if using. Add the nuts and toss well to coat.
3. In another bowl, combine 2 tablespoons of the sugar, the spices, and the salt. Add half the sugar and spice mix to the nuts and toss well.
4. Spread the nuts in a single layer on a baking sheet. Bake for 15 minutes.
5. Remove the nuts from the oven and toss with the remaining sugar and remaining sugar and spice mix. Spread on brown paper or paper towels to cool and blot up any excess oil. When cool, pack into jars or tins.

CHOCOLATE RASPBERRY SAUCE
Yield: 4 half pints

A silken sauce of rich chocolate and raspberries makes a welcome gift, delicious on ice cream or angel food cake, luxurious as a dip for strawberries. Since the recipe is not complicated, older children may be able to make this on their own. Little children can help measure and pour the ingredients and prepare the raspberries. The recipe can be doubled if you wish.

264

You can use any decorative jar for packaging this irresistible sauce. Half-pint canning jars, available in most supermarkets and hardware stores, come in several different styles. Or look for unusual jars at flea markets. A hand-painted label and a square of fabric secured with a ribbon to cover the lid are lovely finishing touches.

4 ounces unsweetened baking chocolate
2 tablespoons butter
⅔ cup boiling water
1½ cups sugar
¼ teaspoon salt
¼ cup light corn syrup
1 teaspoon vanilla
2 tablespoons Chambord or other raspberry liqueur (optional)
12-ounce package frozen raspberries, defrosted

1. In a heavy-bottomed saucepan, melt the chocolate and butter over low heat. Stir in the boiling water. Then stir in the sugar, salt, and corn syrup.

2. Increase the heat and bring to a boil. Cover and boil gently, without stirring, for 3 minutes. Remove from the heat to cool.

3. While the chocolate mixture cools, puree the raspberries in a food processor or blender. Strain to remove the seeds.

4. When the sauce is cooled, stir in the vanilla, liqueur, and strained raspberry puree. Pour into clean half-pint or pint jars. Store in the refrigerator.

LEMON SQUARES
Yield: 35 squares

A luxuriously rich cookie to give, a simple one for children to make. First the cookie base is combined in a food processor and patted into a baking pan. While the cookie base bakes, the lemon filling is whipped together in the food processor (you don't even have to wash out the bowl). The lemon filling is then poured over the cookie bottom and baked a little more. Finally, a sprinkling of coconut gives the lemon squares a festive look.

For gift giving, look for wooden boxes or decorative tins at discount department stores around Christmastime. Line the boxes and separate the layers with colored foil or tissue paper.

Crust
2 cups all-purpose flour
½ cup confectioners' sugar
Pinch salt
1 teaspoon minced lemon zest
1 cup butter, at room temperature, cut into slices

Lemon Filling
4 eggs
1½ cups sugar
1 tablespoon minced lemon zest
6 tablespoons lemon juice
½ cup all-purpose flour
1 teaspoon baking powder

Topping
2 to 3 tablespoons sweetened flaked coconut

1. Preheat the oven to 350°. Lightly butter a 9 x 13-inch baking pan.
2. To make the cookie base, combine the flour, confectioners' sugar, and salt in a food processor fitted with a steel blade. Add the lemon zest and butter, and beat

until thoroughly combined. The mixture will be crumbly. Spread over the bottom of the pan, using your fingertips. Bake for 20 minutes.

3. While the bottom bakes, prepare the filling. In the same food processor bowl (do not wash), beat the eggs until light. Beat in the sugar, a little at a time, until thick and lemon colored. Add the lemon zest, lemon juice, flour, and baking powder, and beat until thoroughly combined.

4. After 20 minutes, remove the cookie base from the oven and pour the lemon filling over it, smoothing the top with a rubber spatula. Bake for an additional 20 to 25 minutes, or until the top is golden.

5. While the cookies are still warm, sprinkle with the coconut. Cool on a rack before cutting into squares.

CHRISTMAS CUSTOMS FROM NEAR AND FAR

You can enrich your own holiday celebration by going global.

CELEBRATE LAS POSADAS In Mexico, Christmas begins on December 16 with the first night of a nine-night festival, Las Posadas. People traditionally traverse their neighborhoods carrying candles and searching for a *posada,* an inn. It's planned ahead that no one will let them in until the host of the evening welcomes them for a party. If you would like to observe this tradition, consider hosting a block party on this evening, instructing everyone to arrive by candlelight (or flashlight). Serve cookies and punch, and break a piñata (see chapter 10).

FIND THE GIFT Follow the Dutch custom of hiding a gift for your child and then handing out clues to its location in fancy wrapped boxes. For an older child, hide the wrapped clue boxes. For a younger child, hand over the clue boxes one by one in order.

PRUNE PEOPLE It's a German holiday tradition to make funny little prune people dolls to use as decorations. For the doll's head, paint a face on a walnut. A fig makes a fine body, and raisins and prunes are attached by toothpicks to form the doll's arms and legs. Add some personality with tiny costumes made of fabric scraps or paper. Arrange them on a table in a cozy domestic scene.

A HEAVENLY DECORATION Follow the Finnish custom of suspending a vision of heaven from your dining room ceiling. Begin by crisscrossing strings across the room, taping them to the edges of the ceiling. Now cut stars and planets out of paper or aluminum foil, and suspend them with threads from your string framework. Put candles on your table to light up the sparkly heavens.

KWANZAA

Kwanzaa, first observed in 1966, is now celebrated from December 26 through New Year's Day by millions of African Americans. *Kwanzaa* is a Swahili word that means "first fruits of the harvest." Families share activities that relate to the seven principles of the holiday: unity, self-determination, working together and responsibility, cooperative economics (or sharing), purpose, creativity, and faith.

LIGHT SEVEN CANDLES On each night of Kwanzaa, one of seven candles is lighted. They include one black, three red, and three green candles; the same colors are used to decorate the house. Purchase black, red, and green candles, and light them one at a time during this holiday.

TELL A STORY Narrate the biography of an accomplished African American man or woman to your child each night of Kwanzaa. You can also tell a folktale or story that illustrates one of the seven principles of Kwanzaa.

MAKE A DRUM The drum, one of the oldest musical instruments, had its start in Africa. Your child can make a drum by removing the top and bottom of a coffee can. Smooth any rough edges. Cover one end of the can with overlapping strips of tightly pulled duct tape. One way to decorate the can is to wrap different colors of yarn around and around the can until it is thoroughly covered. Now the can is ready to be banged on by a child's hand.

TRY AN AFRICAN CRAFT Mask-making is a traditional African craft you can try. Encourage your child to make a colorful mask in celebration of Kwanzaa. She can decorate a paper plate so that it looks like an animal, adding black painted stripes for a zebra, or black spots on a yellow background for a leopard. Cut eye holes. Add paper cutouts of noses and ears, and attach a popsicle stick to the bottom of the mask so your child can hold it in front of her face.

DRINK FROM THE KIKOMBE   The *kikombe* is the unity cup from which family members drink each night of Kwanzaa. Designate a special cup your family uses only on this holiday, and share family stories while you take turns sipping from it.

WEAVE A MKELA   One Kwanzaa ritual is to place items on a woven mat called a *mkela*. You and your child can make a woven mat out of newspaper or construction paper. Place your special Kwanzaa cup on the mat, as well as the Kwanzaa candles.

FIND THE RING   African children play a simple hiding game. Several children make mounds in a sandbox. One of the children then hides a ring or other small object in one of the mounds while the rest of the players aren't looking. Whoever finds the ring first gets to hide it the next time.

RECIPES FOR FUN: FOR KWANZAA

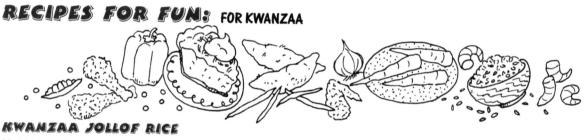

KWANZAA JOLLOF RICE
Yield: 6 to 8 servings

The foods chosen for a Kwanzaa feast usually celebrate the bounty of the land. The dishes are also chosen to reflect the culinary traditions of Africa. This highly seasoned chicken and rice dish is typical of the cooking of West Africa and is a particularly good choice for a celebration because it can be made in advance and kept in a warm oven. It also holds up well on a buffet table.

3 tablespoons vegetable oil
3 to 3½ pounds chicken parts, cut in serving size pieces
2 large onions, chopped
1 sweet green pepper, chopped
4 garlic cloves, minced
2 cups uncooked long-grain rice
¼ cup tomato paste
½ pound shrimp, peeled and deveined
15-ounce can diced tomatoes
2 carrots, chopped
1 cup chopped fresh or frozen green beans
1 cup fresh or frozen peas
4 cups water
1 teaspoon dried thyme
2 teaspoons salt or more to taste
½ teaspoon black pepper or more to taste
½ teaspoon cayenne pepper or more to taste

1. In a large Dutch oven, heat the oil. Add the chicken in a single layer in at least two batches, and cook over medium-high heat until well browned on both sides, moving the chicken frequently to prevent sticking. As the chicken pieces brown, remove to another dish and keep warm.
2. When all the chicken is browned and removed from the pot, add the onions, green pepper, and garlic and sauté just until limp, about 2 minutes.
3. Reduce the heat to medium and add the rice. Cook, stirring constantly, for about 5 minutes, until the grains appear dry. Add the tomato paste, stirring until the rice is evenly coated. Add the chicken, shrimp, and remaining vegetables. Then stir in the water and seasonings. Cover and bring to a boil. Reduce the heat and simmer until the rice is tender, about 20 minutes. Taste and adjust seasonings. Serve warm.

SWEET POTATO PIE WITH COCONUT
Yield: 6 servings

This festive version of the traditional sweet potato pie contains coconut in the crust, coconut milk in the filling, and a coconut topping. The crust is easy to make and requires no rolling out. Making the filling involves plenty of tasks children will also enjoy, including mashing the sweet potatoes and blending all the ingredients. Top the slices with a dollop of whipped cream if you like.

Crust
1¼ cups all-purpose unbleached flour
¼ teaspoon salt
2 tablespoons sugar
6 tablespoons butter
¼ cup sweetened flaked coconut
1 egg yolk
2 tablespoons cold water

Filling
2 cups cooked mashed sweet potatoes
2 eggs, well beaten
1¼ cups coconut milk (regular whole milk or low-fat milk may be substituted)
¾ xcup sugar
½ teaspoon salt
½ teaspoon ground ginger
1 teaspoon cinnamon
1 teaspoon vanilla extract
⅓ cup sweetened flaked coconut

1. Preheat the oven to 425°.
2. To make the crust, combine the flour, salt, and sugar in a food processor fitted with a steel blade. Add the butter, cut in slices, and pulse until the mixture is crumbly. Pulse in the coconut. With the motor running, add the egg yolk and water, and process until the dough forms a ball.

3. Pat the dough into a 9-inch pie pan. Make a fluted rim at the top edge of the crust. Set aside.
4. To make the filling, combine all ingredients except the coconut in a bowl and mix well. If the potatoes are stringy or lumpy, process briefly in a food processor or blender until smooth. Pour the filling into the prepared pie shell. Sprinkle the coconut over the top.
5. Bake for 10 minutes. Reduce the heat to 300° and continue to bake for about 50 minutes or more, or until the filling is firm. Serve warm or cooled.

HINDU FESTIVAL OF LIGHTS

In late October or early November, Hindus in India celebrate Diwali. To light the way for Lakshmi, the goddess of luck and prosperity, they light oil candles. Your family can celebrate this festival of light in your own way.

LIGHT THE NIGHT If your children are old enough not to touch burning candles, arrange and light a group of candles to form a path from the sidewalk to the front door. Then walk along the path, enjoying the light and talking about what good luck means to your family.

MAKE AN OIL CANDLE Your child can make a *diya,* a small saucer with a wick. She can fashion the saucer out of clay. Purchase a candle wick at a craft shop, and add a spoon of olive oil or Sterno cooking fuel. A parent should light the candle. Place the diya in your windowsill.

ANOTHER CANDLE HOLDER You and your child can make a pierced metal candle holder for Diwali or any of the other festivals of light. Remove the label from a food can. You can tape or glue a piece of paper with a design to the outside of the can. Fill the can with water and freeze it (so it won't be crushed by the next step). Then pierce the can following the lines of the design you've made on the paper, using a hammer and nail, a screwdriver, or an awl (the parent or older child should do this part). Be sure not to pierce the can very low to the bottom, where melted wax will be able to escape. Remove the paper and let the water melt. Place a votive candle in the can and light it. Don't touch the sides of the can while the candle is burning, as they get hot.

GOOD LUCK DESIGN As they prepare for Diwali, Indian families decorate their floors with good luck designs made from rice flour. Suggest that your child think of her own good luck design. She can draw it with chalk on the sidewalk, or she can put it on construction paper using paints or a mixture of paste and water in squeeze bottles.

SHADOW PUPPET PLAY Shadow puppets are popular in India and are easy to make. Cut animal shapes out of cardboard and attach them to popsicle sticks, rulers, or yardsticks. Now get between a bright light and a blank wall, and put on a play.

BRINGING IN THE NEW YEAR

The beginning of a new year is an opportunity for families to gaze back and to contemplate the future. Here are some ways to ring out the old and get a fresh start in the new year.

CALENDARS FOR KIDS Calendar making is a craft natural to this time of year. When they use a calendar they've made themselves, young kids learn the concepts of days, weeks, and months. Older kids can learn to use a calendar to schedule their time and plan ahead to reach a goal. Try these calendar activities:

☀ Buy a plain calendar at a stationery store. Your child draws a colorful picture on the back of each page, so that when the calendar is hung, his designs will illustrate the current month. He might like to key his drawings to something special about that month, such as a holiday, birthday, or family event he's looking forward to. If the pages are so thin that marker or paint would bleed through the page, make the drawings on other sheets and glue those to the calendar.

☀ Together with your child, choose a dozen favorite family photos from the past year. Have them enlarged and attach them to a blank calendar, one per month.

KISS IN THE NEW YEAR Some families have developed a bedtime ritual to help their children make the leap from the old year to the new one they'll be waking up to—for instance, kissing their children good night and saying, "This is the last kiss of the year."

FAMILY FOCUS GROUP Before New Year's Day, get together and think back over the past year and ahead to the next. What's important to you as a family? What do you want to have happen in the coming year? Instead of making resolutions, which are inevitably broken and make people feel they've failed, have family members each come up with a few specific things they hope or plan to do: "I hope to learn to play several new songs on the saxophone" or "I plan to do my chores before starting my homework every night." This wording is gentler than "I promise" or "I resolve."

Include some family goals, such as "Let's keep the living room cleaned up so we're always ready for company" or "Let's go someplace new and fun at least once a month."

Next year, pull out your family's goals and talk about how well you all did. Did you reach your group and individual goals? Why or why not? Can you make more realistic goals for next year, or can you work harder or do something differently to ensure that your goals are fulfilled?

GO LOUDLY INTO THE YEAR Noisemaking is a traditional way to celebrate the new year. Have your kids and their friends prepare for a New Year's Day parade around the block by gathering all the musical instruments they have and by making some new homemade ones (see the section in chapter 6 on making instruments). Beat on kitchen pots, or clap two sticks together. Plan the parade for New Year's Eve, or the middle of New Year's Day (so late sleepers won't be disturbed). And don't forget to set a time limit on the whole thing—a full day of noise is too much for anyone.

FIRST FOOTING In Scotland, folks fill their tables with food to offer to the first person who walks across the threshold of the house in the new year. If you tell a few close friends you'd like to replicate this ancient custom of "first footing," you can take turns visiting each other on New Year's morning with a small gift.

TWELVE GRAPES In the Philippines and in Spain, twelve grapes are eaten just before midnight on New Year's Eve to ensure future good luck. Design an equivalent good luck ritual for your own family: Twelve pretzels? Twelve hops on one foot as the clock chimes? Everyone gives a total of twelve kisses to family members at midnight?

WISH BUSH Make a Wish Bush out of a houseplant with sturdy branches and leaves, or a small tree branch placed in a vase or plastic jar. The members of your family write their wishes on slips of paper and hang them from the Wish Bush. The wishes can be for gifts desired for the next holiday, or they can be long-term desires, such as "three new friends this year," "to learn to play the guitar," or on a grander scale, wishes for "world peace" and "thriving rain forests." The slips representing wishes that do come true can be taken down and collected in a little box for remembering. This is a fitting ritual for the start of a new year, or a new school year.

ANNUAL NEWSLETTER Consider publishing a family newsletter once a year at New Year's. Interview each other regarding any new activities or hobbies you've begun in the past year; include an article about your pets; highlight any special events in which family members have participated. Your newsletter can be one sheet or several sheets long. Make copies on your computer, or type or handwrite the newsletter, photocopying as many copies as you need to send to all your friends and relatives.

BE A FORTUNE-TELLER Make a tradition of foretelling the future. Get the family together on or around New Year's Eve and make guesses about what will happen next year. Record your predictions on your calendar. See if anyone correctly guesses what the weather will be on February 12 or July 16. Can anyone predict the day the first flower will bloom in your garden?

Alternatively, compile a list of ten predictions for the coming year on a sheet of paper. Read over the list next New Year's and see how accurate they were.

NEW YEAR'S CELEBRATIONS AROUND THE WORLD

In countries and cultures that don't use the Gregorian calendar, celebrations of the new year take place on dates other than January 1. Perhaps these are traditions from your family's heritage, or ones that your family would like to discover.

JAPANESE NEW YEAR In Japan, the celebration at the start of the new year is called Osho Gatsu. A gong is sounded 108 times, which symbolizes the riddance of the 108 human weaknesses described in the teachings of Buddha. Many Japanese celebrate the new year by thoroughly cleaning their homes in order to get a fresh start while saying thanks for the blessings of the old year. (The Germans believe that the way you live the first day affects all the rest of the year, so they, too, clean house.) A twisted rope decorated with oranges is hung to symbolize strong ties. The oranges stand for roundness and smoothness.

☼ Consider instituting a New Year's housecleaning tradition in your family too. If a total housecleaning is out of the question, you can still spend a couple of hours on New Year's Day with your whole family tidying up, reorganizing your desks, or at least cleaning out a junk drawer as a symbolic action.

☀ Fly a kite with your child, as Japanese children do on New Year's afternoon (for information on how to make one, see page 178).

☀ Japanese children also play with tops at this time, so pull a top out of the toy box.

☀ Make a gong out of a cookie sheet or pie tin and count to 108 as you sound it.

IRANIAN NEW YEAR Now-Ruz, meaning "new day," takes place in Iran for twelve days in March, at the start of spring. Iranians clean house, buy new clothes, and grow sprouts from seeds. At dinner they sit around a special tablecloth that contains seven articles that begin with the letter S in the Iranian language. On the thirteenth day, families go on picnics and toss their sprouted seeds into a running stream to symbolize starting the year fresh and new. Devise a ritual your family can use to symbolize "out with the old, in with the new."

KOREAN NEW YEAR Song Kran is the Buddhist New Year celebrated in Korea. It begins mid-April and lasts three days. Participants have parades and toss water at one another in blessing. It is also traditional to perform kind acts at this time. Have your children think of three kind things they can do either at New Year's or in mid-April for Song Kran. They will also enjoy the water tossing, of course.

INDIAN NEW YEAR Baisakhi is the Hindu New Year celebrated in India. It is carried out in April or May. Colorful saris are worn, and people bathe in the Ganges. Your child might like to take a special bath to begin the new year.

CHINESE NEW YEAR The Chinese celebrate the New Year for several days, beginning on the first day of the lunar calendar, which varies from January 21 to February 19. Red is used in New Year's decorations, candles, and gift wrappings, since it symbolizes happiness. People give money to the children related to them. The numbers 2 and 10 are considered lucky, and 2 is especially valued, so many decorations are hung in pairs. The Chinese set off firecrackers and march in parades that feature dragons, lions, and lots of lanterns.

- If you live near a city that has a Chinatown, visit during the Chinese New Year.

- Hang up some red decorations.

- Your child can make and hang up a good luck sign on a long, scroll-like piece of paper.

- Play Chinese jump rope, in which you raise the rope higher and higher to see how high players can jump.

- Make a Chinese fan by decorating a paper plate, gluing two tongue depressors together, and slipping the plate between them before the glue is dry.

- Attach red ribbons or crepe paper streamers to a piece of wood or cardboard. Put on some music (Chinese, if you can find some in the library), and dance in time to the music while waving the ribbons in circles, swirls, and waves.

JEWISH NEW YEAR In September or early October, Rosh Hashanah is celebrated by Jews around the world. A ram's horn is blown to call the people to prayer. Rosh Hashanah begins the ten-day period leading up to the most serious Jewish holiday, Yom Kippur, or the Day of Atonement.

- The bread traditionally eaten on the eve of Rosh Hashanah is shaped like a ladder, which symbolizes that people can choose to go up or down in the world. Bake a loaf of bread in the shape of a ladder with your child.

- Eat apple wedges dipped in honey, so that the new year may be sweet.

- During the ten days between the two holidays, it is customary to think over your actions for the past year and decide to do better in the next year. Whatever your beliefs, this is a good time for you and your children to ask for forgiveness from each other and from other relatives and friends for anything you've done for which you're sorry.

A WORLD OF TRADITIONS

By sharing with your family some of the customs and rituals practiced by other families, you teach your child respect for other cultures and ways of thinking. Talk about the similarities between your family's values and those of people who are brought up differently. This will deepen your child's understanding and appreciation of others, as well as the connections between all the peoples of the world.

INDEX

283

284

285

286

289

291